American Dreaming

American Dreaming

IMMIGRANT LIFE ON
THE MARGINS

Sarah J. Mahler

PRINCETON UNIVERSITY PRESS
PRINCETON, NEW JERSEY

Library of Congress Cataloging-in-Publication Data

Mahler, Sarah J., 1959
American dreaming : immigrant life on the margins / Sarah J. Mahler.
p. cm.
Includes bibliographical references (p.   ) and index.
IBSN 0-691-03783-3 (cl. : alk. paper). — ISBN 0-691-03782-5
(pbk. : alk. paper)
1. Marginality, Social—United States. 2. Immigrants—
United States. I. Title.
HN90.M26M34   1995
305.5′6—dc20   95-13473

This book has been composed in Galliard

Princeton University Press books are printed
on acid-free paper and meet the guidelines
for permanence and durability of the Committee
on Production Guidelines for Book Longevity
of the Council on Library Resources

Printed in the United States of America
by Princeton Academic Press

1 3 5 7 9 10 8 6 4 2

1 3 5 7 9 10 8 6 4 2
(pbk.)

For the Love of Sophie

———————————

CONTENTS

ILLUSTRATIONS

MAPS AND TABLES

ACKNOWLEDGMENTS

A BOOK, even when it bears a single author's name, is never a solitary effort. Rather, it knits together many people into a network of exchange, reciprocity, and obligation. The scholarly ritual is to acknowledge these ties briefly at the beginning of the work and then, having performed one's duty, march onward with an individual voice. As an anthropologist, I am very supportive of actualizing rituals but will add that my indebtedness is not cursory. There are hundreds of people who have assisted me by providing information, criticism, support, and camaraderie over the past five years since the beginning of my field research. I cannot acknowledge them all; many will always remain nameless or live in the shadows of pseudonyms even in the pages of this text in order that their confidentiality may be protected. And, as always, there will be a few names I should have included but have inadvertently left out, for which I apologize in advance.

Those people to whom I wish to offer my sincerest gratitude first are my informants. I am indebted to them not only for their information but for their friendship and their coming to my defense in times of need. Unfortunately, undocumented immigrants are so transient that I have lost contact with some of the individuals whose experiences are described in this book, but there are twenty or so of my key informants with whom I have managed to keep in contact over the years. I have witnessed their lives settle but not improve very much, a longitudinal look that has given me a deeper understanding of the challenges they face. At this point I would also like to acknowledge all the help and friendship I have received from members of organizations that work with these immigrants, the Central American Refugee Center (CARECEN) in Hempstead, Long Island, and the Center for Immigrants' Rights (CIR) in Manhattan, in particular. At CARECEN, Alizabeth Newman, Esq., Oscar Salvatierra, Arnoldo Lemus, Ken Lederer, Pat Young, and Sue Calvin (whose photographs are featured in the book as well) are just a few of the scores of dedicated individuals who strive to improve the conditions of immigrants on the island and who befriended me.

I am very grateful to a number of institutions and individuals who have supported this research financially. This support includes a dissertation grant from the John D. and Catherine T. McArthur Foundation. I received fellowships from the Anthropology Department and the Center for Social Sciences (CSS) at Columbia University. At CSS, Harrison White introduced me to the wonders of interdisciplinary cohorts, a scholarly paradise that, as I complete this book, I am once again enjoying at the Russell Sage Foundation. My fellow Visiting Scholars this year in the immigration program, Nancy Foner, Victor Nee, Alex Stepick, and Min Zhou, as well as the other scholars, have been wonderful colleagues and friends. The staff and the president, Eric Wanner, treat us magnificently and allow all of us to concentrate on our work with minimal distractions.

I owe a great deal of gratitude to several highly influential colleagues whose commentary and assistance have been invaluable. They include Saskia Sassen, Katherine Newman, and Michael Schwartz. Michael pushed me to focus on the immigrant parallel institutions that have become the core of the book. I am indebted to several colleagues who read and reviewed the manuscript. They include Michael P. Smith, Herbert Gans, David Buchdahl, and an anonymous reviewer. Thanks also to my editor at Princeton University Press, Mary Murrell, to my copy editor, Lauren Lepow, and to the rest of Princeton's staff who have been very helpful. Nia Georges helped me over the rough times by being a wonderful friend and colleague. Mark Stamey, a researcher from SUNY-Stonybrook, introduced me to homelessness among immigrants on Long Island, for which I am very thankful. I have enjoyed the warmth and support of my colleagues in the Anthropology Department at the University of Vermont. They have not only taken me under their wing but have let me test my own wings. Thanks especially to my chair, Carroll Lewin. A UVM graduate, Kate Kenny, skillfully constructed the maps in the book. Finally, my book writing at UVM has been immeasurably enriched by the assistance of Marlo Goldstein. Marlo was friend and sounding board as well as research assistant—and a mighty fine one at that.

It is hard to find the words to thank my family for all the efforts, grand and small, that have kept me going for so many months. My parents, Janet and G. Vicary Mahler, and my brothers, Jeff, David, and Mark, have been enthusiastic fans over the years, kidding me that I must be producing a best-seller. My husband, Boanerges Domínguez, stuck by me through the difficult hours and endured my absences with enormous patience, for which I am grateful. But it was the love of Sophie, the antics and hugs of my toddler, that salted my days and peppered my nights with the devotion I needed to continue and the passion that first inspired me to begin.

Let me end by saying that although I gratefully acknowledge my debt to many other individuals for their assistance, the responsibility for the contents of the book is mine alone.

American Dreaming

Chapter One

INTRODUCTION

THIS BOOK is a narrative of disillusionment. It is the chronicle of the hopes and desperation experienced by a group of undocumented[1] immigrants who have migrated to Long Island in the past decade. These are people from Central and South America who fled dire circumstances in their homelands, sought refuge in the United States, and find little safe haven there, even among their fellow immigrants. Their portrayals of their lives in "America"[2] are full of deceit, dejection, marginalization, and exploitation.

This is not the story I set out to record when I first arrived on Long Island to do fieldwork in the summer of 1989. Rather, as happens to many anthropologists, I found that my informants pulled me in directions I had not anticipated pursuing, or at least following, as far as I ultimately did. The principal force that led me to diverge from my original path was the profound, ubiquitous dissatisfaction these immigrants expressed regarding their experiences in the United States. Though, as I shall argue in detail, they are intensely alienated from mainstream America and its institutions, they focus their resentment on each other, largely exonerating the greater society. When interviewing immigrants regarding their relations with compatriot immigrants, for instance, I was deluged with unsavory characterizations such as the following:

> JUANITA[3]: There's a lot of egoism, jealousy I could say, and it exists between everyone—whether they're Mexican, Chilean, or whatever. Look, the problem arises this way. If I have been here five years and you just came here recently and you have achieved more than I have been able to do in five years, I have to talk bad about you. How can you be winning if you have only been here one year? You are getting more than what I've done in five years. Many Peruvians, many persons who speak Spanish don't understand how someone who has been here only a little time can do better than they can. They have gone nowhere [*se estancan*] and don't want you to get anywhere. Or there is jealousy because of jobs, because some earn more than others. Why do they earn more? That's competition. You feel a lot of competition among those of us who speak Spanish. They comment when you buy yourself some new clothes, that you have such and such.

ALTAGRACIA: There is jealousy, among those here there is jealousy. If someone was promoted but not someone [the coworkers] wanted to promote then they begin to cut him down, calling attention to all his defects. If the [managers] were to promote me because I had been working a long time, the others would still discriminate against me. . . . When I was working as a housekeeper [in a club] [my coworkers] would say, "You do good work," but the same people would always find your hair in the soup. Always! You never are left on good ground with those around you. You have to feel good about yourself.

MARCO: What I know is that there is a lot of jealousy, a lot of jealousy among Hispanics. The fact we are here in this country makes us feel more important because we have more money and are able to do many things with this money, things that we couldn't do over there [in our countries] for lack of money. . . . This fact makes us feel that another person can't have authority over us. They can't do it because I have what I want. And if this person is Hispanic, above all Hispanic, we feel that he is the same as we are but wants to show that he's superior. But I am not going to accept this. I think that being here we ascend rapidly classwise [in the eyes of those at home]. This makes us feel a bit homogeneous because we have money, when we have it. . . . We homogenize ourselves in some sense. Even though I am professional, people call me "Hispanic" and won't accept [my being a professional] easily. Moreover, if they earn more than me they feel above me. You never, never, never hear anything good said by a Hispanic about another Hispanic. . . .

RAQUEL: Hispanics are often egotistical. They don't let you get ahead. When I wanted to begin to work, this Hispanic woman, my landlady, wouldn't let me. She saw that I had a lot of initiative and she tried to keep me from getting access to information I needed. . . . People like that are interested in earning something off of you and I don't disagree with that but you can't abuse others just to do it.

EUGENIA: If I have a true friend, then I would tell her about my problems. But if I know she's going to use the information against me then I wouldn't. Or I would tell her but only to see what type of person she is. . . . Those who come here to this country are not really friends. Only when you're talking with them do they seem friendly, but afterward they turn their back on you. This is the way we, Hispanics, are.

These themes of competition, jealousy, and egotism were so consistent among my informants' testimonies—regardless of their country of origin, aspirations, or class background—that their genesis begged an explanation. To supply that explanation is the principal objective of this book.

There are several other issues I will address in the text, however. One of my chief interests is to provide a longitudinal depiction of an immigrant population in the United States. So often researchers have offered merely snapshots of immigrants after they have crossed the border, and provide little insight into the forces that uprooted them in the home countries. In contrast, I will devote several chapters to explicating why people have abandoned their homelands, how they actually conducted their travels to the United States, and why they migrated to Long Island as opposed to any other area of the country. Why indeed did they migrate to the suburbs and not into the inner city? What interplay exists between global and regional social and economic forces and the lives of individual migrants? The dedication of so many pages to questions often disregarded or underregarded by other migration scholars exemplifies my commitment to representing migration as a process, not as a state of being crystallized in the term "immigrant." Attention needs to be paid to transnational information flows, social status, time, and so forth in the creation, perpetuation, and transformation of migrant streams and migrant identities.

I am also deeply interested in analyzing the opportunity structures migrants encounter in the host country and how they take advantage of them, or not. Though there are exceptions, there exists a tendency in the literature on migrants to homogenize them by nationality, to treat an immigrant group as if it were minimally subdivided by class, ethnicity, or other categories. I challenge this monolithic characterization by documenting socioeconomic differences in status within immigrant groups from the same country, as well as between countries, and by demonstrating that this is significant to their immigrant experiences. Even more important, I will document that heterogeneity exists even among those who occupy the lowest rung of the economic ladder. Immigrants find and exploit an opportunity structure that offers some, albeit modest, socioeconomic mobility. Economic gains are squeezed out of the immigrant sector but not without exacting a price on community solidarity.

Finally, I will weave through the text the argument that immigrants, even highly "unsuccessful" immigrants such as my informants, play an important ideological role in American culture. They contribute to the perpetuation of the Horatio Alger notion of the American dream: that to achieve success in America is largely a function of exercising the "right" values of hard work and sacrifice. My informants are American dreamers; they migrate with the hope that they will, at a minimum, find greater safety and economic opportunity than in their home countries. These dreams drive them to achieve despite the obstacles they encounter, and though most fall short of realizing these dreams, they do not see their efforts as vain. Rugged individualists, they keep the frontier open.

THEORETICAL FRAMEWORK

Mainstream Americans are fond of seeing themselves as constituting a nation of immigrants symbolized by the Statue of Liberty. But their vision is fundamentally assimilationist, not pluralist or multicultural. This unified vision is expressed through a basic creed: *E Pluribus Unum* (from many, one). On each penny, nickel, and quarter this creed is always adjacent to the country's name, "United States of America," as if the two were inextricable. Over the past centuries as different waves of migrants have entered the country, they have been met with this expectation—explicit or tacit—of "Americanization," the shedding of their past and ethnic traditions and their incorporation (at least culturally [cf. Gordon 1964]) into the body politic. Social scientists, most notably the Chicago school of sociology under the direction of Robert E. Park and Ernest W. Burgess, fortified this doctrine by emphasizing in their work immigrants' acquisition of the new culture over their allegiance to their old cultures. The much less dominant paradigm of cultural pluralism, first proposed by Horace Kallen in 1915, did not capture Americans' imagination until the post–World War II era and particularly in the 1960s upon publication of Nathan Glazer and Daniel P. Moynihan's classic *Beyond the Melting Pot* (1970 [1964]).

Glazer and Moynihan acknowledged that many populations in the United States retained their distinctiveness as "unmeltable ethnics." But they saw this as divisive to the nation, propagating the competition between groups and undermining the creation of common ground. Only in the 1980s, two decades after major changes in U.S. immigration law resulted in a radical shift in migrants' countries of origin—from predominantly European to overwhelmingly Asian and Latin American—was cultural pluralism resurrected in a more positive light and given a new name, "multiculturalism." The multicultural movement underscores cultural differences among ethnic and racial groups without ranking them or imposing upon them the expectation of assimilation. Hence, it is quintessentially "postmodernist," embracing fragmentation, ephemerality, discontinuity, and chaotic change as opposed to the eternal and immutable (Harvey 1994). Not surprisingly multiculturalism has its critics who fear for the "disuniting of America" (Schlesinger 1992). The changing demographics of the nation have also been exploited to stir the public's anxiety with such questions as "What Will the U.S. Be Like When Whites Are No Longer the Majority?" (*Time* April 9, 1990). On the academic side, multiculturalism and postmodernism have inspired a new approach to the study of immigrants: transnationalism. Transnationalists (e.g., Glick Schiller, Basch, and Szanton Blanc

1992; Rouse 1992) offer a counterpoint to traditional studies of immigrants that portrayed them unilinearly—as moving from countries of origin to countries of settlement. They oppose this bipolar model in favor of a portrait that delineates "the processes through which transmigrants, living lives stretched across borders, reterritorialize their practices as well as their identities" (Basch, Glick Schiller, and Szanton Blanc 1994:34). For these scholars, as well as for myself, earlier models of indefatigable assimilation need to be challenged and complicated.

Despite scholars' efforts to characterize the multiple allegiances and identities of many contemporary migrants, the American public's support for restrictions on immigration and for several social movements (e.g., the "English Only" movement) reaffirms its assimilationist expectations and its preoccupation with preserving the nation (and its bounty) against an "alien" invasion (e.g., California's Proposition 187). The late 1980s recession accelerated these concerns, spurring researchers to address the fundamental question of whether immigration is essentially beneficial or detrimental to the nation and to its constituent groups individually. It is not my intention to answer this question in this book, nor do I think that there is any definitive answer to be found. However, my work can contribute to this debate by arguing that, while many people—even immigrants themselves—mythologize migration as individuals' search for a "Promised Land," migrations are stimulated and orchestrated by socioeconomic forces much greater than the whims and desires of individuals and their families. By this I do not mean to eliminate the element of human agency; rather, this book is full of stories of human agency, but efforts that are largely conditioned by macrostructural forces over which individuals have little, if any, power. It is my hope that by emphasizing the structural constraints experienced by my informants I will convince readers not to view immigrants as their competitors for scarce resources, but as fellow humans caught up in the difficult project of securing a future for themselves and their children in the unsettling and confusing times of late-twentieth-century global capitalism.

MODELS OF IMMIGRANT ECONOMIC INTEGRATION

One of the most perplexing problems confronting contemporary migration scholars is the arrival of millions of new immigrants in aging industrial areas such as the New York metropolitan region at a time when the manufacturing infrastructure of these areas is eroding. Why would these aging metropolises attract new immigrants when employment opportunities in manufacturing industries—traditional immigrant footholds—

have been disappearing? In the past, generations of immigrant and minority workers provided these industries with cheap labor. Now, the labor continues to stream in while the erosion of the industrial base continues unchecked. Such deindustrialization or "the widespread, systematic disinvestment in the nation's basic productive capacity" (Bluestone and Harrison 1982:6) has been associated with runaway shops, manufacturers who relocate internationally seeking cheaper labor sources. Deindustrialization emerged in the 1960s and accelerated in the 1970s and 1980s. During these decades, migration to the United States skyrocketed from 300,000 to around a million per year. Why would deindustrialization coincide with an *increase* in immigration, rather than precipitating a *decrease*? Numerous theories address this seeming contradiction.

One of the earliest models developed, albeit not specifically to address the problem described above but to characterize mature capitalist economies in general, is the "dual labor market theory." In this model, the economy is portrayed as divided into a core and a periphery, with primary and secondary labor markets corresponding to these divisions. Core industries such as large oil and computer companies value skilled and stable workers. To attract them they offer higher wages, job stability, benefits, and occupational mobility. The core sector is hegemonic, able to influence economic and noneconomic environments to a much greater degree than the peripheral sector (Doeringer and Piore 1971). Peripheral industries are portrayed as more competitive and therefore more cost-conscious. They tend to hire cheap, nonunion labor but suffer a high degree of turnover as a consequence.

In a dual labor market economy, native workers enjoy access to core industry jobs much more readily than do immigrant and many native minority workers, who predominate in peripheral jobs. The latter groups, lacking the skills necessary to perform the core sector jobs (such as computer programming and financial analysis) are "mismatched" to these jobs' requirements (Kasarda 1988). Modern economies are seen as inevitably producing many low-wage, low-prestige jobs; since immigrants are foreign to the prestige hierarchy in the host country, they are less affected by the stigma attached to these jobs than native minorities are (Piore 1979). In this way, immigrants are viewed as an ideal and increasingly necessary labor force as long as the economy produces dead-end jobs. Piore (1979), Sassen (1988), and others have used this bifurcation in the labor markets to argue that native—and, generally, white—workers can access the primary sector while immigrants (and, often, poorly educated native workers) are relegated to the competitive sector. The exigencies of the primary sector generally preclude secondary sector workers from ever being able to access jobs in the primary sector, and two classes of workers become institutionalized.

The dual labor market theory's simple division between economic sectors and their labor markets became accepted dogma; however, more recent empirical analyses suggest that the theory yields inconsistent results (see Lee 1989) and may be too rigid (Nee, Sanders, and Sernau 1994). More germane to the current discussion is the theory's generality. That is, while it provided insight into the dilemma of rising immigration during industrialization, it shed less light on the more micro level of analysis—specific immigrants and their integration into local economies.

During the 1980s a new body of theory emerged that also proved useful to analyzing the economic integration of migrants in postindustrial economies. The concept of the "informal economy" was developed by and attractive to scholars in developing countries who observed how seemingly "unemployed" or "underemployed" individuals generated an income to sustain their families. In contradistinction to the "formal economy," which is constituted by firms and operates within the purview of government regulation, the "informal economy" has been defined as income-generating activities that are unregulated by society's institutions "*in a legal and social environment where similar activities are regulated*" (Castells and Portes 1989:12, emphasis in the original). Lomnitz (1988:43) goes so far as to argue that informal exchange is an integral part of the formal system where it thrives in the interstices, "compensating for shortcomings" of the dominant system. In recent years, the informal economy paradigm has been extended to the examination of informal economies located in the inner cities of developed, particularly postindustrial, nations. Saskia Sassen (1988, 1991), among others, has pointed to the growing informalization of these economies, most notably the reappearance and burgeoning of sweatshops, homework, and low-wage labor in the service sector (often paid in cash). Sassen also explicitly links these structural changes in postindustrial economies to surges of immigrants into these same places, a source of cheap labor to perform tasks natives shun.

Sassen does not limit her model of contemporary immigrant labor-force integration to the informalization of work. Rather, her theory adds two other prevalent trends: (1) the technological downgrading of work into simpler jobs requiring fewer skills, and (2) the appearance of a two-tiered service industry marked by an explosion of high-paid white-collar jobs in areas such as finance, real estate, law, and insurance that provide services to major corporations. At the same time, the demand is fueled for low-paid service workers who cater to the desires of the privileged sector. Examples include workers in boutiques, housekeepers, nannies, dog walkers, and specialty food preparers. Their jobs are characterized by a lack of mobility and job security. Under Sassen's model, "the existence of a major growth sector as is the advanced service sector generates low-wage jobs directly, through the structure of the work process [e.g., sweatshops], and indirectly, through the structure of the high-income lifestyles of those therein employed" (1988:158). Many new, post-1965 immigrants with their minimal skills serve as the perfect labor supply for these dead-end jobs in the United States.

Sassen's model helps explain why areas experiencing deindustrialization, such as New York City, are still the principal ports of entry for immigrants, particularly immigrants with limited skills. Fewer newcomers are being employed by manufacturing companies that offered entry-level jobs and opportunities for advancement to earlier immigrant generations. In Los Angeles, however, Sassen notes that the cheap labor of new immigrants has kept garment industries from relocating overseas in search of less-expensive labor; these businesses have become a mecca for Mexican and Salvadoran women (Fernández-Kelly and Sassen 1991). Sassen's model has enjoyed a great deal of acclaim; what I will examine is whether this model explains migration to the suburbs as well as to the inner cities.

Other models diverge somewhat from the notion that immigrants are economically incorporated into the margins of the greater economy. Several current researchers argue that immigrants find and exploit their own niches, creating sheltered spheres for their economic activity that are often divorced from the mainstream. These theorists are interested in immigrant enterprise—especially the historical continuity of immigrant self-employment in proportions exceeding their percentage of the general population—as evidence that business is key to their success (Waldinger 1986; Waldinger, Aldrich, and Ward 1990; Portes and Bach 1985; Portes and Zhou 1992). According to these theorists, it is not the case (with some exceptions) that immigrants bring entrepreneurial skills or experience with them to the United States when they migrate; rather, they pursue business because they have fewer avenues to success than natives. Immigrants lack the language, the knowledge of how the system functions, the networks and personal contacts essential to obtaining good jobs in the mainstream economy, even jobs they may be professionally prepared to perform based on training received in their home countries.

Furthermore, Portes and Zhou (1992) argue, immigrants experience ethnic solidarity, which these authors label "bounded solidarity." Such solidarity is the outcome of being foreign and being treated prejudicially by the dominant society. Given a cool or even hostile reception by the host culture, immigrants retreat into the familiar. They prefer to consume home country products and to associate and work with coethnics.

This creates a natural ethnic market and fosters an ethnic identity and community, one often bounded by social sanctions against those who attempt to leave or who break the ethnic group's trust (Light 1972:175–76). In a bounded community ethnic markets thrive, providing not only the goods and services sought by the immigrants, but also employment within their neighborhoods and for their coethnics' businesses. Immigrants often tap ethnic sources such as rotating credit unions to pool start-up capital for their businesses (Light 1972; Bonnett 1981); some groups, such as Koreans, tend to bring investment capital with them when they emigrate (Light 1985).

When immigrant enterprise becomes a principal employer, the community is likely to have evolved into an "ethnic enclave." Zhou (1992:4) defines the enclave as

> a segmented sector of the larger economy, a partially autonomous enclave economic structure constituting a distinct labor market . . . [it] is structured in a way similar to the larger economy, but it functions to support ethnic businesses and to help them compete more successfully in the larger economic system. With the existence of such an alternative, immigrants do not necessarily start from the secondary economy or at the lowest rung of the societal ladder. Instead, they can organize themselves to trade exclusively or primarily within the enclave.

Portes (Portes and Zhou 1992:504) claims, for example, that one-third of Cubans in the Miami area work for Cuban-owned businesses; Zhou attributes New York's Chinatown's success to the ample opportunities there for coethnic employment wherein immigrants do not have "to compete with native workers and other ethnic groups for economic opportunities" (1993:5). These authors recognize that immigrants provide cheap labor that is easily accessed through ethnic networks. But they are quick to add that immigrant workers also benefit in the patron-client relationship, enjoying more flexible work conditions, learning the business as they work, and so on (Portes and Rumbaut 1990; Portes and Zhou 1992).

> Enclave employment is advantageous not only for entrepreneurs but also for workers. In Chinatown, low wages are compensated for by the savings of time and effort involved in finding a "good job" in the larger market, the possibility of working longer hours to help contribute more to family savings, a familiar work environment, and for some, the possibility of eventual transition to self-employment. Many business families earn decent incomes, and they earn more money than they would earn from nonbusiness occupations. Moreover, enclave workers can avoid many hassles and costs

associated with employment in the secondary labor market, the most obvious one being labor-market discrimination on the basis of race and national origin. Thus, enclave workers often willingly accept exploitation. They choose to work in Chinatown because they view it as a better option. (Zhou 1992:115)

In the enclave model, ethnic business also offers mobility to people who might not enjoy it in the larger economy. According to Portes and Bach (1985:203), the dynamic ethnic entrepreneurial sector can grow to become organized around class divisions and an ethnic hierarchy. But for this sector to develop, immigrants must have (1) capital—either brought from home or generated in the United States, and (2) an extensive division of labor. This allows for the reproduction "on a local scale, [of] some of the features of monopolistic control that account for successful firms in the wider economy" (ibid.). Enclaves thrive where there is "bounded solidarity" offering entrepreneurs privileged access to ethnic markets and labor that enhance their firms' profitability and hence the entrepreneurs' social mobility.

Roger Waldinger also believes that immigrant entrepreneurship provides a good model for explaining why immigrants have continued to enter the United States despite deindustrialization. Much like Portes and others, he sees ethnic business as a way of skirting blocked mobility caused by a lack of skills traditionally required for job enhancement. He also views group characteristics such as ethnic loyalty and allegiance as linchpins of immigrant business success, qualities traded by the worker to the employer in return for job flexibility, personal loans, and the like. But Waldinger is also interested in exploring how immigrant businesses can extend outside the ethnic market where its growth potential is limited (1986:260). He sees the immigrant market as an "export platform from which ethnic firms can expand" (1986:261) and has developed a model for how immigrants locate and exploit niches in the greater economy. Waldinger argues that there are certain nonethnic niches in Western economies where mass production and distribution techniques "do not prevail" and in which immigrant businesses can flourish. Briefly, these are (1) underserved or abandoned markets, (2) markets with low economies of scale, (3) markets characterized by instability and uncertainty, and (4) markets for exotic goods, such as those which cater to ethnic groups' tastes (Waldinger, Aldrich, and Ward 1990; Waldinger 1994).

The existence of these niches provides an "opportunity structure" to immigrants, but their access to business ownership is dependent upon (1) the availability of vacant businesses with few natives vying for them,

and (2) government policies that may favor (e.g., U.S. programs assisting minority firms) or hinder (e.g., countries with high degrees of regulation) such ownership. Once Waldinger frees his theory of immigrant
business from the confines of an ethnic enclave, he needs to operationalize how immigrants access the available niches in the larger economy.
He holds that ethnic succession is the primary means used by immigrants to achieve this. "Vacancies for new business owners arise as the
older groups that have previously dominated small business activities
move into higher service positions" (1986:46). His quintessential example is that of the New York garment industry, wherein retiring Jewish
owners, whose children disavow the garment industry for higher-status
jobs, open a niche for new immigrants to enter. In general, as a niche
opens it allows a group that normally would be lower on the hiring
queue to move upward. Once a few ethnics can establish themselves in
the new industry, they create social networks and ethnic bonds much as
in an ethnic enclave. However, as the immigrant owners age, their children frequently do not follow them into the business but pursue other
avenues of social mobility open to the native-born. Over time, then, ethnic succession occurs as niches are vacated by one immigrant group and
assumed by a new, incoming immigrant group. For example, Jewish
owners were succeeded by Chinese and Dominican immigrants who
predominate in much of New York's garment industry today (Waldinger
1986).

Waldinger also takes issue with the Sassen thesis. Claiming that New
York's manufacturing sector began to decline in the 1930s, not the
1960s (1986:68), he argues that this decline is a lesser factor in immigrant labor force participation than the succession which occurs when
one immigrant group is replaced by another. Waldinger emphasizes
shifts on the supply side and relies upon a variant of Lieberson's (1980)
ethnic queue argument. According to Waldinger, if nonwhites are low
in the hiring queue, their access to good jobs is greater where the size of
the preferred, white group is smaller. Under his theory, immigrants (and
native nonwhites) do not *displace* other workers but *replace* them as the
native workers retire and leave their niches.

Each of these models has been the subject of criticism, a protracted set
of debates. It is not my intention to engage in those debates but to test
the models' applicability in the micro-context of Long Island. Do any of
these theories elucidate the reasons behind the current migratory wave
of Central and South Americans to Long Island and their economic integration in that local economy? The response to that question will be
the principal theme developed in chapter 5. As revealed by the series of
informants' comments I have already quoted, the notion of "ethnic sol-

idarity" will be thoroughly questioned. Indeed, perhaps the key concern addressed by this book is the comprehension of relationships within the immigrant population. To what degree do immigrants *feel* they are supported and assisted by one another, and to what degree do they express the opposite? Second and equally important, how do immigrants *behave* toward one another, regardless of what they say about these relationships? Anthropologists consistently note that people say one thing and do another; both are important sources of cultural information. I am also concerned about specifying what is meant by "ethnic solidarity." Is such solidarity defined by outside observers, or should researchers also consider their subjects' perspectives—the expectations immigrants have for their coethnics' behavior and the feelings produced by engaging with these people? If immigrants actually do assist one another, what motivates them to do so? For instance, do they assist each other because they are from the same family, town, country, or U.S.-defined ethnic group? Additionally, what types of assistance are involved, and who performs them? These questions must be addressed to make "ethnic solidarity" a more useful tool of analysis. This book is strongly directed toward that goal, though I focus not on how to operationalize ethnic solidarity but on the little-questioned presumption of its existence. More work directed at the problem of operationalization needs to be done on many immigrant populations before the task will be complete.

THE IMMIGRANTS: A BRIEF DEMOGRAPHIC DISCUSSION

As is often the case with ethnography, there is a history behind my coming to conduct a study of immigrants on Long Island. This story begins years prior to the actual research, when I served as a paralegal handling immigration cases for a Manhattan organization, the Center for Immigrants' Rights. During this period I was often called upon to translate for volunteer attorneys who represented Salvadoran clients in political asylum cases. Through this work I became familiar with Salvadorans' experiences, and this background became the platform for a research proposal. Since many Salvadorans in the New York metropolitan area live on Long Island, this area became the locus of my study. Soon after I entered the field, however, I realized that there was a much more complex undocumented migratory flow to the island than had previously been apparent. I began to talk to many Peruvians and Colombians and a few Chileans, Dominicans, Nicaraguans, and Guatemalans as well.

It seemed ironic that Long Island, with its image of classic white suburbia, would attract such a large, diverse group of immigrants. But suburban areas across the country are attracting immigrants, in small part because of the safety and aesthetics of the suburbs as compared to the inner cities, and in large part because jobs have been created in these areas. Long Island is no exception. Many Asians are also moving in, deserting areas of New York City, especially Queens; Turks have come close to monopolizing gas stations throughout the island as well (Singer 1990). As I peered into the inner world of the undocumented Latino immigrants on Long Island, I was struck by the tremendous differences between the Salvadorans I had set out to study and the South Americans I came across because they lived side by side with the Salvadorans, sometimes even sharing the same residences. As a result, I broadened my methodology to include these other informants and developed different networks, primarily among the Peruvians and a few other South and Central Americans.

I realized that I was standing amid at least two contrasting migratory streams flowing into the same place at the same time but propelled by different forces. This disparity between the migrant flows struck me vividly when I attended Spanish-language masses at the Catholic church in Gold Coast (the pseudonym of a town where I conducted intensive fieldwork). The Salvadorans recede to the back of the sanctuary. They are most distinguishable by their dress: the men tend to wear very simple, unassuming clothing—a white fitted shirt, some nice jeans, and boots; the women wear homemade satiny dresses in pastel colors that billow from the waist downward. The South Americans, in contrast, are conspicuous. They occupy the front of the sanctuary, entering from the front as well—in full view of the rest of the congregation. These are people who "dress for success": the men sport tailored suits; the women wear noticeable makeup and debut carefully groomed hairdos and leather jackets over their stylish coordinates.

This group of worshipers manifests the heterogeneity of this population, and the two immigrant groups are distinguished by broad-based demographic characteristics as well as by casual observation. The Salvadorans I met are overwhelmingly of peasant origins, whereas the South Americans come from middle-class or, at least, stable urban working-class backgrounds. Tables 1.1 and 1.2 highlight the differences between these groups. Table 1.1, drawn from 1990 census data, compares Salvadorans with several other Latino groups on Long Island. The Salvadorans earn substantially less, are poorer, and have less education than any of the others. The Peruvians are a highly educated group; over 50 percent of the adult population have at least some college (compared to 20 percent of U.S. natives). The same divergence between Latino groups is reflected in data I collected from 350 adult students in English as a Second Language (ESL) classes located all over Long Island. After comparing several South American groups I found that they were statistically similar enough to combine and compare with a larger sample of

TABLE 1.1
Social Characteristics for Selected Latino Groups, 1990 Census Figures
(Long Island average values)

	Salvadorans	Colombians	Peruvians	Puerto Ricans
Male/female ratio (adults, age 16+)	57/43	46/54	52/48	48/52
Per capita income	$8,561	$11,303	$14,029	$13,108
% families below poverty line	13.5	9.4	6.5	7.1
% speak poor English (> 5 yrs. old)	69.8	47.5	44.9	21.3
Education (adults, age 25+)				
% < 5 years	17.7	4.9	0.5	3.9
% high school graduates	38.0	68.5	85.2	70.0
% some college	16.3	38.3	51.5	36.8

Source: U.S. Bureau of the Census, *Census of Population and Housing*, "Social and Economic Characteristics for New York State" (1990), tables 163, 164, 165.

TABLE 1.2
Social Characteristics for Selected Latino Groups,
Author's ESL Survey on Long Island

	Salvadorans (Total N = 202)	South Americans[a] (Total N = 73)
Male/female ratio	70/30	58/42
Median age[b]	27	33
Median weekly salary	$229	$250
Education		
% <5 years	32.2%	17.8%
% high school graduates	16.7%	33.3%
% some college	5.9%	22.2%
Average in years[b]	6.4	9.5
Median monthly rent	$300	$425
Median monthly remittance[b]	$200	$300
% who remit monthly[b]	83%	69%

[a] Figures combine data for Colombians, Peruvians, and Ecuadorans.

[b] Indicates p<.005 for t-test comparing salvadorans versus South Americans for this continuous variable.

[c] Indicates p<.05 for Chi Square comparing Salvadorans versus South Americans for this categorical variable.

Salvadorans (N = 202). The combined group includes 33 Colombians, 13 Peruvians, and 27 Ecuadorans, for a total of 73 South Americans. As summarized in table 1.2, the South Americans are older than the Salvadorans, are more evenly distributed between males and females, have more education, earn more money (although only twenty-one dollars per week more than Salvadorans, presumably because all these students lack English skills), and have higher expenses than their Salvadoran counterparts.

The information from the census and my questionnaires reflects my own sense of the differences between these two migrant streams. Though there is some overlap, the Salvadorans are principally from rural, peasant backgrounds, whereas the South Americans are overwhelmingly urban and exude the anxiety of the downwardly mobile middle class. I will note briefly that although I have included census information here, I do so with many reservations. This skepticism derives from an alternative enumeration of Salvadorans I performed on Long Island, during which I found that the Bureau of the Census had undercounted the Salvadorans in my neighborhood by over 50 percent (see Mahler 1993). Those missed were primarily poor men with no English skills who lived in unusual housing (basements, boardinghouses, illegal apartments). This leads me to believe that the official count is skewed toward wealthier, more educated and established Salvadorans (a disparity I also suspect is replicated for the South Americans to some extent).

The Salvadorans

In the early 1990s, an estimated 90,000 Salvadorans lived on Long Island. This estimate, provided by the leading agency that works with Salvadorans, CARECEN (Central American Refugee Center), differs significantly from the 19,152 Salvadorans found by the 1990 census (which found another 20,000 in nearby Queens). My research inclines me to agree more with the CARECEN estimate. As map 1.1 indicates, most came from the three easternmost provinces (called "departments") of El Salvador: La Unión, Morazán, and San Miguel, three of the areas most affected by the 1979–1992 Salvadoran civil war.

Long Island's Salvadoran population exhibits a migration pattern which differs from that of other significant Salvadoran populations in the United States, such as those of Los Angeles, Houston, Washington, D.C., San Diego, and San Francisco where more urban Salvadorans live (CARECEN personal communication; Jacqueline Hagan, personal communication; Ward 1987; Chavez 1994; Repak 1994). In general, these cities have received more educated urban Salvadorans and people who are from central and western sections of El Salvador.

A Colombian teaching Spanish literacy to her Salvadoran students.
Photograph by Susan Calvin

The typical Salvadoran immigrant is a male, like Santos Rosa, who is between the ages of twenty and thirty-five, left a spouse and children in El Salvador, and worked as a small-time farmer before emigrating. Santos went to school for only two years and is functionally illiterate in Spanish, with a grasp of only the most essential words in English. In his country, Santos's life revolved around planting corn and beans on a tiny plot of rented land in eastern El Salvador. During the postharvest period he would migrate westward to harvest coffee and sometimes cotton or sugar to earn the hard currency he needed to buy fertilizers for his crops and clothes and medicines for his family. When he was threatened by the guerrillas during the Salvadoran civil war (1979–1992), he fled his country, seeking refuge first in Honduras and later in the United States. He now lives with six other men in a two-bedroom apartment. His wife and children remain in El Salvador supported by the money he sends home from his job as a landscape laborer. He also works nights as a janitor, earning six dollars an hour, but this job is very sporadic. On rainy days and during the winter he idles his time away in his apartment, playing cards with friends or listening to Salvadoran *ranchera* (country) music. He has no money for amusements and he is afraid of being caught by the "Migra" (the Immigration and Naturalization Service, or INS), so he stays at home.

Map 1.1. Map of El Salvador with Salvadoran Towns Sending Many
Migrants to Long Island, New York

The 1994 annual Central American Independence Day parade
in Hempstead. Photograph by Susan Calvin

It is much rarer on Long Island to meet a Salvadoran who hails from
one of the country's cities, such as the capital, San Salvador, but those
migrants from urban backgrounds predominate in the business community and local Salvadoran leadership. A cable channel program, musical
events, and a few local newspapers are the outcome largely of efforts by
this small, elite corps of Salvadorans. This group also organizes the annual Central American Independence Day parade in September in association with a similar elite from other ethnic Latino groups. Among
urban Salvadorans, many were born in the countryside and moved to
the city before coming to the United States, what researchers call "step
migration." Edgar Pacheco is more typical of this pattern. He was born
in San Vicente Department and moved to San Salvador where his father
was a shoemaker. He lived in a *mesón* (rooming house), where each family occupies a room and shares bathroom facilities. Edgar became part of
San Salvador's vast informal economy, producing and selling shoes and
other items on the city's streets.

Regardless of birthplace, Salvadorans migrate to Long Island through
networks of kin and friends. Nearly everyone has arrived since the out-
break of the war in El Salvador, often in surges caused by events there.
My observation is substantiated by (1) my survey, which found that 93
percent of the Salvadorans I surveyed arrived in the United States after
1978, and (2) by a compilation of 1990 census figures for the New York
metropolitan region, which shows that 77.1 percent of the area's Salva-

TABLE 1.3
Latino Population for Selected Long Island Communities by Country of Origin

	El Salvador	Peru	Colombia	Puerto Rico	Dominican Republic	Mexico
Nassau County						
Elmont	59	130	391	977	141	176
Freeport	1,957	102	346	1,423	2,156	210
Glen Cove	245	376	112	742	0	101
Hempstead	3,510	10	610	1,254	328	150
Hicksville	368	16	325	574	94	5
Long Beach	318	296	317	893	89	235
New Cassel	1,165	0	134	64	67	121
Port Washington	362	35	270	127	39	32
Roosevelt	458	0	0	276	61	62
Uniondale	583	22	124	799	224	74
Suffolk County						
Brentwood	1,905	116	716	8,678	1,403	198
Central Islip	1,124	123	337	3,745	255	66
Huntington Sta.	968	0	240	1,267	93	126
N. Bay Shore	652	54	164	3,060	112	23
Wyandanch	71	0	84	361	207	0
Total Nassau	12,437	2,380	6,115	16,688	5,223	2,416
Total Suffolk	6,715	1,236	5,075	42,434	4,979	2,882
TOTAL	19,152	3,616	11,190	59,122	10,202	5,298

Source: U.S. Bureau of the Census, *Census of Population and Housing* (1990). Data based on sample of the population.

dorans arrived in the United States between 1980 and 1990 (Salvo and Ortiz forthcoming). Salvadorans have formed migratory chains that link villages in their home country to villages on the island. The best example is the Glen Cove–Polorós connection; but there are others as well, such as those linking Westbury's neighborhood New Cassel to Concepción de Oriente, and Brentwood to towns in Morazán Department. The densest Salvadoran settlement is Hempstead, located in central Nassau County. Additional areas of significant Salvadoran and other Latino populations are marked on the map of Long Island (map 1.2), and their 1990 census population figures are listed in table 1.3.

The South Americans

In contrast to the Salvadorans, the South Americans can be found sprinkled amid larger Latino populations. They do not have an ethnic concentration like the Salvadorans (or the Puerto Ricans), and their numbers are much smaller. Thousands of Peruvians live in the New Jersey

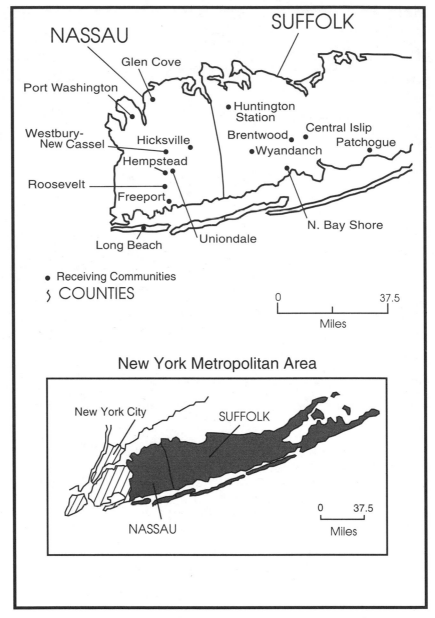

Map 1.2. Map of Long Island, New York, with Communities Receiving
Many Latin American Immigrants

community of Paterson, about fifty miles west of Long Island, and many more live in neighborhoods of Queens, but there is no such community anywhere on Long Island. Nor do the South Americans appear to have developed the community-to-community ties that the Salvadorans exhibit, although people tend to cluster with kin and friends from the same city. Another major difference between the South Americans and the Salvadorans is that there are virtually no peasants or poor among them. "The poor, poor person doesn't come," Pablo Mosquera, a Colombian, told me. "How are the poorest people going to come if they don't have money to pay for the trip?"

Without exception, the Peruvians, Chileans, and Colombians I have met have been from, at a minimum, the most stable strata of the skilled urban working class. This observation is substantiated in tables 1.1–1.3 and by other reports which suggest that poor Peruvians migrate from country to city in Peru and only the middle classes emigrate internationally. "Tens of thousands of peasants have fled to Lima's shanty towns to escape political violence over the past eight years but, in contrast to poor Mexicans and Central Americans who can travel overland to the United States, the cost of leaving here [Lima] has limited the option of emigrating to Peru's middle classes" (*New York Times* January 21, 1989). More often than not, they were professionals with university experience or degrees, small businesspeople, or state employees. Most enjoyed relatively comfortable lives, at least until their countries' economies began to slide downward in the 1970s and 1980s. In general it was declining fortunes, not lack of fortune nor political repression, that drove the South Americans from home. The cost of an illegal entry into the United States from Peru arranged by a "travel agency" currently runs around six thousand dollars. Thus, people must command significant resources to emigrate from a distant place like Peru or Chile. In contrast, Salvadorans need cross only three borders to reach U.S. soil; they incur a more modest travel debt of five hundred to three thousand dollars, albeit this is still an enormous sum for a peasant (see map 1.3).

Juanita Pérez's story is typical of Peruvian immigrants because she emigrated to the United States primarily for economic reasons—her financial security was eroding although not completely threatened. She is one of nine children born to a carpenter who wanted his children to study and become professionals. He died the same year that she left home to study nursing. Her mother then started to work in a monastery, but her role as breadwinner was gradually assumed by the older children. Juanita herself became a nun, living in Colombia for several years, and trained as a nurse. She returned to Peru in order to take care of her mother. After a year of working two jobs as a nurse in Lima yet failing to earn enough to support her mother, Juanita borrowed money and left for the United States.

Map 1.3. The United States and Latin America, Migration up the Isthmus

Among South American immigrants, and unlike the Salvadorans, men and women seem to be equally represented in the migration. According to 1990 census figures for persons over age sixteen (those most likely to be migrants), sex ratios for Colombians and Peruvians, two representative South American populations, are nearly equivalent. Among Salvadorans, however, there is a marked disproportion—nearly 60 percent of all adults are male. There is also a bias toward South American emigrants in their thirties and forties, people who have left families behind or who have delayed having children while they seek their fortune in the United States. Often South Americans have also had English-language classes in their home countries. Although most did not use English there, they tend to pick up at least a rudimentary knowledge of it, driven by the recognition that this skill will open more doors to them. This may account for the overrepresentation of South Americans in the ESL classes I visited all over the island.

Despite their striking distinctions of class and national origin, there are several commonalities between my South and Central American interviewees. First, nearly all of them at the time of my research were undocumented. (This has changed recently, as I will discuss in chapter 7, such that most now have at least temporary permission to be in the country.) Their undocumented status placed them on near-equal footing in the United States, a factor that significantly diluted the role class background could play in their prospects for success. Second, they are overwhelmingly first-generation immigrants. That is, it is they who have migrated, and not their parents or grandparents. Most of my informants have children, but the vast majority of these children live in their home countries. Because both migratory streams are very recent, the children born to immigrants in the United States tend to be very young. The first wave is just beginning to enter grade school. According to New York State public health data, far more Salvadorans will be in this cohort than members of any other group. In 1988, for instance, Nassau County recorded 540 births to Salvadoran mothers (one-sixth of all births to immigrant women), compared to 116 for Colombians, 54 for Peruvians, and 35 for Chileans.

Finally, and most important, regardless of country of origin and class background, all shared disillusionment with their experiences as immigrants in the United States. Most arrived in the country full of optimism—although, as I shall discuss in the next chapter, these aspirations do not explain why they left their homelands, only why they chose to come to the United States over other possible countries. Within a short time after their arrival, however, my informants' optimism waned; they become embittered, angry, and desirous of returning home. The transformation of their perspectives will be documented throughout this text. But before I begin to narrate their stories, I will briefly explain the methodologies I employed to gain access to these immigrants.

ACCESS AND METHODS

Undocumented immigrants live not only in the shadows of the law but also on the margins of mainstream society. Sonia Acevedo lived in the damp basement separated from my apartment by two floors and a rickety ladder; Yolanda Pacheco (Edgar's wife) and I met at an ESL class; and Guatemalan Vidal Portillo helped me buy an inspection sticker for my fieldwork car when it flunked an emissions test. Undocumented immigrants are not the kind of people who can be studied easily through traditional social science methodologies such as random surveys and structured interviews. They carry no scarlet letter to identify them as undocumented immigrants, but they are different from other foreigners—legal permanent residents ("green card" holders), naturalized citizens, and visitors. That is, they do not enjoy legal status to reside or work in the United States, and they often participate in elaborate efforts to avoid detection. Their isolation from mainstream American society has been exacerbated in recent years by the effects of the Immigration Reform and Control Act (IRCA) of 1986. As I shall explain further in chapters 5 and 7, IRCA was passed as a measure to thwart undocumented immigration through restricting employment opportunities. Before IRCA, foreigners who lacked work authorization could not legally obtain jobs in the United States; if they found work, however, their employers were not liable, only the immigrants themselves. IRCA imposed sanctions on such employers to close this loophole. After IRCA, fewer employers were willing to risk sanctions by hiring undocumented workers, and this pushed these workers still further from the mainstream economy. Consequently, one of the areas where undocumented workers concentrate, in part because they are less likely to be found by the INS, is in domestic employment. Even if they work for Americans, however, immigrants enjoy little exposure to the life of Middle America, because they retreat to ethnically segregated neighborhoods after work and remain there when they have time to socialize. To study them requires finding them; to find them requires patient, exhaustive networking; to understand them requires entering their communities and earning their trust—a result that I achieved by building social ties of mutual interdependence.

Since the immigrants had information I wished to gather from them, I approached them with the hope that I too had information which would benefit them. Principally I could offer them my skills as a bilingual interpreter, my knowledge of immigration law and practice from my years of casework, my services as chauffeur and translator, and my general knowledge of the way things work in the United States. I typically found that as soon as I spoke to people in Spanish, they were so pleased to be able to speak to a "real" American that they were quite willing to speak freely. On several occasions my motives were questioned—not by the immigrants, but by others who worked with them— and I was ultimately redeemed by my connections with well-known organizations serving the immigrant community, as well as by my own reputation as a person knowledgeable of immigration law.

I began the preliminary stage of my fieldwork in early 1989 by contacting several formal and informal organizations working with undocumented Salvadorans on Long Island. As previously mentioned, I decided to focus my study on Salvadorans because I had worked closely with many in the preparation of their asylum claims and knew that they had compelling personal experiences. I also knew that little research had been conducted on Salvadorans to date and felt my work could contribute new dimensions to the immigration literature. Although my fieldwork would carry me in directions that I never imagined at this point, the approach I originally proposed, a threefold field methodology, was executed largely as planned. First, I decided to spend a large amount of time scouring Long Island's two counties, Nassau and Suffolk, to learn where Salvadorans lived and the basics of their lives. I used this time to locate and interview members of organizations working with them and to determine whether there were any voluntary associations such as clubs or athletic organizations that the immigrants had formed themselves. During these months I went to numerous ESL classes, church events (both Catholic and Evangelical),[4] dances, parties, and so on. I collected 350 anonymous questionnaires, primarily from students at ESL classes, and I informally interviewed hundreds of other immigrants at these gatherings. This information was used to explore hypotheses about their experiences as well as to identify concerns of theirs that I had not thought of previously.

The second phase of the methodology was to conduct extensive interviews among informants with whom I had developed strong relationships during the first phase. A few of these interviewees were found through the "snowball" method (Cornelius 1982): I would interview a person with whom I had developed a trusting relationship and that person would associate me with other people. I completed forty-two interviews, as well as six with immigrants who had been among the first to come to Long Island. These interviews, all conducted in Spanish and later translated by me into English, often lasted five or more hours and required several reschedulings owing to my informants' demanding work schedules. The third prong of my methodology was an intensive community study. After many months of preliminary research, I relocated to Gold Coast on the North Shore of Long Island in the winter of 1990. I moved into a Salvadoran settlement neighborhood, living and working there intensively for six months. The formal period of field research ended in the late fall of 1990, some eighteen months after I had begun. I remained in Gold Coast until the summer of 1992 and have maintained my contacts since then through phone calls and follow-up research conducted in 1994–1995.

Before closing this discussion of the methodologies I employed in my research, I feel compelled to address the issue of representativeness. I have written this book as a case study of immigrants living in a particular part of the United States. Any arguments I put forth that are extendable to other immigrant groups or to the immigrant experience as a whole are welcome but not explicitly proposed. However, I am responsible for the representativeness of my informants vis-à-vis the universe of undocumented Latino immigrants on Long Island. The extensive interviews provide the voices most frequently heard throughout this text. This is due in part to the difficult and time-consuming task of arranging for, conducting, and transcribing interviews. I also rely strongly on them primarily because this format empowers immigrants to speak for themselves as much as possible in this book. They communicate their experiences most vividly. The interviewees were not selected randomly, although they were consciously selected from different immigrant populations and from various communities on Long Island. Nor are the questionnaires I collected at ESL classes representative in a statistical sense because they were not drawn at random and because they were self-administered (students illiterate in Spanish were assisted to the degree possible by me and ESL teachers).

What gives me confidence that the stories told on the following pages are representative is my contact with thousands of immigrants over many years. Each counseling session or casual encounter was treated as an opportunity for asking basic questions about family, occupation, and place of origin. The five or fifteen minutes were tapped for testing hypotheses and other immigrants' stories. When, after dozens of conversations, however brief, I received similar responses, I felt confident that the story I had heard from *Fulana* (a "name" meaning So-and-so) was accurate. When I had received conflicting responses, I used those minutes to clarify them. And when this did not resolve the confusion, I consulted other immigrants or people with long-standing contact in the immigrant communities. Consequently, the detailed ethnographic evidence offered in this book has been selected to shed light on common experiences and dilemmas my informants faced. But as much as possible I have them communicate their stories unmediated except by translation.

The Scope of the Book

This book is the outcome of my quest to address several theoretical questions while providing a holistic and intimate account of immigrants' lives before, during, and after their journeys. Chapter 2 begins their saga by presenting the historical background leading to their decisions to abandon their homelands. The detachment process is documented in their words in chapter 3 as they travel to the United States and to a new world. In chapter 4 I juxtapose their expectations for life in the United States with their early disillusionments, particularly the treatment they receive from their compatriots in their first days here. This chapter introduces their alieneation from home country traditions. Then in chapter 5, I detail how these immigrants are marginalized from mainstream American society as well. Consequently, many immigrants' needs are not met by mainstream institutions. The marginalization buffers the mainstream from criticism for these deficiencies and also opens up niches of opportunity for immigrant entrepreneurs to fill.

Undocumented immigrants find their greatest opportunity for socioeconomic mobility within their ethnic community. Where the greater society fails to meet the needs of immigrants at affordable prices and with a modicum of convenience, immigrants step in to meet their own needs. They learn how to squeeze profits out of their communities by operating as informal entrepreneurs providing services and products to coethnics, though these efforts do not evolve into ethnic enclaves or business niches in the mainstream. In so doing, they generate institutions largely parallel to the mainstream society's where a small group of entrepreneurs can profit. For instance, when immigrants discover that they have to pay rent in the United States—an expense they never faced to the same degree in their homelands—they devise ways to organize the rental of housing to minimize their payments or, in some cases, actually to make money. When they discover that private cars are essential to transportation on Long Island, they offset the maintenance costs by using these vehicles as informal taxis for their compatriots. As I will detail in chapters 6 through 8 of this book, these activities rarely constitute what we normally think of as "businesses." They are little more than imaginative strategies for achieving goals immigrants find difficult to meet, given the limited opportunities available to them. Though these efforts become institutionalized as many immigrants copy them, they do not result in the formation of a true ethnic enclave because these people are still critically dependent upon the larger society—for jobs in particular but also for many services.

An examination of this construction of their own institutions offers insight as to why my informants hold their coethnics in low esteem.

Through the process of acculturating to their new lives, what I call the acquisition of "immigrant capital," they learn that people take advantage of them in ways generally prohibited in their homelands. They arrive expecting to be exploited by "Americans" but find that they are also victimized by their own. Everyone comes saddled with the burden of generating significant income—more than needed for their mere sustenance—in order to pay off travel debts, send money home, and accrue savings for the return to their countries. These pressures lead to the suspension of many social rules that conditioned life before migration. These immigrants thus come to the United States expecting to find their old community solidarity, but encounter a competitive, aggressive subculture instead. American dreaming becomes American disillusionment. This is the *immigrants'* perspective on their experience, and I feel it must be voiced and explained, but not uncritically. As an outsider, I frequently witnessed acts of cooperation and generosity among these people. Theirs is not a Hobbesian world; neither is it a Promised Land.

Chapter Two

LEAVING HOME

BENJAMÍN VELÁSQUEZ is from Chalatenango Department in El Salvador, an area that borders Honduras. Now in his forties, Benjamín has never married; he has dedicated his life to assisting his family. In Chalatenango, he and his family owned a parcel of land on which they grew corn and beans. Benjamín supplemented their income by selling cattle. Their lives were harsh but survivable until two events changed them forever. First, Benjamín was falsely accused by the Salvadoran National Guard of collaboration with antigovernment rebels, jailed, and nearly killed; shortly afterward, their village was burned to the ground in a military confrontation between the guerrillas and the Salvadoran Armed Forces. Benjamín and his family lost everything they owned, and they were not allowed to go back to their village. When I asked him what made him decide to leave his country, he responded, "When I was let go, it was then that I became convinced that many others had died in the same way that I almost died—because the *guardias* [National Guardsmen or rural military force] didn't bother to investigate accusations. I was deeply shocked and as soon as I could, I left to come to the U.S."

As illustrated by this vignette, migration is preceded by a process of uprooting. Once people are wrenched from the familiar, they face the task of deciding where to go. It is important to recognize that migration has two essential components: leaving one area and going to another. Oftentimes people conflate these two distinct movements, assuming, for instance, that everyone is anxious to come to the United States and that this is sufficient reason for them to leave their homelands. Scholarship on migration once took a similar, simplistic focus. The "push-pull" or equilibrium model focused on individuals, how forces pushed them out of their homelands and pulled them toward certain host societies. The equilibrium approach has been criticized by many scholars, often referred to as the historico-structural school, who argue that it ignores supraindividual factors that influence the initiation, direction, and termination of migrations. I take up this discussion at the end of the chapter, linking U.S. foreign policy and aid toward El Salvador to the eventual exile in the United States of one-sixth of that country's population.

For now, I will argue through personal testimonies that there are complex and compelling reasons for why people abandon their homelands. Few of my informants, for example, stated that they came to the United States for fun or adventure. The journey was too expensive to be undertaken whimsically. Nor did many come with the intention of staying permanently. They told me that they wanted to go home when conditions there improved. In fact, most described their lives in their homelands as much happier and more satisfied than their lives in the United States—at least until significant events changed these home lives for the worse. It took enormous political and economic changes to get them to abandon their countries, phenomena that I will describe in detail after depicting my informants' lives prior to these changes.

MEMORIES OF HOME

Since El Salvador is one of the poorest countries in the Western hemisphere, readers might expect to hear someone describe a peasant life there in unflattering terms. Contrarily, Salvadoran immigrants of peasant roots rarely do so. Rather, they reminisce fondly about life in their small *caseríos* or hamlets, often employing the Salvadoran saying, *Donde deja el ombligo, nunca se olvida* (You never forget the place where you left your umbilical cord). High population density ensures that many relatives live close by and that there is little privacy in the countryside. Consequently, relationships are reinforced daily. Interdependence is not only commonplace but a necessary means of assuring everyone's survival, given the marginal living that peasants scratch from the earth. Most of my informants from rural El Salvador look back upon this life as very hard but much more rewarding than their lives in the United States because of the strong sense of community people shared. Reminiscence often casts a favorable light on the past, and there is no bona fide ethnography of rural Salvadoran life prior to the civil war against which I can compare my informants' recollections. However, the theme of community sacrificed in the migration process arose so repeatedly among my informants that it seemed unlikely to be merely an artifact of reminiscence. They felt strongly that the common courtesies and reciprocities of their home country lives had not migrated to the United States with them. Sister Maria Villatoro grew up in a tightly knit village with her large family. Everyone worked together and helped each other, she remembers fondly. "It was a very small village where we lived," she began. "Everyone knew each other. Over there, any one person's problems were shared by the rest. It is a community. Even now I know that people help each other out economically. Sometimes my mother didn't have corn to make tortillas to give us and an aunt would lend her corn or, if we didn't have beans to eat with the tortillas, other people would give them to us. It was really nice this way.

"There are no *milpas* [small garden plots] in this area, only coffee plantations. Thanks to God my father had a place for our house but nothing more. Others didn't have even that. But they helped each other to give them a place to build their house. They also shared their lands because my father gave several of my uncles land to build their houses on. They made them out of *bahareque* (wattle and daub), which is the way they are built over there. They are very humble houses made of earth and with only one room. Some people had half a *manzana* [0.7 hectare = 1 manzana] of coffee land. They picked this during the harvest season of November and December. They'd pick their own and then go and work on other farms, farms that were much larger and where the harvest lasted longer."

People such as Don José Prudencio describe Salvadoran town life in similar terms of reciprocity and neighborliness. Now in his forties, Don José owned a store in Usulatán Department. His middle-class status there earned him the patronage title "Don," which he still carries in the United States although he has worked here only itinerantly as a laborer. He recalls innumerable family and friends, even strangers, who would stay with his family and receive unrestricted hospitality indefinitely. He could not help comparing his past with life in the United States. "Here things are very different," he explained. "In El Salvador a peasant has his own house; he's a peasant but he has his own house. He has a cow to give him milk. He doesn't use oil, he doesn't pay for fuel because he has firewood. . . . Everyone collects firewood. . . . So you don't pay for the wood; you don't pay for water because there is a tank and you go and get your water. . . . You don't pay for light, you don't pay any type of taxes. You plant beans, rice, corn, and feed for the animals and chiles. You also have your own chickens, pigs, cows; you have your own horses and so you don't have to buy anything. . . . So those people who are not lazy always have enough to live on. They can always survive even if they don't have a salary. . . . People live, yes they live poorly, logically, because if they have no salary then they will live poorly. But they live. Here they can't live; if a person here doesn't have a salary then how is he going to live? There aren't any charitable institutions to help people. The Catholic Church helps in some areas but not in all areas nor in all the cities here on Long Island. That is, here things are very different. Life is very hard. You feel the change. Anyone will give you a place to stay for a night or two and sometimes more but here no one can really give shelter freely if they are paying rent. They don't want to have any freeloaders because this is too expensive. This is the problem. There is a big change here; the willingness of Hispanics [to help each other] always exists, the brotherhood to help each other . . . Thus, help exists when you can help. But there are times when you can't help. And that's the reality." Just before coming to the United States Don José used his pickup truck to ferry dozens of families who were fleeing the violence in the countryside. He received death threats for doing so, but he continued undaunted until another man, driving his truck, was ambushed and killed. This event convinced him to flee his homeland.

Pablo Mosquera also could not resist comparing his new life in the United States with the one he had left behind in Colombia. Pablo and his wife, Raquel, came to the United States over ten years ago. They came with their young son who is mentally retarded, seeking treatment for him. But they started out living in dilapidated apartments, working two or three jobs and leaving the boy with strangers almost all day. Lacking health insurance, they could get few services for him. They subsequently became legal immigrants and a few years ago bought their own house, although the mortgage payments require that each works long days and their son still comes home to an empty house. Pablo misses the family togetherness that characterized their home life in Colombia. "We lived very well in Colombia. We lived very well. That is, we worked five days per week, eight hours a day. We lived together. We spent time with the family; we had time to enjoy ourselves, to go out and travel to places—to enjoy life. Not here! [He laughs.] Here it is very different; here there is no time to be together. There we lived well, ate well, and we earned good money, enough to live off. I like life here a lot but life is very different. Here you have to have two jobs in order to survive and, many times, you have to work a different shift than your spouse. Many times husbands and wives don't see each other at all or very little. Many times, as in my case with [my wife], I have to work Saturdays and Sundays and Fridays and she is in the house alone with [our son]. This has been going on for ten years. And life is limited. I am looking for another job because [my wife] can't stand this life any more, nor [my son]. He's always alone. My job demands it."

Manuel Sosa, his wife Berta, and their good friend Alfredo Pineda also shared with me reminiscences of their past lives in the northern Peruvian city of Trujillo. Berta and Alfredo were schoolteachers; Manuel held an office job in a telecommunications company. Their lives were intertwined as *compadres*, or fictive kin (godparents to each other's children). During several long conversations with them I learned how Alfredo would zip by Manuel and Berta's house and give her a lift to school on his moped, sometimes dropping off fresh milk as well. On weekends their families socialized, and they could never be absent from each other's birthday parties. After years of hard work and patronizing the Peruvian bureaucracy, each family had bought a modest, government-subsidized house in the same neighborhood. Theirs was a neighborhood of hardworking dreamers, people laying claim to middle-classdom during the early 1980s. They shared the buoyancy of social mobility. But in the mid-1980s an economic crisis shattered their vision and threatened their status as homeowners. This is what motivated them to come to the United States, Manuel explained. But he quickly regretted his action when he learned that "life here is a life of fantasy, no more. . . . It's a life of work more than anything else. In our country there is time to do other things."

Many of my informants could not describe their past lives without quickly jumping to the changes that had disrupted those lives. Gilberto Canales remembers life with his family in rural La Unión Department of El Salvador as tranquil, at least until a wave of repression hit at the end of the 1970s. His life, heretofore hardscrabble but happy, would never be the same. Gilberto lost his father and a brother to the war; he himself was tortured. He recalls how conditions changed irrevocably: "I remember that before when the moon was out as it is today it illuminated everything and you could walk peacefully. You slept in the fields, watching over the cows. If you stayed out at night with friends and came home late, no one said anything. But afterward the guerrillas and the army started fighting. The worst thing was when the army started taking people out of their homes. After that no one would go out, or if they went out it was difficult to know if they would return. And if they returned, it wasn't good for them to go out. They would arrive and accuse you of being a guerrilla, even if you weren't involved in anything. How could you challenge that? . . . They would throw out bodies, without heads, without hands, without feet. You would go outside and find dead bodies, with the hands tied, heads missing or stuck on top of poles. Sometimes you would find five or ten, two or four bodies. Sometimes they had been killed by the military, sometimes by the guerrillas. . . . In our case, they killed my father and my brother. So some, those who had courage, they joined the guerrillas. And if the guerrillas killed someone, then the victim's brothers joined the army. That's why there have been so many attacks. . . . That's why this war escalated so much."

Gilberto's rapid shift from fond to morose memories was commonplace among my Salvadoran informants, perhaps because I asked informants many questions about their hometowns and then posed the pointed question, "What is your strongest memory from your life in this place?" The word "strongest" initiated an introspection I had anticipated, one that served to open the topic of the civil war. But for each of these informants it also served as a starting block from which we would run through the factors leading up to their emigrations.

By and large, my informants left their homelands reluctantly because of dire circumstances. Salvadorans invariably were quick to insist that they did not want to leave their homeland. "I came here *por la situación*," they would invariably say, "because of the situation." In my former capacity as an immigration counselor preparing asylum claims, I had learned how to get past this noncommittal euphemism. The phrase "I came here because of the situation" reflects people's adaptation to a war in which they had to actively profess neutrality. "The people could favor neither side, not even think about leaning toward one side," Nicolás Guzmán told me. At fifteen, he came to the United States because the military were trying to recruit him to fight the guerrillas. He had no interest in fighting for either side. "People had to stay in the middle. Because if they sided with one group then they would die, they'd be killed. So they had to be really calm, *tranquilo*. . . . My fear was finding myself in the cross fire between the two groups and, in the middle of them all, dying. . . . I didn't want to serve in the *cuartel* [garrison] nor alongside the guerrillas. *El miedo mío era que no morir ni de yo matar* [I feared killing or being killed]."

Any identification of a person with either the left, the guerrillas, or the right, the Armed Forces and elite families, would invite retaliation. In many cases, as Don José testifies, innocent people were fingered for personal retaliations. "Those who have had enemies have sought revenge against them because those who had enemies used to, as we say crudely, 'point the finger' at someone. They would point someone out as being a guerrilla when he really wasn't a guerrilla. 'So-and-so is a guerrilla; so-and-so helps the guerrillas.' So then the authorities would take this person away. And in the beginning they didn't get testimonies or give the captured person a chance to defend himself. Instead, without justifying these claims some people were decapitated. So people would be found dead and, perhaps, with a flyer stuck in his pocket that the guerrillas use as propaganda. So when they want to kill someone they plant one of these papers on the person so the people will say, 'That guy was a guerrilla,' but it's not true. For this reason, of the 70,000 deaths that there have been in El Salvador, 10,000 were guilty but 60,000 were innocent. The vast majority were innocent. Also, in some cities there have been people who are paid to point the finger at others. So someone who didn't want to get his hands dirty would pay another. In the city of Suchitoto, there is a woman named 'the one who wears makeup' who, according to a story I was told by the inspector of electrical systems, had fingered 60 people and all had died."

El Salvador: Roots of the Civil War

The reign of terror that characterized life in El Salvador from 1979 to 1992, when a peace accord was signed, coincides with a massive refugee flow out of the country and into Mexico and the United States. Current estimates of the number of Salvadorans resident in the United States hover around one million; one in every six Salvadorans now lives in the United States, and the majority of them arrived after the beginning of the civil war.[1] Some researchers have even correlated escalations in the violence there with surges in apprehensions of undocumented Salvadorans in the United States (Stanley 1987). Of course many factors produced the civil war; although an in-depth discussion of them lies outside the scope of this book, many are linked to my informants' experiences as root causes of their decisions to leave El Salvador.

El Salvador's violent history has been and continues to be the saga of an export oligarchy and a powerful military coupled with the ongoing disenfranchisement of the vast peasant majority from the land. Perhaps the most fundamental problem facing El Salvador is that of land. It is a tiny country with a large population. Additionally, it is a very poor country where most people are subsistence peasants, semiproletarianized rural workers, or urban shantytown dwellers. About the size of Massachusetts but with close to six million inhabitants, El Salvador is densely populated (Woodward 1985). Population density is not the key cause of poverty, however; highly inegalitarian land tenure and cash crop production are (Santana Cardoso 1975; Armstrong and Shenk 1982; Durham 1979).[2] Since the nineteenth century, most of the best agricultural lands have been held by fewer than fifty powerful landowning families who use them to grow crops for export such as coffee, cotton, and sugar (Barry 1987). The peasantry was systematically pushed off these lands and concentrated in less productive areas. Many peasants became landless and were forced to work for the oligarchical families as *colonos*, or day laborers (Hamilton and Chinchilla 1991). The Armed Forces, including security police and the military, were formed in the late nineteenth century to enforce class divisions and the subservience of the peasantry (Armstrong and Shenk 1982).

Land ownership concentration and the development of cash crops squeezed the peasantry off most of the land and many into a seasonal migratory lifestyle. This was the first stage in their uprooting. During the planting and harvesting seasons for food staples they would live in their small villages and grew their own crops on small plots of land that they owned or rented. During the fallow months, peasants would migrate to the coffee-, cotton-, and sugar-producing areas and harvest these crops, for which they received modest cash wages. Any attempt by these peasants to improve their working conditions on the large farms was thwarted by the Armed Forces. The most famous example was the 1932 *Matanza*. In that year—a year during the Great Depression when world coffee prices had plummeted and with them workers' wages—coffee workers protested and were slaughtered. Thirty thousand are estimated to have died, and a great lesson was imprinted on the minds of the peasantry (Anderson 1971).

During the years between the *Matanza* and the start of the civil war, conditions continued to deteriorate as the population grew and more lands were put into production for export. A solution to the crisis was sought through urbanization and industrialization, but this sector never became as highly developed as anticipated (Pearce 1986; Gordon 1989). In fact, urbanization in El Salvador never even approached the rates achieved in much less densely populated countries in Latin America (World Bank 1979). Some people sought to improve their economic conditions by emigrating to neighboring Honduras, others intensified crop production on their small lands (Hamilton and Chinchilla 1991), but few emigrated to the United States. Peasant informants explained their reluctance to migrate to the cities, saying that in those areas they would have to pay for everything. "Things are difficult for you on your *rancho* [little farm]," Santos insisted, "but you have enough with your few beans and little corn—at least this is guaranteed. But to go to a town where you don't have anything, that's hard because in a town you have to buy firewood, you have to buy *everything*. And the government is not going to help out."[3]

But where urbanization existed, it catalyzed the formation of labor organizations and unions, which militated through the 1970s for improved wages and working conditions. Salvadoran governments maintained a policy of repressing such initiatives, and during this period several resistance groups—both urban and rural—were formed (see Cabarrús [1983]; Armstrong and Shenk [1982]). The resistance did not become unified into the FDR-FMLN[4] front until 1980, a year after the civil war formally began following a military coup. The FDR-FMLN represents one side, or *bando*, of the conflict and the Salvadoran Armed Forces (including police units, the National Guard, and the army) represent the other. During the 1980s, the war also began to disrupt the delicate cycle of survival that the peasants had created over many years of deteriorating land tenure conditions; no longer was it possible to produce subsistence crops peacefully since combatants on both sides of the conflict either burned them or ate them, and the cash crops, the one source of hard currency, became too dangerous to harvest. Consequently, some peasants began to abandon the countryside, and, as a second stage in their uprooting, they sought refuge in small towns. This was not wholly satisfactory because these people possessed few marketable skills and had little money to buy food and other necessities. Others began to populate refugee camps both inside the country and along the Honduran border, and a steady stream migrated northward into Mexico and the United States. The closure, mandated by the war, of internal migration as an economic strategy translated into international migration. Already accustomed to a transient lifestyle, such migrant laborers had to extend the distance of their travels and the duration of their sojourns.

Salvadorans Describe the War

The brutality of the civil war, which left some seventy thousand dead—one of every one hundred citizens—is often noted. But the conflict tends to be presented facelessly, such that it is difficult to picture its impact on ordinary Salvadorans. One individual caught up in the clash was Sister Maria. She grew up as the oldest child of a large colono family. Like many of my rural informants, she spent many years migrating with her father to the coffee harvests in western El Salvador. "We used the [coffee] season to make money to buy our notebooks, our uniforms, pencils—that is, to pay for school or to buy a new piece of clothing," she told me. "This was the only time when you could earn money. . . . You became very happy because you were going to go pick coffee with your whole family. It's like a holiday because everyone gets happy because they are earning money—sometimes to pay what they have borrowed during the winter when there is no work." But later, she said, "it changed because it got very dangerous to be on the farms. . . . The guerrillas held strikes so that the salaries would be raised but the soldiers would arrive to guard the farms and then they'd end up fighting. People were afraid of dying and so it was better not to go. . . . And then they didn't have enough to live on." One year her family had to stop going to the harvests altogether. "We wanted to go to a place to harvest called *El Tigre*," she recalled. "We had to go there by car and bus because there wasn't any other transportation. They didn't let you pick. I don't know if they were guerrillas or soldiers but they told us that if we picked them they would cut off our hands. He who continued would have his hands cut off. That was when we were at the coffee farms. Some men came and told us, 'No. Today you are not going to pick.' So we paid attention and we didn't pick so that we wouldn't have problems. I always want to avoid problems. But those who insisted on picking had their hands cut off. I saw this myself. Two had their hands mutilated because they didn't obey. If a worker on a coffee hacienda resisted they tied his hands. He had to stop working. . . . [The next year] my father was so fearful that the guerrillas would take us with them that we stayed at home. We didn't work. That was when I had to leave school. I couldn't go to school because my father didn't have the money."

The guerrillas tried to stop the coffee harvest because it was the oligarchy's principal source of income. But they cut off the poor migrant farm workers as well; this often produced resentment against the guerrillas. Another source of resentment was the constant demands made by the guerrillas and the military upon the rural folk like Maria's family: "My mother would have to make tortillas two times a day. As soon as the subversives [guerrillas] would arrive, you had to give them food because if you didn't they would make you do it. A little while later the soldiers would come: 'Señora, we are hungry. We haven't eaten today.' My mother would make them all tortillas. And they would ask, 'Haven't the subversives been here?' And my mother would say, 'No.' No one was able to say anything." The peasantry also suffered because the war made it difficult to sow and reap their crops. Sometimes the government bombed their villages or harvests, accusing people of collaborating with the guerrillas. For many Salvadorans, particularly heads of households, these conditions made it impossible to sustain their families, and they contacted relatives or friends, borrowing money with which to leave the country.

In Sister Maria's case, the war only convinced her further that her mission in life was to help others. She took her vows to become a nun and set out to work with families displaced by the war. This is her story:

"I asked to work in rural areas. It was there that everything, everything changed. . . . In 1985, I [was working with a group of people who had been displaced by the war and] would give catechism to the children. I'd go to their houses to talk to them about God because owing to the conflict people had lost faith in God. They would ask where he is. If God existed then this wouldn't be happening, they'd say, they wouldn't have to live under the rug. Because many of these people lost their own homes when they left, they made their lean-tos and that's where they lived. They didn't have anything to eat and we [nuns] would go and bring them things. I admired these people. I was very happy. Serving others I felt happy, full of enthusiasm until 1986.

"I was assigned to study teaching during the three months of vacation in 1985. The next year I was placed as a kindergarten and first grade teacher. I was transferred to Usulatán and I was there for one year between 1986 and 1987. . . . While I was there I was happy working with the children. I taught them. But on Saturdays I would always leave to go to the *cantones* (rural townships) to give catechism to the children. These were children who couldn't come to the city because it was too far or because their mothers didn't want to bring them. We made a place on the side of the road and we would give them the catechism and then play with them. We made them happy. It was then that the men came. I had the habit of always traveling in the religious community's car. Two men [flagged me down one day and] told me to give them a ride to the other side of town. They stopped me and so I stopped. And they said to me,

'Take us over across town.' It was a difficult route and very far. If I took them I would not arrive home to my community on time. (It was five in the afternoon and at six I had to be with my community because this was the norm there. All of us sisters had to get together in the sanctuary for the mass.) So I told them I couldn't do it, some other day perhaps, but that I didn't have permission. And I couldn't without permission. So I told [the men] that I couldn't take them home. [I was wary of them] because I knew of a doctor who had been kidnapped and had been ransomed for a lot of money. So these might be the same men who had kidnapped this man. [It turned out that they were the same men and] purely by chance I had run into them on the road. So they said, 'Remember this. We are going to keep you in mind. You are going to regret what you have done now.' And I said to them, 'Please. If you are helping the poor as you say, let the doctor go,' because I recognized them. . . . I don't know if they were from one bando or not, if they were guerrillas or soldiers. . . . I didn't do what they wanted me to do [give them a ride] because I couldn't. But about four months later the doctor was let go; when they let him go he was half dead. His ransom had all been paid. His house had been sold and he was practically on the streets. He was a very fine man because he helped the people. At this point I had forgotten the problem I had [with the two men].

"But another day in September I was met by the same two men. They didn't speak; they only grabbed my hand and said, 'Follow me.' . . . And I was dressed as a nun but—I don't know if they were waiting for me or not. They just said, 'Come.' 'Don't say anything,' they told me. 'Don't look back. Don't worry, only follow us.' And so I followed them. I asked them, 'What do you want?' 'We don't have to tell you. You are going to come with us.' 'I'm not going to go with you,' I thought, 'They are probably going to kill me if I do.' 'Take this,' one said, 'so she can't see who it is.' And there was another man with them. By now I had been blindfolded so that I couldn't identify them.

"They took me to a farm where they had other captives. And they said to me, 'You don't want to follow us [join our bando].' 'Ah! Well, kill her then!' the other said. 'No,' he said, 'I will make her be my woman because nuns are only the priests' women but they don't want to be for us.' And I still had the courage to speak and I said, 'When you make me your woman you are going to find out who I am! Because we aren't what you say, we aren't the priests' women. You are going to find out but it will be too late.' This was the only thing I said. Then another man told them, 'Go. You take her.' And they threw me down and covered my mouth. They killed me. Another said, 'Go and make her your woman.' And I heard them. 'No,' he said, 'She is a nun and you can't make her your woman.' [Crying.] And the man just said to me, 'Forgive me,

Mother, for what I am about to do. We are saving our own lives.' He was the one who raped me. After that I don't know what happened to me. I was not myself in that moment. Because I—[crying]. Then they let me go. They said, 'We are going to let you go just for fun. Afterward, if you speak one single word we will kill you and your family too. You, yourself, will go and kill them.' These are the things that they told me.

"After that day my whole life changed completely. In the convent I spent my time crying; I was sad. I couldn't confide in anyone out of fear. [My attackers] would call me on the phone saying that they wanted to talk to Sister [Maria] and what they wanted was to tell me, 'We know. If you leave we will know. You know what you have to do. Say nothing or we will go and get you and we will kill you and everyone in your family, your father and his children.' This is all that they would say. They would call, if it was possible, two or three times per day. And the nuns didn't know anything. And I tried not to show my pain to anyone but when you have something like that inside you, you will always show it. I didn't eat. I thought and thought and the Mother Superior asked me, '[Maria], what is the matter with you?' 'Ay! Sister,' I would say, 'I don't know if I am going crazy.' I didn't want to lie, but who was I going to tell? How could I tell them? Until one day, when I was with my students one child said, 'Mother I have a note for you.' 'And who gave it to you?' I asked. 'A man told me to give it to you.' According to the children it was a note from a friend who was going to come to the school. But for me it was only a [death] sentence. Since the children couldn't read, the men had only told them to bring the note to me. It was [a death threat]. I then asked for a transfer from this convent. I told the Mother that I wanted to move, that I didn't feel good at this place. And they sent me to San Jacinto in the capital to a school. The note was from the same men who had threatened me and it said that if I spoke they would find me.

"But I never thought I would become pregnant. It never, never occurred to me. But when it was time for my period to come it didn't come. And I began to cry and cry—and I said, 'Why? Why? This child will be born but not of love but of violence.' And I didn't want to live. I didn't want to live. Until I got to the point that I lost all faith in God. That God had abandoned me. Why had these things happened? Since I couldn't talk, I couldn't tell the truth, I only told the Provincial Mother that I wanted to leave the convent, that I didn't want to go on. She saw this as very strange. She didn't want me to go. She wanted to get the truth from me. 'Don't do this, Maria. We'll send you to Peru, we'll send you to Africa. But don't leave, you are very good. You are a religious.' I said, 'Mother I can't continue; I don't want to continue.' And this was a lie because it wasn't like that, I wanted to continue. I was very happy there. But the pregnancy made me flee. How was I going to say that I was pregnant? How? And to whom? But I couldn't.

"I left secretly in the morning because they wouldn't give me permission to leave. Since I had taken my vows and was a religious the General and Provincial Mothers had to give me dispensation. But since I didn't wait, they sent it to me here. I just couldn't continue; I was pregnant and I couldn't wait because I would show. But during those three months I always received *anónimos* [anonymous threatening messages]."

"They knew that you had moved?" I asked her softly.

"They knew it very well," she responded.

"And you never found out who they were?"

"I never—I think that they were people I knew."

"Why do you think they selected you?" I inquired.

"Because I was very attractive—not physically but because I motivated many people. I had a lot of responsibilities. [The people] don't know why I left but many lament my having left. And I don't know who, why, nor to what end."

"And your daughter was born last year?"

"She was born in July." [Begins to cry.]

"When you left could you confide this to anyone?"

"No. Not even to my mother. My mother found out only two months ago that I have a daughter."

Maria borrowed the money for her trip from a cousin living on Long Island without telling her or anyone else why she was leaving El Salvador. When she was reunited with her family in the United States after an anguishing trip, her cousin spied her bulging abdomen and asked, "You came out of the convent pregnant? What happened?" Maria begged her not to tell anyone the story. Several months later Maria's daughter was born, but the hospital delayed her departure because Maria, penniless, had no clothes to dress her in.

Jesús Argueta is also a peasant from El Salvador. His story illustrates how difficult it is to separate out political from economic factors in refugees' decisions to flee their countries. Jesús is the only person who openly confided to me that he had unwittingly collaborated with the guerrillas. He is in his late thirties and has distinctly Indian features. His wife and six children live in El Salvador, and Jesús returned to rejoin them in early 1993. He, like so many others, has tried to return to the United States but has been unsuccessful owing to his detection in Mexico and subsequent deportation. Jesús was abandoned by his parents at birth and raised by his grandmother, only to be disinherited by her when he reached adulthood. Landless, he struggled to buy property, often spending months picking coffee in Santa Ana Department. "After about four years I had paid off all of my loans and had a house, and I began to work more and more for myself," he told me. "I planted three manzanas of corn. I got some big harvests and a hell of a lot of corn—twenty or thirty sacks of corn. I had enough corn to sell and to eat with. It was then that things started to go bad for me." About this time, in the early 1980s, Jesús was forcibly recruited to serve four years with the local Civil Defense command. (The Civil Defense was a paramilitary force that conscripted local men and pressed them into service, primarily to defend their local towns against the guerrilla forces. In El Salvador, as elsewhere in Central America, the Civil Defense has been used to control the peasantry and to actively discourage peasant collaboration with the insurgents.)

After fulfilling his active service term with the Civil Defense, Jesús was required to pay five colones (Salvadoran currency) per week in lieu of service. Shortly thereafter, the guerrillas came to his home demanding that he pay them a "war tax" or join their forces. Jesús believes that they targeted him because he had personal enemies who had already joined the guerrillas. "There were some guys who were with guerrillas and they were my enemies," he explained. "It was because of this that they started to attack me because they said that I was ambitious. What was I going to do? There was no other way but for me to collaborate. I was aware of the war and politics because it was necessary but I never treated anyone like they treated me. They came by my house one night, some forty armed men, to take me away and kill me. And I was about two minutes from being killed. My oldest boy and my oldest girl, who was about five months old then, were home too. *Púchica!* You feel it deep down! They asked me where I had a pistol hidden. This was their method to make me nervous. How was I going to run around with a *pinche* [damned] pistol, I said. They had the idea that I had been given this gun by the army and I was serving the commander [of the local militia]. 'What are you doing with a pistol? You can help out the war [i.e., join the guerrillas],' he said.

"I had a lot of bags of beans, about eight sacks of beans, and they started to search the sacks with their hands looking for this pistol. And I had sacks of corn too, some of it hadn't been stripped from the husks yet. 'You have the means to pay a war tax. Why don't you collaborate?' they asked me. They hadn't talked to me about collaboration, about justice, I said. 'I don't have to pay something I don't owe. I have a right to the land,' I said. Then they hit me with the first war tax, 150 pesos [colones]. I had to borrow them. This was in 1983. After that they began demanding a monthly 'collaboration.' At the very least I had to give them 25 pesos. Afterward it wasn't just the war taxes I had to pay but I had to do other things as well. Well, I wasn't dumb; I had talked to others about the war, about politics, and I wasn't afraid. But later on,

I couldn't find a solution because they were taking a lot of money from me. They 'visited' me too much. Sometimes people would hear about it and I feared they'd tell the Guardia [National Guard]. They're going to find a way to do away with me or—I don't know what. . . . I decided that I had to help them in another way, so that's when I started to buy them things but I didn't want them to come to my house."

After several years of paying war taxes to the guerrillas, Jesús could no longer afford them. When he stopped paying, the guerrillas forced him to pay his taxes in labor and he began work as a "mule," transporting food to the guerrilla camps at night. He told me that for over a year he went virtually without sleep because during the day he had to work his own land and at night he would have to carry heavy cargoes for the guerrillas. The lack of rest damaged his health, causing him to lose twenty pounds. Ultimately he was exhausted to the point that he became too ill to work.

During his service to the guerrillas, Jesús lived perilously close to death at all times. He could not work for the guerrillas during the day because he might be seen—either by the military or by his neighbors—denounced, and killed. But the guerrillas would kill him if he stopped helping them or joined the military. At one point the danger came to a head. "I was detained by the military," he recalled. "I was carrying a sack of corn when the military detained me. In those days it was hard because the mere act of going to another town was enough to incriminate you. They accused you without your having committed any crime. When I was carrying that sack of corn a soldier said that I was taking it to the guerrillas. I told him that I was not a guerrilla." Jesús says that boys (under the age of twelve) were frequently recruited as runners for the guerrillas because the military were less likely to bother them than older youth. Consequently, they could successfully get messages through areas controlled by the military.[5]

His direct experience has taught him a lot about how both sides work. He says that you have to be astute, that "if you aren't real sharp then you can fall into the trap in a lot of ways. If it isn't with the guerrillas then it's with the soldiers. So you have to know each side's politics. I know the politics of each side; I know how each side maneuvers. But there are times when it's the fault of the people. Because they hear a little bit of noise and they say, 'So-and-so is a guerrilla!' And you have to tell him to be careful because both sides are the same. Because someone who knows the politics has to tell the others so that not so many die. If not, one single person can cost you the entire caserío." Jesús's experience was especially harsh: he lost an agricultural cooperative he had started with other peasants, he lost most of his crops, he lost his health, and his children grew malnourished.

Jesús was repressed by both bandos, from the left and from the right, over the course of several years. Despite losing his health and his land, Jesús withstood the pressures until 1988 when his crops were destroyed by a drought. At the end of that year, unable to feed his family or travel to the coffee harvests to earn money, and fearful for his own life, Jesús finally contacted a friend who had already traveled to the United States, borrowed fifteen hundred dollars, and left. Leaving was very hard. His twin daughters were only a year old, and one of them was very sick. But he knew he could no longer provide for his family by staying in El Salvador.

"Why do people leave El Salvador?" I asked him, and he responded: "If you get involved with the military, you die; if you go with the others, it's the same. This makes you think about coming here; perhaps to help your children too. Sometimes you don't have any way to help them, give them vitamins, buy them clothes, shoes. If there were no war there, there would be no reason to come here. Because you can produce a lot in El Salvador, it's a good place to work."

To this point I have selected only rural Salvadorans to give testimony; this does not mean that urban El Salvador was spared by the violence. Quite to the contrary, urban informants such as Edgar Pacheco and his wife Yolanda offer gripping confirmation of the war's devastating impact on their lives. Edgar is the son of a shoemaker, now in his late twenties. He was born in the countryside but moved to San Salvador at a tender age. He met Yolanda there, and they fell in love despite her family's objections. Yolanda is from a middle-class family and was trained as a secretary. Both had children by other common-law spouses before they met and married in the mid-1980s. Yolanda's mother migrated to the United States shortly thereafter and found a job working as a live-in domestic. As Yolanda's descriptions of life in San Salvador became more horrific, Yolanda's mother encouraged her to leave. But Yolanda was less worried about herself than about her husband and brother, who were constantly at risk of being recruited by the military in the city or by the guerrillas if they traveled to the countryside. "You can be in your neighborhood," she explained, "and see that a truck has pulled up and has started to recruit, and what the military does is wait for the youth to return to their houses from work. They catch them when they get off the buses coming home from work so that their own communities don't find out that they have been taken off. So what you have to do is get very close to the truck and watch to make sure that no one that you know has been taken and, if so, to see what you can do to get them out. They take them and then they don't give them enough training before they send them to the front lines and they come home with their legs mutilated because they haven't gotten enough training to know how to defend themselves. And this is something that you have to be constantly worried about. In my case, I would come home from work and would hear that they were recruiting nearby, and I would run out of the house fearful for my brother and husband. When I would meet one of them coming back I would say 'Thank God. Go back home and don't leave!' Then I'd go out again until I met the other and if it got late and I still hadn't met him I would start wringing my hands and thinking, 'What might have happened?' And I'd wait a little bit more and worry because they never tell you when they are going to recruit. It's really difficult, it tortures you psychologically. You're never at ease. When they leave the house you never know if they will return."

As if the mental strain of the conflict were not enough, the civil war also brought further economic pressures. The company where Yolanda worked began failing, and she worried about losing her job. The economy in El Salvador plummeted during the civil war in the 1980s, and work became very scarce. During these years the United States sent a billion dollars of economic and military aid, but the poor benefited least and suffered most under the military repression that this aid supported. At this time, Edgar found it more and more difficult to make a living selling shoes. I asked him when things started to deteriorate, and he replied, "Since 1978, 1977, and then afterward. I remember perfectly. Before, there were possibilities to work. We had opportunities. For instance, in my case I worked making shoes. We made shoes to send to different parts of El Salvador. We worked seven days just to get the products out, before the conflict. When I was learning the trade, and I started working when I was about eleven or twelve years old, I would accompany one of my boss's sons to deliver the boxes of shoes with the bus. And we would come back with money in our pockets and nothing ever happened to us. That was before this war situation. When the war started we could no longer do that. We only worked about four days; now there was no night work and the work was very unstable. And there was a lot of unemployment. People wanted to buy the cheapest things so you had to find a way to produce things cheaper. So labor began to lose ground and pay went down. I'm talking about earning 150 to 180 colones when there was no conflict. Now, if you earn 150 or 180—really, if you earn that it's not much and maybe it allows you to cover 40 percent of your needs. Now you can see the big difference. Before you worked, exported your products, and there was no problem. You worked at night and the authorities came by and they didn't do anything. Now, after eight at night you can't work because there are problems. . . . Because if it gets to be eight at night, let's say ten at night— you can go out before ten at night but after then you can't even put a foot out into the street. . . . If you leave after this hour, because of martial law and the *toque de queda* [curfew], if the army finds you, you will disappear. You understand? If you leave after this hour, they don't ask you anything, not even about what you're doing or for your documents, or anything. They have to 'pull the kitten'; that is, they have to shoot you and it's not a problem if they kill you because the toque de queda is in effect."

The curfews and martial law imposed by the government throughout the capital city in an effort to curtail guerrilla activity devastated many businesses. Edgar, who often toiled in his small workshop in the evenings, found out that the cover of night also served to hide many violent deeds. One time he observed a pickup truck laden with bodies being brought to the funeral parlor next door. "Imagine," he implored me, "a pickup with an extended bed with wood planks to make it higher. We call them *pantes de leña* when the bed of a pickup is full of firewood. But on this occasion it wasn't firewood [that they were carrying]. It was cadavers, half-destroyed cadavers. Imagine adolescents, boys between fourteen and twenty or twenty-one years old, half-mutilated with only half of their faces left. Some were naked. Others only had on their underwear. Women in their panties only. Women without bras on and with bullet wounds in their breasts. Imagine, imagine what a situation—so upsetting, so *turbe*, as we say. You are working but your mind is thinking that next door is a funeral parlor and that over there they are preparing all those cadavers. Someone said, 'Look! They're bringing some cadavers.' We went over because we were curious. They opened the tarp. Imagine that the bed of the truck is so high [pointing to ceiling] and it's completely full of cadavers. This time there were about forty, maybe more. All of them were half-destroyed. With these parts [arms and legs] missing. Part of their faces was missing. Their hands were tied behind their backs with *cintas*, which is tape. And on [their backs] they were cut along the spine, like meat. All the way down the spine. Their ears had been cut off. It was horrible. They had brought in two that same night and their genitals had been cut off and stuffed into their mouths. Imagine it. Women, with only their underwear on, and bullet holes through their nipples. Really, it's unimaginable."

Edgar describes life in El Salvador as living with a constant pressure, "pressure to preserve your life. You are always worried that in one moment or another anyone who has a weapon will kill you before you can kill him—because of a misunderstanding or a mistake. But, sincerely, you can't subsist. It's not so much the economic situation but the pressure that you feel." He left El Salvador a year after Yolanda's departure. A friend of his agreed to make the trip with him but decided against it at the last moment, and Edgar, with only fifty dollars in his pocket, left alone. The trip, as described in the next chapter, took him several months and required much cunning. He is one of the hundreds of thousands of Salvadorans fleeing the war who entered the United States but were never accorded refugee status. The U.S. government could not define Edgar and his fellows as refugees without admitting that it had been funding an illegitimate war.

Crises in Peru Spur Emigration as Well

Salvadorans I interviewed always attributed their flight from home to "la situación," and most readily agreed that if it were not for the war they would not have come here. In contradistinction, South Americans readily conceded that they came to the United States for economic or family unification reasons—even though many of them came from Peru, which has itself been experiencing a civil war since 1980. The war in Peru has also been conducted between the military and a guerrilla group, the latter known as *Sendero Luminoso* or "Shining Path." Most of the fighting has taken place in the countryside, displacing many peasants. They have fled into the coastal cities, but they lack the resources to leave Peru since the passage to the United States costs many thousands of dollars. Nationally, violence escalated for a decade until September 1992 when the group's leader, Abimael Guzmán, was captured and jailed. Shining Path pursued a scorched-earth policy, destroying much of the country's infrastructure and so disrupting the Peruvian economy that the conflict is estimated to have caused $16 billion in damages—equivalent to 85 percent of Peru's GNP during the 1980s (*Wall Street Journal* July 20, 1990). Inflation soared during the height of the war to 7,650 percent in 1990 (*New York Times* January 31, 1995). But Peru's economic crisis goes back to fiscal policies begun in the 1970s (Thorp 1983). Greatly affected by this crisis were the salaried workers in the cities. Between 1973 and 1978, real wages fell by 40 percent, and as of 1984 the minimum wage workers received constituted only 20 percent of the amount needed for subsistence (Stein and Monge 1988:32, 33).

Despite Peru's political turmoil, close informants described their reasons for leaving the country in exclusively economic terms. Manuel and Berta had achieved middle-class status through their salaried jobs. But by the mid-1980s these salaries could no longer support their five children and high mortgage payments even if they pared their expenses back. Berta started buying and selling goods over the Ecuadoran border on weekends to supplement their income, but it was still not enough. "Most people come [to the United States] because of the economic crisis," Manuel said, "and for no other reason." "If there weren't an economic crisis, I don't think that anyone would come. What you earn [in

Peru] is not enough to live on. Sometimes you don't have enough even
to buy clothes. My concern was that there was enough to eat; you can
sew the clothes and if they rip you can sew them again and you can put
up with it. But you can't do that with your stomach. Medicine also became too expensive. The medical appointments for my children were
very costly even though I had two insurance policies."

Berta had always dreamed of visiting the United States and taking her
children to Disneyland. But slowly this dream was transformed into the
idea of emigrating "to work and earn more money to help our family."
"Between the year 1980 and about 1985 or 1986, the economic situation wasn't horrible. There wasn't a very bad crisis. But later what I
earned and my husband earned wasn't enough to cover our necessities.
So we started thinking that we had to go to some other place, like this
country. We thought that if things went well or at least okay for us we
would stay but if things went badly then we would have to go home
again." At first Manuel was reluctant to abandon the family, so, in 1988,
Berta decided to find a way to the United States by herself. "It was the
only way to save our house," she said. "If we hadn't gone to the United
States we would have lost our house because we couldn't pay the mortgage on our hundred-dollar-per-month salaries." When Berta received
her tourist visa from the U.S. embassy, Manuel acceded to her wishes by
accompanying her. They left their children in the care of their eldest
son, then only sixteen years old, and they arrived in the United States
with the idea of staying only six months, working, and saving up some
money that they could take back with them to Peru to invest in a small
business. This was their scheme; they hoped that the business would
allow them to weather Peru's economic storms, especially the galloping
inflation.

At about the same time that Manuel and Berta decided they no longer
had a future in Peru, Juanita came to a similar conclusion. She is the
woman who was trained as a nurse while living in a convent in Colombia. Juanita returned home to Peru to help care for her sick mother and
disabled sister. She arrived to find that the sheltered life of the convent
had hidden her from the crises facing South Americans every day. "The
economic crisis has been tremendous," Juanita explained. "People only
have enough money to eat. . . . There are families who only have tea,
bread, and rice [to eat]. No meat, no fruit, no vegetables, no nothing.
I was working in the poor, poor neighborhoods and there were children
whose stomachs were distended owing to the malnutrition. They have
no shoes, their stomachs are swollen with worms, and they have *granos*
[boils] on their heads and all over their bodies. It's atrocious." And
when I asked her what effect the crisis in Peru had on professionals like
herself, she said, "I bet you that a professional, a teacher, now earns

about $70 per month, maybe $80. The lower-level professional gets $70, and if they are higher they earn a little bit more. But the money you earn doesn't even go far enough to pay for you to eat. I was working as a technical nurse and before I came here I was working two shifts and earned about $50. That's two eight-hour shifts! By day I worked in the hospital and at night I worked with private patients. Fifty dollars *per month*. Look, I earned $50 for sixteen-hour days. And here I am earning $1,500 or $1,800 per month. Do you see the difference, Sarah? You see the difference and you think that I will think about going back to my country? Of course, here life is much more rushed. But it's the opportunity. I see that here there is opportunity. Over there life is relaxed. Eight hours seem very long. But here it's different; here you run, run, run. But I don't know, I like the *ambiente* [atmosphere]. Other people I know say no. It's mostly those from El Salvador whom I hear saying no. But I have never heard a Peruvian say, 'Now I'm going to go back to my country.' They say, 'I'll visit but then I'll return to the United States!'" She rationalizes this by arguing that "even if you have money it's not worth anything there. If I start up a business there, the inflation will eat it. I could go out and buy some goods and sell them. How am I going to invest more money in buying more goods if the inflation there is so high that prices rise every few days, or daily? So practically all my money would be wasted and I wouldn't have anything to work with. No business is worthwhile in Peru, not even one. When I left [Peru in 1988] the inti [Peruvian currency] was at 250 [per dollar] and now it's at 17,000 [in 1990]."

Juanita has no plans to return to Peru except to visit even if she obtains legal residency. Although Juanita left no children back home, she has been busy financing her siblings' emigrations. Over four years she has brought in two brothers and three sisters. All of them work to contribute toward the construction of a new house for their mother and sister in Lima. Many other Peruvians and other South Americans told me similar stories. Most, like Juanita, arrive with the burden of providing for the livelihoods of families as well as supporting themselves. If they are unable to survive and send money home, then their families' livelihoods will deteriorate—and they know it.

These vignettes illustrate how difficult it is to distinguish between political and economic factors in migration, although this complexity is not acknowledged by policymakers. Jesús's life was directly threatened, but this was not enough to make him flee his homeland. He left only when a drought destroyed his means to support himself and his family. Is he an economic or a political refugee? Similarly, the civil war in Peru destroyed the country's economy. Even though my informants were not themselves persecuted in this war, it was directly responsible for the deterioration of their standards of living. Are they economic or political refugees? Although the U.S. government contends that it fairly applies international refugee standards to all, its policy has been to deny status as political refugees to nearly all Salvadorans and Peruvians. Despite much criticism, as I shall explain in chapter 7, U.S. refugee policy has long conflicted with law. A glaring inequity has resulted; for example, when, until recently, Cubans who flee in boats are picked up by the Coast Guard, they are given immediate safe haven while Haitians in similar circumstances are repatriated or placed in camps. In sum, the conditions that precipitate migrations are only one factor determining the status of many undocumented immigrants and hence their futures. Politics plays an extremely important role as well.

WHY DID THE IMMIGRANTS CHOOSE THE UNITED STATES TO COME TO?

Informants offer many reasons for having left their homelands, but why did they choose to enter the United States, especially since they would not enjoy legal status? (I will address what attracted them to Long Island specifically in chapter 5.) Scholars answer the question of why people choose one country to migrate to over another in a variety of ways. Some suggest that migration patterns reflect economic and foreign-policy links between countries (e.g., Mitchell 1992; Sassen 1988; Sassen-Koob 1984; Rodriguez 1979). This helps explain why people living in colonies of former empires tend to migrate to the mother country of those empires; for example, Barbadians migrate to England, Algerians to France, and Curaçaoans to Holland. The pattern also applies to countries within the United States' sphere of influence. Thus, Puerto Ricans, Dominicans, Colombians, Salvadorans, and other peoples from the Americas tend to migrate to the United States over other countries. Additionally, industrialization in the country of origin appears to exacerbate, not reduce, emigration. For example, Korea's rate of emigration to the United States rose at the same time that the country became an economic power (see Sassen 1988).

Another frequently cited factor determining the destination of migrants is networks (e.g., Mines 1984; Lomnitz 1977; Pessar 1982a, 1982b; Dinerman 1982; Garrison and Weiss 1979). Networks involve linkages between people. Sister Maria fled to the United States primarily because she had a cousin there who could finance her trip. Similarly, Alfredo headed for Long Island where his friends Berta and Manuel had already settled. They themselves had selected Long Island because it was the home of a compadre, a godparent of one of their children, who had encouraged them to leave Peru. On Long Island, a perfect example of this phenomenon can be seen in the network that interconnects the town of Concepción de Oriente in eastern El Salvador and Westbury, Long Island (see map 1.1). By all accounts, it was begun by Don Miguel Yanes. Don Miguel was the head of sanitation and public health in the small rural town of Concepción de Oriente in La Unión Department of El Salvador. In 1971 a high-school friend from the city of San Miguel helped Don Miguel get a visa to the United States through government contacts. The two went to live on Long Island, where Don Miguel's friend had relatives. Don Miguel then found a job quickly at a plastics factory in the Westbury, Long Island, neighborhood called New Cassel. (After two decades he still works at the same job.) Eight years later, just as the civil war in El Salvador was escalating, he returned to Concepción de Oriente with a green card, which he had obtained by marrying a Puerto Rican woman. He told his family and friends—a group comprising nearly the entire population of the town—about his good fortune and the opportunities for work in Westbury. Shortly after he returned to Westbury, *Concepcioneros* started streaming in, most staying a few days or months at Don Miguel's home while they looked for housing and jobs nearby. When I went to interview the "godfather," as he is called, Don Miguel told me that so many, perhaps as many as a thousand, of his townspeople have come to the United States that he no longer even knows them all.

Don Miguel's history illustrates how emigration to places offering the possibility of better material, if not social, lives also fosters chain migration. This is a complicated phenomenon akin to "Keeping Up with the Joneses." It also functions, as I shall explain, to create among people who have not migrated the illusion of an easily achievable American dream. This process begins when a few individuals migrate and either send home news or return to visit. These are the "pioneers" who lay down the first network links. Generally it is the successful who return, and they return laden with gifts for their friends and family. The gifts serve as symbols of their success and foster an American dream vision among other community members. In many cases, the lives the immigrants lead in their host countries are miserable, even worse than those left behind. But an immigrant who has such an experience is particularly anxious to recoup his or her social status upon returning home (see Piore 1979; Massey et al. 1987). Their gifts and other material displays are used to achieve this. Everyone else observes the bounty flaunted by the returned migrant, and many, particularly the young whose dreams of social mobility have been stifled, are smitten with the idea of migrating themselves. They leave, using the guidance of the pioneer and often staying with him or her in the host country. Then the cycle is repeated with more players.

Networks are constantly evolving as the players and conditions of travel change. Their dynamism makes them difficult to study although they are known to facilitate migration. Like paths in the forest that become weathered and worn with the treading of feet, they make it easier and sometimes less risky for people to travel. Of course, migrant networks can wear out when they become so institutionalized that they are detected by authorities. But new networks or pathways are continually being devised to take their place.

Networks explain how migrations grow but tell us less about why they link two specific countries. For instance, many Salvadoran informants were persecuted in their homeland and, like Gilberto, fled to the United States because family and friends were living there. But why had these earlier migrants chosen the United States? Why not Guatemala, which borders El Salvador (see map 1.3)? The answer to this question hinges on political, economic, and social relationships mentioned above. However, the single most important force of attraction is the likelihood of finding social stability and economic opportunity. That is, everyone, regardless of background, wishes to provide safety and well-being for their families. This is why far fewer Salvadorans migrate to Guatemala than to the United States or even Mexico. Guatemala, engaged in a virtual civil war for decades, is hardly a hospitable site for relocation. Because people fleeing persecution do not necessarily relocate in the nearest country but often head for countries offering economic opportunity and social stability, they tend to be labeled "economic" and not "political" refugees. This argument has often been utilized by the U.S. government to justify excluding many groups, especially those, such as Haitians, fleeing right-wing regimes friendly with the U.S. government. Haitians have been labeled "economic" migrants in part because they tend not to flee into the Dominican Republic, which shares the island of Hispaniola with Haiti. Instead, they launch boats into the Caribbean with the objective of landing in the United States. To bolster its position, the U.S. government disregards the fact that Haitians have been summarily deported from the Dominican Republic and that the two countries have had very poor diplomatic relations during the past two centuries.

People tend to migrate to places that offer the possibility of economic success, as well as political stability, even when they have migrated from countries whose political crises have imperiled their lives. This can easily lead to the assumption that these people left their countries solely to seek economic opportunities. Many Americans make this assumption, confounding migrants' reasons for abandoning their homelands with their reasons for choosing a specific country as their destination. Such confusion fosters the American dream image of immigrants, that of people coming to seek their fortune in the land of milk and honey. For instance, when I asked students in a course I teach on the immigrant experience, "Why do people leave their homelands?" I was immediately deluged with responses like "They come for greater opportunities." I then told the class that people do come to the United States seeking opportunities they do not enjoy in their homelands, but this does not explain why they are uprooted. Only in the direst of circumstances—such as the 1994 war in Rwanda—does nearly an entire people flee their country. In most cases, certain sectors of the population are dislodged from their customary forms of life and they then become likely candidates for migration. Direct labor recruitment by U.S. companies has been the method most commonly used in the past century. Most turn-of-the-century European migration and later Mexican migration was begun this way (Piore 1979). Even some pioneer Salvadoran migrants were recruited in the 1960s. Though a crucial element in most contemporary migrations, recruitment is rarely acknowledged publicly. I believe this is ideologically convenient; immigrants portrayed as American dreamers detract from the fact that they primarily serve the interests of capital, not their own.

For uprooted peoples, the United States is an attractive destination because they earn their salary in dollars, a currency whose buying power rarely diminishes vis-à-vis the home country's currency. Particularly during periods of inflation, people who earn an income, or can save their assets, in dollars are less likely to become impoverished. This fact is well-known even among the poorest and least educated. The quest for hard currency, however, all too frequently leads to a miscalculation of the dollar's value in the United States, a miscalculation that fuels emigration and results in great disillusionment once migrants realize their mistake.

Sonia described the dollar craze to me one day. "It's the vision of dollars that carries people away!" She is a slight women whose deeply etched face readily communicates the difficulties of a small agriculturalist's wife. She migrated from the rural Salvadoran town of Polorós in the late 1980s after watching dozens of her friends go off before her. "In El Salvador people earn ten or twenty colones *per day*! And it's not everyone who earns twenty colones per day. And while the workday there is from 6 A.M. to 4 P.M. and you are paid ten pesos, here you work from 6 A.M. to 4 P.M., or, as in the case of landscape workers, you start work at 8 A.M. and finish at 4 P.M. and earn fifty dollars. Over there you can't earn that kind of money. Here the same money you earn [dollars] is the money you spend; but over there it's different. Not even a government official or an attorney earns that much in a day. Anyway that's what I think. . . . Women who are here and who used to work [in El Salvador] would earn—at the most—three hundred colones per month. And they would only get two days off per month; sometimes they'd get more for vacation but only after working at least six months. . . . But here you can earn in one day what it takes you a month to earn over there. This is the craziness of coming here," she added.

Sonia describes how people get swept up by American dream fever because of a simple miscalculation. They see the value of the U.S. money in terms of how it "multiplies" in their country, and they calculate their potential earnings as migrants using this multiplier effect. This is not unusual; people who live in unstable countries generally learn the value of holding on to stable currencies like the dollar. But such estimations frequently lead to inaccurate assumptions about the cost of living in the United States. Miscalculations, as Sonia hints, are commonplace because the dollar is estimated out of context: people at home hear what the standard wage for workers is in the United States—five dollars an hour for workers on Long Island. They then translate a day's salary, forty dollars, into what that would buy in their own country where the minimum wage is about four dollars per day. By this comparison, a miserable wage in the United States sounds like a king's ransom. It may be difficult to believe that people can make these calculations without figuring in the cost of living in the United States, but this is precisely what happens. I will return to this theme in chapter 4, where I discuss the immigrants' early disillusionment.

Most Salvadorans in particular emigrated because their lives were in danger, not because they were smitten with the dollar craze Sonia describes. But they immigrated to the United States because it promised opportunities for socioeconomic mobility that were unavailable in their country owing to the long-standing class divisions of a rigid social hierarchy (see Suárez-Orozco 1989). These people did not come to the United States having made detailed estimates of nest eggs they hoped to save, the mark of "target earner" immigrants. But, like Cándido Cruz, they did perceive the availability of economic opportunity in the United States. Cándido was a landless peasant in El Salvador; when I asked him what his life's goals had been there, he laughed: "Over there you don't achieve anything, you don't reach any goals. Because over there you don't accomplish anything." In El Salvador, getting ahead had become entirely impossible. He could see, however, how the small amount of money he is able to send home multiplies there: "The little bit of money you make here feels abundant over there. If you send two hundred dollars or five hundred dollars, the money grows. . . . My objective is to buy a place for my children to live so that they don't move around anymore." Cándido's outlook has been transformed in the United States;

he now thinks prospectively, but not about his life in the United States—only about his life in El Salvador if he returns.

Both migration and the uprooting that precedes it are complex social *processes.* As will become increasingly evident in the following chapter, migration evolves through the development of transportation and other social capital links from the host to the home country, links that open new opportunities for economic survival or betterment (Mines 1984; Portes and Walton 1981; Piore 1979). Whereas at first only the more fortunate are able to migrate, these pioneers widen the avenues, making it easier for other social classes, especially peasants, to undertake the journey (Piore 1979:138–40). This pattern fosters competition in local communities in the sending country: families prosper in comparison to their neighbors when they have members taking advantage of the new linkages, and this intensifies the neighbors' desire to immigrate to achieve similar results. As local political or economic conditions deteriorate, the pressure builds; people come to believe so fully in this new "El Dorado" that they refuse to hear the downside of migration, or they underestimate it. Like adventurers generations before them, their heads filled with American dreams, they will risk what little they have or can borrow to chase after these illusions. Whether their dreams are fulfilled or vanquished is the subject of the following chapters.

Chapter Three

THE TRIP AS PERSONAL TRANSFORMATION

THROUGHOUT many literary traditions, journeys are metaphors for personal transformations. The travelers are heroes-in-the-making; the trip tests their character to see if they are worthy of the hero's honors. The voyagers return home transformed: strengthened, matured, and rejuvenated. When the Israelites wandered in the wilderness, they went into nature to seek culture, to have God communicate his laws to them. Stripped of the diversions of "civilized" life, they were in essence defrocked of their old culture in preparation for their rebirth as a new, or at least redirected, people. Similarly, Odysseus embarked on many years of voyages and personal tests against creatures representing nature, culture, and sometimes both. His journeys brought him wisdom; when he returned home, he was able to assume a new identity as his people's leader. For my informants, their journey to the United States is also a rite of passage. They do not emerge, however, as heroes but as outlaws, as outsiders in a foreign land. Their trips transform through subtraction, not addition; through exhaustion, not rejuvenation. Undocumented immigrants' journeys signify a separation from the past, a breakage of social customs, a challenge to their past identities, and the preparation for rebirth in the United States. But rather than maturing through this process into full-fledged men and women like cultural heroes, they emerge from the border wilderness as children again. They must learn a new language, a new culture, and how to play many new games in which their old traditions will assist them little.

Immigrants tell different stories about their trips, but several experiences are shared. All describe the trip as an ordeal, one that cost them an innocence that can never be recovered. Second, the trip serves as a great leveler. Undocumented immigrants must cross the border with little more than the shirts on their backs. They leave behind the accoutrements of the lives they are also shedding—often dumping passports and other personal items within yards of the border. They bring with them only the abilities and knowledge accumulated in the past, human capital with which to start their lives anew. The trip also creates new conditions of existence, such as indebtedness, that will play key roles in migrants' experiences in the United States.

Why are these migrants' trips ordeals? Largely it is because they are undertaken illegally. Coming to the United States as an undocumented immigrant entails borrowing large sums of money, facing dangers and insufferable treatment, leaving behind family members unlikely to survive the trip, and assuming chameleon identities. Most people who arrive as undocumented immigrants would prefer to migrate legally and avoid the travails of crossing borders without authorization, but are prohibited from obtaining legal visas because the United States restricts their distribution carefully through its consular system. Consulates tend to grant tourist visas only to those people who are at a low risk of using the visas as stepping-stones to a permanent migration—people who leave assets in the home country that would serve to guarantee their return. Don José explained to me that the only way for most Salvadorans to get a visa is fraudulently. This is because, as he says, "if you go to the U.S. embassy to get a visa you have to have a good job, a bank account, and the title of a house. And if you present yourself for a visa at the U.S. embassy with these things, then they will give you a visa so you can travel as a tourist. But if you don't have this, they won't give it to you. It's true too that not everyone will get a visa even if they have all of the requisites. Two to three hundred persons go to the U.S. embassy every day and they may give a visa to twenty or ten. Of these two hundred people, perhaps 10 percent will get a visa. It's almost a loss to go to the U.S. embassy. So people come *mojado* [as a wetback]."

The irony is that legal migration, which among my informants is considered "high class" and out of their reach, tends also to be the least expensive form of migrating. According to information from my ESL survey, undocumented travelers pay an average of six hundred dollars more for their trips than those who arrive legally; this figure rises to sixteen hundred dollars more for Ecuadorans and Peruvians. Most Salvadorans do not even bother to apply for a visa since they know that they will not meet the stringent economic solvency requirements. Only a lucky few migrants in general clear this hurdle, Berta and her husband among them. Berta explains the criteria she had to meet to get a visa from Peru to the United States. "They required that you worked for some time in your job and had a large quantity of money to afford the trip. Because supposedly I was asking for a tourist visa, I had to show what property I had, how many children, and all of these things so that they would give me the visa. The requirements were from my job—I showed I had nine years of service. I showed pay stubs, bankbooks, and the title to my house, and titles to our two cars—which we were able to get through major efforts by taking out loans from the bank—and the birth certificates of my children, our marriage certificate, the certificate of my husband's job. Also, the title to some land my mother had given me, which was about three and a half or four hectares. All of these documents I took with me to the consulate. And in the first interview I had, they gave me the visa." According to an INS employee I spoke with, country-by-country records kept on numbers of people who overstay tourist and other nonimmigrant visas are not used by consulates in determining who is granted a visa. However, it is clearly much more difficult for people from Latin America and other Third World countries to obtain visas than it is for Europeans. Many Europeans now do not even need a visa to enter the United States as tourists. Consular discretion in granting visas is not a new practice, but the nationalities targeted for special scrutiny have changed. There was, for instance, a time-honored tradition of denying visas to certain groups, such as Jews, after World War I (Szajkowski 1974).[1]

Thus, for many aspiring immigrants, legal entry is not an option. In past years it seems to have been easier; pioneer migrants I spoke to told me that they were able to obtain visas relatively easily if they were of middle-class status or had contacts with officials. But for the poor, a tourist visa is a pipe dream—most do not even take the trouble to apply. How then do people arrange their trips? Alternatives include buying or falsifying visas, traveling by air to the Mexico-U.S. border and crossing by land, or traveling by land from point of origin to final destination. The option chosen is determined by price, and price depends on two factors: the distance between the country of origin and the Mexico-U.S. border, and the level of convenience or security of the trip—whether one travels by ground or air, alone or escorted by coyotes (organized smugglers). Smuggling has become an industry in Latin America; coyote services are advertised openly in the classified section of many newspapers, often promising "door-to-door" service (Schoultz 1992).

Since the money spent on migration is almost invariably borrowed, the type of undocumented journey chosen (if there is a choice) depends in great degree on how much one is able to borrow and how deeply one is willing to go into debt. But whatever type is chosen, prices increase with distance; Mexicans seem to arrive the cheapest because of the proximity of their country to the United States[2] and the fact that they are less likely to have to bribe Mexican officials or their bribes are lower. According to the ESL survey I conducted, undocumented Salvadorans spend an average of $1,796 for their trips, Colombians $1,738,[3] Ecuadorans $2,880, Peruvians $2,620, and Mexicans $664. Additionally, both Salvadorans and South Americans borrow an average of $1,319. This means that Salvadorans have fewer capital resources they can liquidate to pay for their journeys than do South Americans.

The high travel prices and ever-increasing demand have spawned an illicit travel industry that facilitates undocumented travel. For example, Salvadorans often claim that the Armed Forces enjoy a special relationship with the U.S. embassy in San Salvador and that many military officials exploit their ability to get tourist visas, selling them to the highest bidder. A similar situation occurs in Peru, as has been documented elsewhere (*New York Times* August 8, 1990). In Peru some professionals who are able to overcome the solvency hurdles at the embassy sell their credentials to individuals who need visas. The recipient presents the other's information with his or her own photo, is granted a legal (though fraudulently obtained) visa, and travels freely to the United States. The price tag for this type of service? About six thousand dollars, which includes one to two thousand dollars for the professional; the rest covers travel and intermediary costs. Juanita, the Peruvian nurse, confided to me that she bought one brother a visa, then lost eight thousand dollars trying to get another brother into the country, and finally financed another sister's visa for another four thousand dollars—all within a year and a half! To accomplish this she had to work nearly fourteen-hour days for the entire period. Brígida Manzanares told me that she bought illegal visas for each of her three children, who had stayed behind in El Salvador when she migrated. Each visa cost her three thousand dollars or more. One child's visa was detected as fraudulent when it was presented to INS officials in New York, and she was returned to El Salvador. That cost Brígida another three thousand dollars. This woman spent so much money reuniting her family that, had she been spared this expense, she commented laughingly, "people have told me that I would have had a lot of money by now." But she feared that if she had not sent for her children, they might have been killed.

For most people, these prices are out of reach. If a visa (legal or fraudulent) is not an option, what other alternatives are available? In El Salvador, coyotes (*polleros*, in Mexican lingo) or their underlings circulate among even the tiniest villages, seeking out potential travelers. Crucial to the institutionalization and expansion of transnational links, some coyotes specialize in serving certain communities or provinces; those who achieve good reputations for safe overland journeys and evasion of the U.S. INS are rewarded when families return to them with new business. Yolanda, for instance, had her son and brother wait several months while the coyote she trusted felt that passage was too difficult and delayed their departure. On the high side of sophistication, entire "travel" agencies have arisen that offer elaborate networks of services: clients are provided with passports, fake visas, and intricate travel agendas often involving several countries. A Peruvian told me that these agencies are very competitive, and that when one is rising in popularity its competitor will denounce it to the government. When it is investigated and shut down, the competitor takes over. Why the rivalry? The business is extremely lucrative. The typical price for a Peruvian rose during my fieldwork from around four thousand to six thousand dollars; a Salvadoran might spend as much as thirty-five hundred. The migrant (or his sponsor) usually has to pay a portion of the trip's cost to the coyote in advance. The rest is paid in full once the person is safely within the United States.

The size of the groups escorted by coyotes varies enormously from small packs of about a half dozen to hundreds leaving together in several buses. The trip is usually initiated by a local coyote who travels with the group, facilitating its passage by offering bribes to local officials. If the trip is by air, coyotes travel independently to avoid detection at customs. Similarly, coyotes will distribute their group inside buses among other passengers so that if some are caught most will still get through. Once the travelers reach Mexico—generally, but not exclusively, Mexico City—the local coyote shifts responsibility for the group to a Mexican coyote who passes them across the Mexico-U.S. border. Many times, however, this connection, or *conecte*, is never made, and people are abandoned in Mexico to find their own ways of continuing. Sometimes this is due to problems in payment along the coyote network, or migrants may fall prey to *mordidas*. A derivative of *morder*, "to bite," this term denotes searches by Mexican and other nations' immigration officials, as well as by the Mexican Federal Judicial Police (*federales*) and narcotics police (*narcóticos*), performed in order to collect bribes from travelers.[4]

THE TRIP: DÓLARES, CONECTES, GARITAS Y MORDIDAS

I turn next to the narration of several actual trips taken by informants, highlighting the significance of the journey for undocumented immigrants. I begin with those who went "first class," continuing with an examination of the "economy class" method, and ending with the more harrowing experiences of those who left "*sin cinco*." To travel "sin cinco" is the modern-day version of steerage, those who leave "without even a nickel" in their pockets.

First Class, Undocumented Style

The idea of coming to the United States occurred to the Colombian Pablo when his son's doctor recommended that the family find medical treatment there for the retarded boy. Pablo did not really consider it seriously until some friends raised the issue with him and encouraged him to go. That was in 1978. After discussing the idea with his wife, Pablo recounted, he contacted a cousin living on Long Island, took some money out of the bank, and contracted with a "tourist" agency.

"In the town I lived in, I heard talk about a lot of people who were coming to the United States. In those days, they were called excursion trips. But in these excursions, you paid someone to include you in the trip."

"With the intention of coming here?" I probed.

"Yes, to come here. Everyone [in the "excursion"] was coming here [to stay]. So, I made contact with one of these people and he told me that the route was through Panama. You fly from Medellín [Colombia] to Panama; from Panama you change planes and fly to Nassau, Bahamas. From the Bahamas you travel by boat to a beach that they had in Miami. I got the money I had to pay this person from the bank. . . . It was at that time about ten thousand Colombian pesos. I'm talking about ten or twelve years ago and this was a lot of money. . . . I remember now. It was twenty-five hundred dollars."

"And did you have to pay this all up front?"

"Yes, but they said that if you were caught they'd take you over again. It was guaranteed."

"So you flew?"

"Yes, from Medellín to Panama. I went from Panama to Nassau, Bahamas. I stayed in the Bahamas three days, paying $2.00 for a can of soda! A banana cost $1.50 then. We stayed inside in a room in a hotel—some twenty persons. All of us from Colombia. We were there four days during which we couldn't continue because the weather was very bad. We started to get *desesperados* until one day, a Sunday morning, we all got into a boat and we got to Miami. . . . We arrived in four hours. It was a motorboat for five, and twenty or thirty of us were aboard. . . . We couldn't bring our suitcases with us, they arrived afterward. We call it a suitcase, but it was more like a briefcase with a pair of pants and a shirt and nothing more." Pablo got a job working in a restaurant; after only a year he was discovered by the INS and he left the country. Some nine months later he made the same trip and has remained in the United States ever since. In 1981 he spent forty-five hundred dollars for his wife and son to come over. They took virtually the same route but flew the last leg by plane. Scheduled to last only a half hour, the flight took four and a half hours because their tiny plane flew into a hurricane and they were nearly lost. This was only the beginning of what would become a life of disillusionment for Pablo's wife, Raquel.

The advantage of traveling first class is that the agency will generally take care of all the contacts, pay off all the bribes, and leave the traveler with an almost effortless trip. Things do not always go as planned, however. During her trip from Peru, Juanita obtained a visa to Mexico and got through the Tijuana airport by hooking her arm around a Mexican woman as if she were her daughter. But after she left the airport, her taxi was stopped by the federales, who wanted a bribe. Juanita's coyote, who was with her, dashed out of the taxi as it came to a stop and hid in a nearby house. The federales demanded five hundred dollars. When Juanita refused to pay, the federales forced the taxi into a remote area and searched her and her companion, ripping open the seams of their clothes looking for hidden money and harassing them until they produced the money demanded. The travelers were released, furious, only to find the coyote calmly waiting for them when they got back to the taxi. Stories like Juanita's are commonplace.

Economy Class

Economy class generally means traveling by ground from the home country, such as El Salvador, through Guatemala (although some also go through Honduras and Belize) and into Mexico. South American travelers may begin their ground travel in Mexico after entering that country with a tourist visa, typically fraudulently obtained, but others fly to Guatemala or other Central American countries and then, picking up the ground-travel routes, journey up the isthmus (see map 1.3). When South Americans go directly to Mexico and then cross the border, their trip usually costs them a minimum of four thousand dollars, while traveling completely overland costs them at least a thousand dollars less. Salvadorans who travel by land usually pay five hundred to three thousand dollars for their trip—again, some portion is usually paid in advance and the remainder is paid once the immigrant is safely across the Mexico-U.S. border. In Mexico the routes diverge. Many take the long route into San Diego, while others split off and head toward El Paso or Brownsville, Texas. A few informants told me that they were able to reach the United States from El Salvador in two days and that they encountered almost no mordidas, no stops for bribes. Most, like Sister Maria, are not so fortunate and endure at least one harrowing moment.

Maria's came when she was crossing the Suichiate River between Guatemala and Mexico. The trip so far had been easy since Salvadorans have not needed a visa to enter Guatemala. After that, the winds changed for her, she said. "The only thing we had with us was a change of clothes, nothing more. One to wear to cross the river and the other to change into. But when we were crossing the river the thieves came out. They would throw stones at us. If we didn't give them money they'd let the river carry us away. They were on horses and we were on foot. If they found anything on us they would take it all away. They searched us when we crossed the river and were putting on our shoes. They took everything and left us only with the clothes we had on. . . . They took the money from the coyote first because they knew he was the one with the most money. But what I had done in El Salvador was to sew the money into the sleeves of my shirt. For as long as they searched me no money fell out, they didn't find anything. They searched me in my underwear, in my bra, everything. But they didn't find money. I was carrying one hundred dollars. One hundred dollars that my cousin gave me, saying, 'Don't give these to anyone! Take these with you. They're going to help you.'"

Even though the practice of sewing money into one's clothes is common and well-known to coyotes, federales, and thieves, Maria's money was not detected; with it she financed the group's trip as far as Matamorros, Mexico. In Matamorros the group met another coyote who demanded five hundred dollars to take them across the border. If Maria delayed paying her, the consequences, the coyote promised, would be dire: "She said to me, 'I can throw you out here in Texas,' she would say all the time, 'I can leave you here so that the Migra [INS] finds you. If you don't pay me the five hundred dollars I will leave you here. . . . I can dump you wherever I want to.'" Maria desperately called her cousin on Long Island. After several days' wait, Maria's cousin finally sent the money, which she had to borrow from her husband's family, and the small band headed out for the Rio Grande the next night. "We crossed the river and had to cross running so that the Migra wouldn't catch us because there were helicopters all over. . . . When we were on the flats and a helicopter came by we would throw ourselves on the ground. . . . We ran and hid from about nine o'clock to about two in the morning. . . . The helicopters have a light but they didn't see us because when they came by we would hide in the bushes and when the helicopter had passed we would run to the other side. When the helicopter would return we'd run into the bushes again."

Maria, several months pregnant by this time, felt cramps as she ran, but could not stop. Once safely across the river the travelers were sheltered in the coyote's safe house, a tiny room with a couch, a large mattress on the floor, and a small kitchenette. Safe houses are used to sequester immigrants and hold them until their sponsors send the second portion of the trip's price to the coyote. Waiting for the payment to be made so that one can be released is always stressful. For sponsoring relatives it can be harrowing. After weeks of waiting for her six-year-old son to cross Mexico on his trip from El Salvador, Yolanda was not allowed to talk to him when he finally crossed the border and was being held by his coyotes. She had to send money without being able to confirm that he had arrived safely.

Risking Your Life "Sin Cinco"

Pablo, Raquel, Juanita, and Maria all have one thing in common: their trips were financed in one way or another. Edgar's and Marco Peña's trips were similar but more perilous because they traveled with minimal

resources. Edgar was effectively penniless for most of his journey's duration. His story involves ingenuity, persistence, and a bit of luck. Edgar's
wife left El Salvador a year and a half before he did. When he decided he
could no longer stand the pressures of life in San Salvador, he called her
and asked for money to make the trip. She had little to spare and sent
him only a hundred dollars. That night he took his son to his grandmother's to leave the boy with her, but the grandmother had passed
away suddenly and Edgar had to spend half of his travel money for her
burial. With a close friend of his, Edgar mapped out a strategy to travel
until the money ran out, work awhile, and then continue the journey.
The friend dropped out at the last moment and left Edgar alone. Determined to go forward with his plan, he took a bus to the Guatemalan
border. Once across, the bus stopped, even though it was supposed to
take him directly to Guatemala City. Not knowing what to do next, he
watched a coyote pull his group into a taxi and head away. Edgar decided to follow him and asked a taxi driver how to get to Tecúm Umán,
the Guatemalan town on the Mexican border. The driver suggested he
take a bus from the nearby bus station; while the two were in the taxi,
Edgar took advantage of the moment and probed him. "So I started to
talk to him and I told him baldly about my situation. 'Look. This is the
first time I am traveling and I don't know how things work. I would like
it if you would help me.' 'Why?' 'Because I don't know anything.' 'Let's
see what I can do,' he said. So we talked for some time and we got to the
bus terminal and he introduced me to a guy who is the ticket taker on
the buses. And he told me to talk to him, that he was a good person.
And I told him that this was my first time traveling and I would like his
help. 'I'll give you a few pesos when we get over [the border],' I told
him. So he told me, 'It's okay. You can accompany me.' And the other
coyote arrived and when he got into the bus he stared at me. It was like
he was following me. So the ticket taker told me, 'When you see one of
the Guatemalan immigration officers getting in, get up and sit down
next to the driver. Later, stand up and take the tickets like you were the
ticket taker and I will sit down in your seat.' 'Okay,' I told him. So
whenever I saw that the bus was going to stop I would get up and walk
over to talk to the driver. And this guy would go and sit in my seat and
everyone would watch me. I did this about four times until we got to
Tecúm Umán."

Once Edgar arrived in Tecúm Umán, he found out quickly that the
situation in Mexico was *fregada*, very complicated. Each night several
busloads of people were deported into Guatemala, many had been
robbed, some had died when the trucks they had been riding in flipped
over, and so on. He was weary and penniless, so he began looking for a
job to finance the next leg of the trip. After a couple of days of asking

people, he got a tip about some farm labor. The next day he arose at dawn to look for the bus. "I got a hat and put on the most wrinkled shirt I had," he explained, "and I flagged down the bus and the driver asked me where I was going. 'I'm going to—to look for work.' 'Okay,' he said, 'Come on up.' He gave me a ride and I saw a whole group of peasants on a huge hacienda where they cultivated some [plant] to make oil out of. And they also cultivated cotton. So I arrived and I asked for whoever was in charge. I said, 'Excuse me. My name is so-and-so. I'm from such a place. And I need to work because I was deported the first time I went across [the border to Mexico] and now I'm going back and I don't have money to pay the bus. I'd rather work than steal so if you could give me an opportunity. . . .' And so she asked me if I had worked in agriculture and I said, 'Really, no. I've never worked in that but I'm hungry and I'm sure that the necessity will make me learn.' So we talked and at the end she said, 'Okay. I'm going to give you the job. Come back tomorrow and bring a *cuma* [machete].'. . . . The next day we went back. . . . And we went to an immense farm, so big that it didn't end at the horizon. 'Look,' she said, 'I'm going to give you a chance. You are going to order these people around. You are going to be the *caporal*, the foreman.' 'Wow. Magnificent.' 'You like it?' she asked. 'Of course, it's fine and many thanks.' And I stayed working there for two months. During this time I looked around for a way to get across, talking to friends and watching the situation."

During the day Edgar worked at the farm, and at night he searched for a coyote. There were many coyotes in Tecúm Umán, he says, of "every nationality." Each had a slightly different system of conectes, including many that required paying off Mexican immigration officials to facilitate passage. But the prices for these services were high: twenty-five hundred dollars to escort you to the U.S. border, fifteen hundred to hide you in a truck carrying fruit.[5] "Free" passage was available only to those who would carry packages of cocaine over the border. Edgar opted against them all. After some time he found an older Cuban coyote who had a good reputation, and began to negotiate with him. Edgar promised eleven hundred dollars at the end of the trip, and the coyote ultimately agreed to the deal as long as there was no *turbiada*. A turbiada is a disquieting situation, as when the client gets to his destination and refuses to pay. The Cuban told Edgar that if he tried this he would be killed.

So, exactly two months after arriving in Tecúm Umán, Edgar, along with the coyote and a few others, crossed the river between Tecúm Umán and the Mexican town of Tapachula. They crossed on rafts made of inner tubes, then walked an hour around the first *garita*, or Mexican immigration post. There would be thirty-six garitas between Tapachula and Puebla, Mexico. I asked Edgar how he managed to get by them. He told me that the Cuban was an excellent forger, and while in Guatemala he had prepared for him a set of forged student identification cards. Edgar was to pretend to be a university student from the Autonomous University of Mexico in Puebla. To accomplish this feat, the coyote held training sessions for his *pollos* (charges, but literally chickens). "When I was in Tecúm Umán," he said, "they taught us how to answer a bunch of questions, like 'Who is the president of Mexico?' and 'Where are you going?' or 'Where are you from?' He also taught us the address of our destination, a few historical facts like names of governors and so on. You had to memorize this so you would have it on hand whenever necessary. And you had to try to imitate the Mexican accent." I asked him if this was enough to get by the Mexican authorities, and he answered, "In part, but we came *costeados* also." He defined *costeado* as "pre-paid," explaining, "Despite the fact that we had our documents, [the coyote] had his conecte with Mexican immigration and he paid a percentage for each of us. The only thing we had to do was talk like real Mexicans. It didn't have to be perfect but we had to try."

Using these techniques the group reached Puebla, but the uncertain situation forced them to wait there for two weeks. Edgar got restless and decided to head on alone. Two Peruvians from the group convinced Edgar to take them with him, and he became their pseudo-coyote although he had no experience. The three pretended to be university students who had just finished their studies and were beginning research for their theses. En route to Mexicali they hit more garitas; each time, their student documents were checked and they were interrogated about life in Puebla. Each time, they barely got through. The worst moment came in Reynosa, Mexico, Edgar said. "It was about three in the morning. Immigration forced us out and we had to put ourselves against the wall. They made us kneel down by the bus because one guy started running. He was even a Mexican but he didn't have any documents. Because of him, I thought that they were going to kill us all." After some time they were released and proceeded to Mexicali, only to find that the relative of one of the Peruvians who met them there had no money—no money to pay Edgar for his service or to get them across the border. So they walked over it by themselves. Edgar describes the border as a mad throng of migrants, motorcycles, cars, helicopters, and dogs. Edgar and his companions were fortunate because they crossed near some others who sent one Mexican out as bait for the U.S. Border Patrol to catch. In this common coyote strategy, the bait person seizes the INS's attention; while officials are preoccupied with capturing this sacrificial lamb, dozens of migrants slip through. Edgar and the Peruvians waited for the decoy to work, then ran a distance until they found a car graveyard. There they negotiated a ride to Los Angeles in the trunk of a car. Edgar's wife then sent him some money and he flew to New York.

Rough Passage from Peru

Marco Peña and his wife, Patricia Quiroz, are university graduates and trained social scientists. Romantics, they had both worked as organizers: she organized peasants, and he worked with factory laborers in the northern Peruvian industrial city of Chimbote. But their love for this work was stifled by the miserably inadequate wage it paid. They got an idea: Go to the United States for two years, save some money, and come home with the resources to start a family and continue their lives. This dream fortified their courage and belief so that they could *saltar al vacío*, as Marco told me: "I think that people who emigrate. . . . saltan al vacío [take a leap of faith] because they are at the edge of an abyss. They are the only ones who will dare themselves, who will jump into emptiness, knowing that they could fall into water or onto a pillow. We do it out of hope. Maybe we know that below there is water, but we jump hoping that there is a mattress below to cushion our fall. If we fall onto the mattress, then nothing happens when we jump into the vacío [nothingness]. And this is the image we have of the United States, that the United States is a pillow, a cushion that—when we jump and with a little help—we know will keep us from dying. But it is a jump into nothingness, motivated by being on the edge of the abyss. For me, to be in the Peruvian middle class and only earn a hundred dollars a month, which was only enough to eat with, was being on the edge of the abyss. And I knew that each day as things got more expensive I would eat less. I think that we [Peruvians] come here not because we have nothing to eat, but because we are eating less now, because we can't buy many things. . . . He who wants to survive, risks the little that he has."

Patricia was readily granted a visa because she had been in the United States before, but Marco's application was denied and he could not afford the three thousand dollars for a travel agency to get him to Mexico. So he decided to risk traveling overland. With nine hundred dollars in his pocket (small change for the trip from Peru), he told his family not to worry because he had three advantages: (1) a rational mind, (2) enthusiasm born of innocence, and (3) belief in God. From Peru he took a bus through Ecuador and into Colombia. From Colombia he flew to San Andrés island, a Colombian territory in the Caribbean near the Nicaraguan border. On San Andrés he met many Peruvians who were stuck there because no country on the Central American isthmus would give them a visa. Many had been jailed for using fake Colombian passports. But after a week, Marco arranged a visa to Nicaragua. When he arrived, he says, "there were groups of Peruvians who would be in the airports to receive you and would say, 'Look. I will teach you how you can leave this country. Do you want to leave by plane or by land? If you want to go by land it will cost you so much and by plane so much.' That is, they sold information to us Peruvians who would arrive there. But that's because they couldn't leave themselves. They didn't have any money. They were there already and they couldn't do anything and there wasn't any work. And so I found out that the Salvadoran consulate gave out visas. Moreover, the consul was a mafioso and he lived off the visas. It was because the Cristiani government was taking over and his government was going out and he was a consul under [then president Napoleon] Duarte. These were his last days so he was selling visas for his own pocket. And he sold me a visa for twenty-five dollars. This was the next step forward. From San Salvador you would go through Guatemala."

Marco actually bought a visa to El Salvador only after trying to leave Nicaragua for Honduras and being deported back again. When he flew to El Salvador, he only had $120 of his original $900 and the Salvadoran immigration officials demanded more than this amount to admit him to the country. When he could not produce the sum, they put him back on the plane with the intention of deporting him back to Nicaragua. But the plane first had to land in Guatemala, and Marco, thinking quickly, asked immigration officials there to let him through. Miraculously, one official granted him a thirty-day transit pass, and Marco got out and headed for the Guatemala-Mexico border. He was stopped twice for mordidas. Once he reached Tecúm Umán, the border town, Marco received $700 from his wife and paid $500 to a Guatemalan coyote.

By night Marco and the other pollos crossed the Suchiate River by floating on inner tubes; then they paid 43,000 Mexican pesos to a travel agency in Tapachula to take them to Mexico City. En route Marco and others in his group were caught by federales and held three days in a shack. The Mexican police told Marco that he was being held until enough Peruvians were caught for a group deportation. "They wouldn't let me go," he explained, "because I committed the error of saying that I was Peruvian. If I had said that I was Guatemalan they would have thrown me over the border and that would have been it. But as a Peruvian they told me that I had to wait until there were more South Americans so we would be sent by bus to Mexico [City] and returned to our countries. I was there three days until I got very tired because I didn't change my clothes or eat. So I offered $40 to a man, not to the chief but to a subordinate. We were in two rooms without windows. And with those $40 I got out. He told me to go to another town and to take another [bus] to another town until I got to the capital." Marco's original coyote had long since vanished but had left word that he could be contacted in a certain town. When Marco was released, he took a bus to this town and the coyote was astonished to see him. The coyote then sent him to Puerto Vallarta, a Pacific coast tourist town, where Marco took a flight in a tiny airplane to Tijuana. But the federales again caught him as he disembarked, and they held him in a room, demanding $250. He had only $125. Consequently, he was placed in a holding pen where unfortunate travelers are kept until another means of getting them across the Mexico-U.S. border can be found. If Marco had paid the $250, he would have been escorted across, he says, because the whole system is completely orchestrated by Mexican authorities and coyotes. His lack of capital at the airport ended up costing Marco more money—and nearly his life as well.

Marco was ultimately charged $800 to cross, $200 more than the others because he was Peruvian. Once again, he contacted Patricia for the money. It was several days before she sent it because she had to borrow from her relatives in New York. His captors were unconcerned; they knew he was more vulnerable because he would not risk being deported to Peru. After payment, he was whisked across the border in a truck, then transferred into a tractor trailer with 182 other people and no ventilation. Observing how smoothly the transaction was conducted, he reasoned that an army of collaborators must be involved. But they were not losing money, he asserted to me. "If Mexico weren't on the border with the United States, if Mexico were in Central America it would be very poor. . . . The mafia there earn about $60,000 or $70,000 daily. And if they only pass people through three times per week that's close to $200,000 per week. In one month, imagine, they get close to $1 million. This is good production, a good service industry. And they say that the police receive $100,000 per week because I talked to some of the people over there."

For Marco, the border networks signify an institutionalized mafia with no scruples and no concern for their human cargo. When he discussed his experience, he told me that our conversation helped vent his anger. "If we had been inside [that trailer] ten minutes more, people would have started dying. There were children crying—babies in their mothers' arms." He calculated that the officials made over $70,000 in that one trip: 183 people paying an average of $600 each.

Marco's story of near suffocation is not unusual. At least two other informants had similar experiences, and countless others have faced death crossing the Mexico-U.S. border (see *New York Times* November 12, 1988). This stage of the trip may be the last big hurdle, but it can also be the most daunting. Altagracia Sánchez's common-law husband, Edmundo Granados, lost a brother who drowned in the Rio Grande near Brownsville. Another man I met told about "losing" (*se perdió*) his wife to the border. She left El Salvador four months before our conversation, disappeared with another woman, has not been heard of since, and is presumed dead. Other horror stories abound. Oscar Zelaya crossed into Arizona only to walk three days without food or water and with only a dollar in his pocket. Cándido Cruz rode through the INS checkpoint at San Ysidro, California, hidden in the back of a pickup. Later the truck was chased by the U.S. Border Patrol. The driver stopped suddenly and shouted at everyone to bail out. Cándido was the only one to escape being caught by the INS, but he found himself alone in the California desert, knowing nothing except that he was in the United States. Juanita was forced to run across the six-lane highway leading to San Diego where 227 undocumented immigrants have been struck since 1987, 127 of them killed (*New York Times* January 7, 1991). Sonia traveled miles in the Texas desert without food, and Carmen Rivas collapsed on a neatly groomed lawn after walking all night. She awoke to find that a startled suburbanite had called the INS and turned her in.

"WELCOME TO AMERICA"

One-third of my interviewees were caught by the INS after crossing the border into the United States. Two managed to trick the immigration officers into believing that they were Mexican, not Salvadoran, and were "deported" into Mexico, then immediately reentered the United States. Though they see this circumvention of the system as a great triumph, it does not necessarily work to their best advantage. Technically, anyone who makes such an illegal entry[6] has the right to a deportation hearing regardless of his or her legal status. An important Supreme Court decision in 1987 guaranteed this right to all Central Americans and forced the INS to stop pressuring these people to sign "voluntary departure" forms to get them to leave the country without having had their cases heard before the immigration courts. Thus, a Salvadoran who enters and is captured by the INS has the right to apply for political asylum and, in most cases, can be freed on bond.

But these concerns are not on the minds of the newly incarcerated. Indeed, most have no knowledge of their rights and are only aware of the freedoms that have been taken from them. First they are interrogated so that the INS can gather the evidence it needs to make a deportation case against them. Immigrants have a great deal to say about how frightened they felt during interrogations. Sonia's younger brother was so petrified that he completely forgot his name and his destination. He was released because he was a minor, and only that night, when he took off his clothes, did he remember that his T-shirt carried the logo and telephone number of the restaurant where his brother works on Long Island. After processing, some undocumented immigrants are released on bond while others are kept in *corralones*, or detention centers. Some corralones, like Oakdale in Louisiana and Port Isabel in Texas, hold many thousands under questionable conditions. At Port Isabel detainees sent a list of grievances to authorities, complaining about insufficient food and time to eat, lack of legal representation, and harassment by INS guards. Most of my informants found the corralón prisonlike. Tina Vega, a diminutive but extremely spunky woman from Nicaragua, was picked up by the INS and held in a corralón for five months. This is how she describes being incarcerated there. "You despair there. You look out the window. You look at the birds and you want to be a bird so you can fly away. Everything there is *enterrado* [like underground], only rooms, only women and children. The food was so horrible. It was too much. There are moments when you cry; moments when you write, moments when you go into the bathrooms to clean them and then in your room. It's so *desesperante*, so horrible, so sad to see only four walls. I didn't know what to do. I would walk back and forth, then lie down or take a shower. . . . The question you always ask is 'When? When am I going to get out of here?' 'When are they going to take me out? What is going to happen to me?' I used to say [to my attorney], 'Take me away from here!. . . . I don't know what I have done to be here!' There was one woman who grabbed the walls and said, 'I don't want to be here anymore!'"

Time spent languishing in the corralón is torturous not only because of the conditions inside but also because detainees are prevented from fulfilling their responsibilities to their families. They feel pressured to get jobs, send money back home, and pay off their debts. Tina was held until she was five months pregnant. During those months she received no prenatal care. But her primary concern was for her family in Nicaragua, especially for her two-year-old son whom she had left in the custody of her mother and sister. "The conditions there weren't bad, they were okay," she recalled. "But the thing is that you come here with the desire to work hard so you can send your family [money]. And to come here and spend so much time without doing anything is what makes you so desperate. All this time without doing anything and me alone. Every day I would lie down on the bed and hide my head and I wouldn't get up for anything. . . . I felt bad that my family would find out and I also felt bad that they didn't know I was in jail. Because I knew that they would think that something had happened to me." When Tina was finally released, one of her friends from the corralón who had already been released borrowed money and sent it to her. That is how Tina came to Long Island; she had always planned to go to Miami, which has a large Nicaraguan community.

Detention has deep psychological as well as economic costs. When people are released on bond, the cost of their trip escalates wildly since most bonds are set at a thousand dollars or more. If they present themselves to INS court, as required, they may not lose their bond money. But few understand the court system or the deportation process; they think of bond money as unrecoverable, just another expense. Tina herself said that when she was told she had to appear in court, this frightened her more than the likelihood of being deported. She said, "I was afraid of the court because, even though I'd seen pictures of it, I didn't know exactly what a court was. . . . I didn't feel afraid to cross the river but I was afraid of going to court!" In the long run the cost of capture may easily outrun the short-term gain an immigrant obtains by applying for political asylum. Once they have applied for asylum, people gain protection from immediate deportation and they may be able to acquire work authorization while their case is adjudicated. This provision, although stated in INS regulations, has not always been followed to the letter. In summary, the benefit of being discovered is that a person may be able to get work authorization, and through this a Social Security card and other necessary documents with which to begin to establish a life in the United States. On the other hand, falling into the deportation process can signify enormous new costs—attorney's fees, lost work time when INS hearings are scheduled, and, of course, the near guarantee of having one's case denied and then facing deportation. This is complicated by widespread rackets set up to trick Central Americans into applying for asylum, as I will show in chapter 7.

As Maria's and Yolanda's stories reveal, those who are able to get across the border without being detained are normally held in safe houses by their coyotes until their sponsors pay the remaining part of the coyote fee. After that they also face the possibility of being caught while moving from point of entry to their final destination. In 1989 the INS increased its inspections of planes leaving border areas (*New York Times* February 28, 1989; March 1, 1989; March 15, 1990). In Texas, for instance, INS activity is concentrated on finding and deporting undocumented immigrants once they have crossed the border and are trying to find transportation elsewhere (INS, personal communication). If migrants are fortunate, they arrive without incident and are met by friends or family and taken to their new home. Some arrive to no welcome and, with no other recourse, hire taxis to take them where they have to go. Taxi prices to Long Island from New York City start at around sixty dollars. Those arriving in New Jersey face the added obstacle of an INS program set up to identify and arrest people who come to meet incoming undocumented relatives and friends. One person told me that his car with all its contents was confiscated at Newark Airport; he was not allowed to recover any of his sequestered belongings.

The Journey as Personal Transformation

The individual who emerges from a tunnel or trailer or trunk of a car and steps onto U.S. soil is not the person who left Peru or El Salvador or Colombia. Her identity has become the near antithesis of the woman left behind. She has gone from citizen to foreigner, law abider to lawbreaker, legal to illegal, independent to dependent, social member to social outcast; and her personhood is degraded. Fragments of her previous self remain, but they lie scattered like shards of broken glass. The trip strips her naked, and from her nakedness she is expected to clothe herself in the American dream. And people at home are depending on this anticipated metamorphosis, keeping her from dwelling on her newfound confusion.

The changes migrants initiate during their journeys are rich anthropological veins to be mined and interpreted, a task that the proponents of a transnationalist framework for international migration implore us to pursue (Glick Schiller, Basch, and Szanton Blanc 1992) and one I can only begin to perform here. Perhaps the most obvious of the changes is the migrants' loss of personal integrity. Undocumented travelers are a very vulnerable group. As foreigners who travel with all their possessions on their persons, they are easy targets for predators who extract everything they can—cash, clothes, mementos, and personal dignity. These assaults occur every step of the way, but they are particularly notorious within Mexico (e.g., USCR 1991). Abuse along the Mexico-U.S. border is commonplace as well (Bouchier 1978; Juffer 1988). Some are lucky and avoid discovery—like Gilberto, who traveled from El Salvador through Guatemala and Belize to Mexico. On the way he befriended a family, and by playing with one child each time they encountered a garita he was able to evade detection. Several of my informants were not so lucky. Lorenzo Ramos was strip-searched in Mexicali and beaten. Another informant was frisked; when no money was found on him, he was pistol-whipped, stripped, and beaten. "It's then that you wished you had money on you to give them," he said. Carmen hid behind a door while the federales raped and beat several women who were caught with her. Other women told me that although they had not been harmed, they had heard many stories of others who had suffered horribly in both Guatemala and Mexico. What fuels the corruption and abuse is the enormous flow of money traveling with the migrants. Officials and others who are conveniently situated siphon off a good share, stripping their victims not only of their possessions but of their dignity as well.

It is ironic that the pursuit of illegal status should carry such a high price tag. Not only does the cost of an illegal entry tend to be far higher than that of a legal entry, which involves only the cost of transportation and perhaps some fees, but much of the added cost goes to further other illegal activities: bribery and extortion. There is so much money traveling along the isthmus that a veritable corruption industry has developed over the years. The industry has evolved into a complex giant with many layers, each exacting its own mordida. Feeding off the migrant stream proves to be much more lucrative than most jobs in Mexico. Thus, while Mexicans can travel more or less freely within their country, documented reports show that conditions have deteriorated for other migrants in Mexico. It used to be that migrants in transit could simply pay bribes and move on. Now they are robbed, detained, and deported without any administrative or judicial hearing (USCR 1991). When people are turned back once they have reached Mexico, they have to begin the entire trip over again and incur extra debt. Many spend up to several months in Mexico or Guatemala waiting to travel on; some are turned back several times before they are successful.

To avoid being caught and deported, immigrants must become chameleons, developing acute cunning and deviousness much as Edgar did. They are aided by coyotes and other members of the illicit travel industry who provide "sensitivity" training to their paying customers. The smugglers give the prospective migrants a crash course in what the trip will be like, the kinds of transportation to be used, and how to deal with Mexican immigration and other authorities. The pollos are often given quick lessons in Mexican accents and slang. Sometimes facts about Mexican history, elected officials, and the like are taught so that travelers will be able to "prove" they are Mexican. Jaime Hernández, a Peruvian from Lima, revealed to me that he was told to act Mexican even though his African features made this seem almost ludicrous. A Honduran man said that he hired an agency to train him on how to present himself to the U.S. consulate after his visa application had been denied twice. The third time he applied he showed great knowledge about the type of machinery he was supposedly traveling to buy—and was given the visa. The coyotes also tell their pollos to lie about their nationality if they are picked up by the U.S. Border Patrol—the feared Migra. They are told to insist that they are Mexicans, shout "pinche" (Mexican slang swear word, roughly equivalent to "damn") a few times, and give a Mexican hometown.

Coyotes capitalize on the fact that when Mexicans are detected and detained (which is generally within seventy-two hours of crossing the border [Reichert and Massey 1979:613]), they are taken back into Mexico and released just across the border. The next day or the next hour they can try to return. Thus, coyotes teach their non-Mexican pollos to feign Mexican nationality so that if they are caught the pollos will get a second chance. The coyotes also insist that their clients throw away their passports and other identifying documents before crossing the border. This advice puzzled me at first, but after talking with Don José I realized that this is the coyotes' ingenious way of ensuring that they will be paid the second half of the contract price. If a Central American is picked up by the INS and can convince the officers that he is Mexican, he is thrown back over the border and is free to come in again the next day. But if a Central American admits to his nationality and is detained, he will be processed and kept in a corralón or jail for some days until a court hearing is held or scheduled, or he can post bond. The coyote loses money each time this happens. "The coyotes make you lie to the INS," Santos said, "because the coyote told me, 'You are going to say that you're Mexican. You're not going to say that you're Salvadoran.' . . . He told me, 'If you fall in [the INS's] trap, then we'll just try another trip.'"

Pollos are taught to toss away their documents but these are now merely symbolic of the identities they have already relinquished. The institutionalization of undocumented travel has spawned a set of practices, deceit and exploitation among the most notorious, that pollos learn—or endure—along the way. Many Salvadorans had already learned to beguile authorities and hide their identities during the civil war, but during their trip to the United States these skills are honed in a different way. The knowledge they acquire is embedded in the language people have cultivated to describe themselves: coyotes feed upon chickens (pollos) but must dole out mordidas, or bites, to the federales. It is the cultural construction of a "natural" food chain.

Introduction to the New Set of Social Rules

What is perhaps most amazing is that people pay dearly for their own exploitation. Indeed, one of the principal consequences of their journey is the descent into dependency. Most become indebted to people who were their social peers but are now more like patrons in a patron-client tie. The rules of the new game require that a proportion of the trip's cost be paid prior to embarkation. In order to raise that capital, many migrants sell their worldly belongings; that is, they divest themselves of the fruits of their past labors. Their home or small farm gave them social standing in their community, social membership. This is now bartered for an uncertain future, and the money generated in the sale becomes a kind of "life-price." The price is set by institutionalized figures and forces far away who view the migrants as little more than chattel. Their life-price is based on the distance they must travel to the United States, and the relative luxury and security of the accommodations. For many, particularly the poor, they will see more hard currency pass through their hands during this transaction than at any other time in their lives.

Selling one's worldly belongings rarely covers the entire cost of the trip; inevitably, people must borrow money to cover the rest. As I have said, the average indebtedness of the undocumented immigrants I surveyed was $1,326. For peasant Salvadorans and even urban South Americans, this sum represents at least a year's income. Numerous authors have noted this indebtedness among the migrant populations they studied (e.g., Samora 1971; Gibson 1988; Ewen 1985; Fitzpatrick 1987). But what are its implications? The frequency with which immigrants spoke about the pressures they felt to repay this travel loan convinced me that this indebtedness was qualitatively different from neighborly indebtedness. I have described how these people often reminisced about sharing food and services with friends and extended family in their homelands. But the travel loan broke these standard social rules for generalized reciprocity. Why?

Latin American immigrants come from societies with rigid class hierarchies in which subordinates are used to being indebted to superordinates. Peasants owe landowners money borrowed for seed, fertilizer, and other supplies. Urbanites develop long-standing relations with shop owners who extend credit and are repaid when the workers cash paychecks. But this traditional patron-client relationship is not preserved in the financing of trips to the United States. Rather, the *prestamistas*, the people lending the travelers money, tend to be friends and relatives of the migrants who are already in the United States but nonetheless are from the same social class. This means that, according to the rules of reciprocity, the moneylenders should be patient about being repaid and should not charge interest. New migrants such as Edgar find that while they are infrequently charged interest, most are pressured to pay the loan back shortly after arrival.

Edgar's case highlights the stresses such indebtedness places on relationships. He borrowed his travel money from his wife Yolanda, who borrowed it from her employer. As they were beginning to pay this debt off, Yolanda's son by another relationship and her brother began their trip north. Yolanda's boss, knowing that Edgar was now in the United States, demanded quick repayment, but Yolanda needed money to finance the others' trip. She applied pressure on Edgar to pay back his debt immediately. Edgar, expecting some leeway from her, particularly since she had a steady job and he could find only day jobs, told me he felt "squeezed of everything I have." When they lived together in San Salvador, they had shared all expenses; it angered him that they now paid their own expenses separately. Also, because Yolanda was working for an American family as a live-in domestic at the time and Edgar was renting a room, he felt that he bore a disproportionate amount of their total expenses. To make the situation worse, Yolanda's mother, who is also in the United States, refused to help finance her son's trip. Yolanda finally turned to her employers again. Shortly after her relatives' arrival, Yolanda was docked $50 from her $150 weekly salary toward repaying her debts. With the new expenses she incurred in caring for her son and brother, Yolanda pressured Edgar even harder to pay off his debt. This friction nearly cost them their marriage.

Yolanda and Edgar's example illustrates that the exigencies of life in the United States strain the type of social reciprocity characteristic of life in the homeland. The travel debt begins an ever-escalating cycle. Because the sums required are so huge—particularly in relation to people's salaries—relatives and friends of the traveler often tap multiple contacts to come up with the necessary funds. The traveler and the sponsor are obligated to many other people, and if any one of the lenders requests repayment, the pressure passes from shoulder to shoulder and stresses each relationship in between. In sum, people are willing to help each other with monetary loans and do so frequently. But while such transactions reinforce social ties in their homelands, in the United States they also become the source of much friction, jealousy, and disillusionment. These distresses are qualitatively different from strains felt at home because the sums transacted are much larger and because there is no safety net to catch migrants if they fall. The travel debt thus introduces immigrants to a new social system, one that requires people to break traditional social rules. This brusquely introduces them to the commodification of social relations.

Not only does the journey to the United States involve breaking rules of social reciprocity, it also entails breaking rules of social organization. The arduous challenges migrants face during their trips act as screening mechanisms. Many people are not willing to submit themselves to these terrors and challenges; many would not survive them. Children and the elderly tend to be left behind. Often men travel first and only later send for their wives and, less frequently, their children. For people accustomed to a life that knew no privacy, the separation and isolation from family is overwhelming. Paradoxically, it is precisely in the name of preserving the family that so many people leave their homelands. For many Salvadorans, the government and guerrilla practice of forcibly recruiting males for military service spurred the separation, but it was the cruelty of the borderlands and the price of travel that prevented families from leaving together.

The traveler is exiled from her native culture, and the journey introduces her to a new type of social system replete with rules for behavior. But, as travelers learn en route, these rules—driven by monetary, not humanitarian, interests—often conflict with their homelands' prescriptions. The trip serves to introduce them to a new world of highly monetized social relations. Travelers, like Sonia in the following story, come face-to-face with this attitude. She and several other Salvadorans had just crossed into Texas with their coyote when they ran into two abandoned children who had fallen asleep beneath some sagebrush. "By chance we ran into those children and they were huddled under a bush. One had fallen asleep but now was crying. . . . The other child said that . . . his aunt had been picked up by Immigration and in that moment the children were separated [from the aunt] because some other members of the group [they were with] were holding them by the hand. But when Immigration took the aunt these people let go of the children's hands and they were lost. . . . So when our group came by, one of the men begged the coyote to take the children along. . . . They were very young. One was very, very young and the other a bit older. The younger one didn't speak very well. So when the person begged the coyote to let us take the children with us, he said, 'No. It's going to be a problem for us, [they would slow us down].' Our group didn't know what to do; but we knew that if we could only get them further along we would be able to find out who their [parents] were. But one of the children was very alert and had his mother's telephone number memorized. So we took them along with us and we got [to the safe house] but we didn't find the mother. No one helped the man who had taken it upon himself to bring the children because the coyote had said no. This man carried them, saying, 'I have children. I can't leave them here, abandoned. They must be taken to Los Angeles.'" In order to save the children, the pollos had to break the rules of passivity that dominate the coyote-pollo relationship. They were very conscious of this break because of their dependence on the coyote for their own safety and destiny. Raw courage, duty, and a sense of compassion convinced them to take a risk—doing something that would never have required a moment's hesitation back home. This story has an unfortunate ending since only one child reached his mother. The other was lost later at the INS detention center when she was separated from the man who had rescued her.

The journey of undocumented immigrants to America is cultural as much as physical. By selling their worldly goods to finance the trip, divorcing themselves from their families and the reciprocal bonds of friendships, breaking many rules of proper behavior, and falling prey to abuses that humiliate even the most steadfast, these immigrants must shed much of their past identities. They take on new identities as debtors, passive chickens in the clutches of coyotes, beguiling chameleons who assume new personae to test wits with seasoned predators, and finally illegals, wetbacks, or merely outlaws in the Promised Land. They approach their last crossing, the Rio Grande, with little more than the shirts on their backs. They have come to nature virtually in a state of nature.

The waters of the Rio Grande are their baptism to the new land. There is a new language, a new culture, customs, and games to be learned. Still glistening from the crossing, they have little idea of the fresh perils awaiting them. Altagracia made it safely to the Brownsville airport with a friend after crossing the border unaided. They needed to find a flight to New York, and she was selected to inquire. "I walked over to where [a Spanish-speaking woman stood] but my blue jeans were still wet from crossing the river. How would they not notice that I had just crossed over the river? The secretary spoke Spanish and she told me that the plane had already left but that there was another plane which left in an hour. So we . . . sat down and then three men from Immigration came by. 'Good afternoon, good afternoon.' How awful it was! 'Would you show us your papers, please?' Papers, what papers!" The INS took her to the corralón, the detention center. "Ay!" she recalled, "I felt as if the Migra and death had come upon me. All night I couldn't sleep thinking about being deported."

Immigrants speak about their journeys as ordeals, rites of passage they would prefer never to repeat. Generally, like Santos, they want their relatives and friends to be spared this experience. "Perhaps you have a friend and you tell him that life here is very hard," he explained. "But that person will not believe you. . . . I have two younger brothers and I have written them that I don't want them to come—it's too hard. . . . The trip for me was a nightmare. I would never want my brothers to make the same trip to come here. The trip is very hard and you are almost assured of losing money." Probably because they pay so much more for their trips than do their Mexican counterparts—more money,

time, distance, and security—my informants have not elevated undocumented travel to the venerated piece of folklore it is for Mexicans (e.g.,
Massey et al. 1987; Mines 1981). For many Mexican men, the trip is
tantamount to achieving manhood; for many of my informants, the trip
extinguishes much of their personhood. This comparison is perhaps
communicated best through a *corrido*, or ballad, often played among
the Salvadorans. It is called "Tres Veces Mojado" (Three times a wetback), and it chronicles their journey:

> When I left my land, El Salvador,
> with the idea of going to the United States,
> I knew that I would need more than bravery,
> that the best would await me along the way.
>
> I had to cross three borders,
> and I traveled undocumented through three countries;
> I had to risk my life three times
> and this is why they call me three times a wetback. . . .
>
> For Mexicans the steps are few,
> if they're deported the next day they return;
> this is a luxury that I don't have
> even though they may kill me or take me prisoner. . . .
>
> (Los Tigres del Norte [my translation])

Chapter Four

GREAT EXPECTATIONS, EARLY DISILLUSIONMENTS

UNDOCUMENTED IMMIGRANTS' journeys to the United States are sobering, not only because of the danger, humiliation, and sacrifice they entail, but also because for a great number of migrants they provide the first of many jolts that shock them into the reality of their new lives. That is, virtually all of my informants left their homelands with idealized visions either of the United States itself or of the lives they would lead there, only to realize shortly thereafter that these visions were fantasies. Manuel's utopian fantasy is illustrative and evocative of previous generations' dreams. He told me that when he arrived in New York, he expected to find so much money for the taking that he could literally "sweep it up off the streets." In his American dream, the streets were not paved with gold, but dusted with dollars ready to be swept into his arms. This vision may seem naive, even incredible in this day and age, though it captured the imaginations of earlier generations of immigrants (e.g., Gold 1930:102). But beliefs held by fresh waves of immigrants to U.S. shores are not so surprising when understood as one of many manifestations of the material fetishism that erupts when people from commodity-poor societies enter consumptive, industrialized ones. The classic example of this culture clash is the cargo cults that formed in the South Pacific during World War II. These cults worshiped planes because the cargo they carried to the islands seemed to be a divine creation—like manna from the sky. Knowing nothing of the human manufacturing processes that created these objects, the people in the cult attributed them to the gods. Similarly, the material goods migrants send or bring home have fostered a fetishism that mystifies the human efforts which produced them. The bounty defies commonplace explanations. For example, if a peasant's neighbor with no more than a second-grade education returns home with gold jewelry and money to build a cement house, this peasant will likely conclude that money is easily made in the United States, so plentiful that anyone can pluck it off the streets.

THE CONSTRUCTION OF ILLUSIONS

The illusions migrants bring to their U.S. lives arise from the fact that information about the United States received in the home countries is generally distorted; if information does arrive in a pure state, people do not accept the bald truth. To begin with, information people receive about the United States is generated almost exclusively by two sources: earlier migrants and the media. Both sources offer much biased information and foster unrealistic dreams. The U.S. films and television shows that circulate in Latin America reach primarily the urban lower and middle classes, not the peasantry. These media offer a window into the American middle-class lifestyle, one that many would-be immigrants aspire to but are unlikely to attain for reasons I will develop in the following chapter. Several middle-class informants arrived in the United States carrying the expectation that they would find, in their words, *el país de las maravillas* (the land of marvels), an expectation based on the media images they had been exposed to as well as information they received from migrants. They expected to find a developed and sophisticated land, but were quickly disillusioned. Berta flew into John F. Kennedy airport, and her compadre drove her to Long Island along the Long Island Expressway. The pavement was so potholed and riveted that the car bounced and jerked just as cars do on Peru's thoroughfares. Her dream immediately deflated.

Alfredo explained his experience to me. "There is a curiosity about the United States as the land of marvels," he began. "This impression comes from the newspapers, the television, the movies—the media. They create this curiosity. For instance, in the programs on television you would see something that for me was strange, those skyscrapers in Manhattan. The programs said that there were buildings so high, so high that the clouds run into them. And I said, how could that be? When I got to Manhattan [with my friends] the first time, I found that the skyscrapers weren't so interesting, because they were high but not much higher than [those in Peru]. The building materials were the same. It was disillusioning for me. . . . I had the feeling that everything was okay until I saw the people lying in the streets, drunks and so on. It was disillusioning. I don't know, other states might be different. But New York is the capital of the world. And I don't see anything different here than you see in Peru. As I've told you, I'm not involved with the North American society, at least with the middle class or upward. Maybe that's different. But from what I can observe, things are pretty much the same as in Peru." Similarly, Don José, the Salvadoran merchant, recalled that his first impression of the United States "was bad, negative. I had had a dream before coming to the United States and a negative panorama had appeared to me. I was walking in a park and I saw the houses like the low ones around here and I said, 'This is the United States that I thought was full of skyscrapers like New York.' And when I got to California with all its small houses I thought, 'Is this a house? There are houses everywhere in El Salvador like this one.' This did not fulfill the reputation of the United States. What happened in my dream happened in reality too. When I got to California I viewed Los Angeles like a large village. There is a very small zone where there are high buildings and it looks nice. But the rest of it is just old houses. It's like a giant village. It's not a real city, big and beautiful. Secondly, I arrived and it was really hot; it was August. On a couple of days the temperature rose to 112 degrees. That was terrible! And I spent the first month without finding work. All I wanted to do was go back to El Salvador. Everything was negative. My brother lived in a tiny apartment and in El Salvador I had lived in a large house and I felt like I was in this teensy-weensy place and given the heat—I felt like I was going crazy. When you first arrive everything is negative, completely negative. I don't think that anyone comes and is received with open arms and feels like he has leapt into heaven or a paradise and feels happy. Definitely no. That happens maybe many years down the line when he now has settled in and has his car, his house, and many other things to make himself feel comfortable. Then he feels good. But when one just arrives it's all problems. Totally horrible."

In contradistinction to urban informants, peasants formed their ideas about life in the United States almost exclusively on the basis of others' accounts, those of friends and relatives who had already migrated and sent home the news. Sometimes, as I will explain shortly, this information is an accurate depiction of migrants' hardships. Frequently, however, migrants embellish their descriptions, emphasizing the positives (or even inventing them) while downplaying the negatives, and misleading their listeners. This is precisely what happened to Altagracia, who decided to leave El Salvador because she had heard that life was so much better in the United States. After arrival, she felt deceived and even embittered. "Ah! They painted it all rosy-colored. No!" she responded when I asked her how her friends had described the United States. "They said that life here was very nice. You know, they tell you a lot of lies."

"What type of lies?" I pressed.

"They told me that you earned a lot here and worked very little, that you worked very little and earned a lot. [Laughter.]"

"And how is life here?"

"Oh, it's different. You work a lot and earn very little. Because, Ay! everything is very expensive, you have to buy everything [not make it yourself] and you can't save very much."

"Do you think that they were just saying these things or because life really was rosy for them?"

"For me what they said was purely imaginary. They like to make people believe that they live in a castle here [in the United States], that things over there aren't the same."

"Why do they do this?"

"To make themselves be big people, big economically. To show that they live well here and that their lives are good even if that isn't true. The person who listens to them, who doesn't know better, is someone who believes in fantasies," she concluded.

Most immigrants insisted that they suppress much of the grim reality of their experiences in the United States (and of their journeys) in order to keep their families from worrying about them. I suggest that another factor comes into play. This is migrants' desire to counter the attacks to their social esteem that they encounter in the United States by recovering or enhancing their social status at home. The pressure to appear successful is pervasive as well. By borrowing enormous sums of money and abandoning their family for an uncertain future, migrants put their families and their reputations at risk. Success, expressed through remittance payments, goods sent home, and even inspiring pictures, helps alleviate these stresses. I found that the need to justify the risks taken escalated in proportion to the magnitude of those risks, and that the more migrants' status was lowered in the United States, the more they felt compelled to buttress it at home. Middle-class migrants who became blue-collar workers in the United States rarely admitted this fact to their loved ones at home and often bent the truth to fellow migrants. It was too painful to admit that in order to preserve their families' status and lifestyle at home, they had to perform duties they would never have condescended to in their homelands, work such as cleaning and cooking. This theme often arose during conversations with South American informants, like Felipe Rodríguez. Felipe is in his thirties and is from a moderately wealthy family in Chile. He spent years in Spain, then decided to rebel against his family by migrating illegally to the United States. He has been employed principally as a landscaper and church custodian, occupations that his fellow Chileans deem unworthy. Felipe brushes their criticisms off, joking that their occupations are no better, no matter how much they try to cloak this fact. "There was one man who spoke to me last Sunday at church," Felipe recounted. "We always say hello to each other. His family always goes to mass. He told me, 'I lost my job in the bank today.' 'Yes,' I said, 'but you were working there doing cleaning, no?' He was trying to paint himself as a banker with this 'my job in the bank' comment as if he was something else. When I asked him if it was a cleaning job, he said, 'Yes, that's right.' But he was taken aback and then he made excuses, 'They hired a new [cleaning] firm.' He was presenting himself as if, for instance, I would say to someone that I have to go to work in the office. 'I'm going to my office,' as if I was going to work at a white-collar job and not as a night cleaner."

Middle-class migrants were also most likely to appropriate symbols of

affluence, cars in particular, and transmit evidence of them
and friends at home. (Felipe himself acquired an old MG (
he frowned on ostentation by others.) I say most likely beca
from peasant roots also engaged in this ostentation, but it was
fervent and more delayed. The elevation in status is easily achieved
through "doctored" photographs, as Alfredo explained to me. "Among
those who come here the first thing that they buy is a car because people
want to be noticed," he began. "They send photographs back to their
country to show that they have their car now, and so on. I see this in the
feelings of my friends. In my case, Sarah, I am a person who doesn't like
to show what I have. . . . I have not even sent back one photograph to
show what is happening here. Not even one. . . . I can't give them [my
family] illusions. But my friends can. They buy several rolls of film and
take photographs of their cars, the flowers, here and there, and they
send them back home to Peru—here is the bridge, the skyscrapers, and
so on. What are they doing? They are giving their [kids] a fictitious
world. I have told Berta and Manuel that they are people who like to
appear what they are not. I don't know how many photographs they
have taken of their car to show their children. . . . But these kids are
getting used to something that in any moment will not be possible for
them to provide. They think that [their parents] are perfectly okay.
Look at what has happened lately to Manuel. He has been without work
for one month. He's been disabled. What will happen is that soon his
kids will ask for money, 'Father, we need four hundred dollars.' They are
going to think that [their parents] can send it but they definitely cannot.
This is the fictitious world. And the first thing that the majority of people do when they come here is buy a car if possible. To *lucir bien* [look
good]."

On several occasions I myself was pressed into service as a photographer. My subjects would comb nice neighborhoods looking for the fin-
est, sharpest car and pose in front of it for me to snap their pictures. For
a few moments they would appropriate the car, and the American dream
it represented, for themselves. But the image imprinted on the film was
permanent and real to family and friends at home. "Look at that car!
Fulano [Mr. So-and-so] has really made it in America!" I can imagine
them exclaiming, seduced by the invented success. Such images foster
emigration at the same time that they repair or bolster migrants' status
at home. "There are many people who are deceived because they receive
letters from people who are here and they are jealous of them," Yolanda
told me. "The people at home think that the people in the United States
are living well in this beautiful country. This country may be beautiful
but you don't come here to enjoy the beauty. You come here to work,
work, work, and the time you have to enjoy it is very minimal. But there

Homeless Salvadorans invent their success to send to family at home.
Photograph by Sarah J. Mahler

are a lot of people who have gone back and they make it their business to paint a rosy picture—that you earn a lot, that there are tons of things to buy, and that everything is inexpensive compared to El Salvador."

The importance of this illusion is further illustrated by a casual conversation I had with an acquaintance about a business venture Don José told me about. Don José's idea was to videotape immigrants and then have the tapes played to relatives back home. José was enthused by the plan although daunted by the logistics of transporting VCRs into the Salvadoran countryside. When I mentioned this entrepreneurial idea to another immigrant, he scoffed at the idea, saying, "That will never work because no one wants their relatives to see how they *really* live in the United States." I countered by suggesting that immigrants could tape themselves in fantasy environments, much as is done with photographs sent home. But he rejected the enterprise again as too costly. Needless to say, I have yet to hear of this proposition's taking root on Long Island.

The Unacceptable Truth

This cycle of deception, whether intentional or not, is difficult to stop, primarily because people in the home country do not accept negative depictions of el país de las maravillas. This leads me to the second reason why informants migrated with inflated aspirations for their lives in the United States. They literally could not entertain the prospect of failure. The Nicaraguan Tina told me that if you told the truth about how you lived in the United States, no one would believe you because "they [would] say that you are egotistical. . . . No one, no one accepts you telling them that things in this country are hard. Because the first thing they say about you is that you are egotistical or that you don't have money here; that you don't want others to prosper. They would say that you don't want them to get ahead, to make money [like they have]."

I was so struck by this response that I specifically asked dozens of people what they told people back home and what effect the information had. Invariably I got the same response: they won't listen to you if you tell them the truth. When accurate information is communicated to aspiring migrants, as in Berta's case, it is so overbalanced by the rosy-colored depictions that people deny the reality until they see it with their own eyes. Berta's compadre drew an authentic but grim picture of his day-to-day world for her. "He told us that you work hard here, that it isn't what we think [in Peru] that everything is easy and that we would have easy office jobs. No. He always told us that people come here to work like robots. From your job to home and home to work, and that weekends you have to go to the supermarket and laundromat. You have to spend those two days doing what you can't do during the week. He told us what things really are like. But you always have to see it, live it to believe it. Sometimes you say, maybe he is telling us this so that we won't go. But now that we are here we can say that things are the same way that he painted them."

The construction of an imagined world that, along with structural forces discussed previously, propels people into the migratory stream has serious implications for policy makers interested in stemming the tide of illegal migration into countries like the United States. The information traveling along migratory networks may paint an accurate picture of life in the United States, but the material fetishism fostered by migration is more powerful.[1] Consequently, migrations gain force and volume like a snowball rolling downhill.

DESCENT INTO DISAPPOINTMENT

More often than not, the brooms migrants imagined using to sweep up dollars turn into the brooms that they toil with in the rest rooms of restaurants or kitchens of the middle class. Reality swiftly eclipses their visions. Even those who had been well-informed by their relatives about life in the United States still did not anticipate how they would have to realign both their expectations and their strategies after arrival. During their early days and months, migrants' eyes are opened. They learn that the rules of life are different in the United States from what they were at home. As innocents and greenhorns, they often learn these lessons through victimization. But once having paid their dues, they also learn to play the new games to their advantage. Among the lessons migrants learn in the days following their arrival, three play crucial roles in re-aligning expectations with reality: (1) learning how difficult it is to pro-duce and safeguard surplus income, (2) understanding that the drive to produce a surplus commodifies most relationships, and (3) realizing that opportunities for producing that surplus lie primarily within one's com-munity and not outside it. To tap these opportunities, migrants must recognize and utilize their community's resources for their own benefit. As I will explain in the next chapter, intracommunity strategies become immigrants' primary avenue to socioeconomic mobility because they are largely excluded from mainstream America, its economy and opportuni-ties. They live segregated from the mainstream by structural forces be-yond their control, forces that limit their opportunities for success. Most stagnate within this restricted sphere but some advance, learning to ex-ploit resources found mainly within their immigrant communities.

From Subsistence to Surplus

The majority of my interviewees arrived in the United States mired in debt from their trips but with great expectations of returning home in a few years with a nest egg—several thousand dollars—in their pockets. Yet nearly everyone told me that within days of arrival they wished they had never come and wanted to go home. Most felt like Don José, who was ready to leave the United States after only a month. Their debts, their pride, and the burden of providing for their families keep them from turning back. In their first months, they swallow their disillusion-ment and despair because they face the daunting task ahead of finding ways to meet their obligations. In order to understand these people's despair, one must comprehend the magnitude and complexity of immi-grants' financial obligations relative to their capacity to generate in-come. Second, it is critical to recognize that the immigrants under-estimated the difficulty of meeting their obligations owing to a simple miscalculation and to the fact that most would not listen to seasoned immigrants who sent home bleak information about prospects in the United States. The miscalculation, as I mentioned in chapter 1, involves estimating earnings in U.S. dollars but failing to account for the costs of living in the United States.

The first task immigrants face following arrival is to find employment and to work as long and as hard as they possibly can. Work becomes life's fulcrum in the United States, qualitatively different from its function in migrants' home countries. Gilberto had known long days as a peasant in El Salvador, but he found that work there was much different from work in the United States. "There you're not obligated to work," he said. "You work out of *cariño* [love]. Sometimes you work hard but you work with more cariño because it's your own. Yes, I mean you work with more *voluntad* [willingness]. Because you work for yourself, you are happy with the work you're going to do. But here, no." "Why do you work here?" I asked him, and he responded, "Because if you don't work you won't have a place to stay, even though you don't live comfortably anyway. Sometimes you don't even earn enough to pay the rent."

When Gilberto says he feels "obligated" to work in the United States whereas at home he willingly went off to work, he articulates the dilemma facing all of my informants. Though they earn salaries that classify them among the working poor (typically four to seven dollars per hour), their incomes must stretch much further than mere survival. They are obligated to produce a surplus from their meager salaries in order to (1) repay their travel loans, INS bonds, and any other debts they incur as they start their lives in the United States, (2) remit monies homeward to sustain their families left behind and finance investments there, and (3) save a nest egg to return home with. Additionally, immigrants hope to have some savings on hand in case of an emergency or the loss of their job. Undocumented immigrants qualify for no government public cash assistance, and in only a few states do they even qualify for Medicaid to pay for emergency medical treatment. They have little if any institutional safety net (the church, soup kitchens, and a few other charities are the only sources of aid I have found) to fall back upon if they cannot meet their own needs, let alone meet the needs of their dependents and creditors.

It is difficult to convey how pressures build on immigrants, driving them to assume the nonstop work lives that they are famous for. Cándido's early experiences are illustrative. He crossed the Mexican-U.S. border in the back of a pickup truck that was detected by immigration officials who gave chase. The driver stopped the vehicle and ordered his human cargo to jump out; there was screaming and shooting as people ran for their lives into the surrounding desert. As the migrants ran, the INS officers shouted at them to stop or they would be shot, but Cándido kept running. "Me, I didn't even turn around to look at him," he said. "I said to myself, 'I owe all this money and how am I ever going to pay it off if they deport me, if they catch me?' So, I ran by myself into an area covered with vegetation and I escaped. But the rest were captured and put in the corralón."

Even when the pressures to repay their travel debt become less acute, their void is filled by responsibilities to families at home. When Tina was languishing in the detention center, for instance, she was beset by guilt for not being able to send money back to her family. Her sister was caring for Tina's young son and would send her letters begging for help: "'Things are worse now than when you left. Just to buy milk is so expensive. If you don't send me money how will I be able to buy a tin of milk?'" Her sister thought that she was working; Tina had not had the heart to tell her the bad news that she had fallen into the hands of the INS. But she had no job and no income except a few dollars that she received from friends who had been released. She would send off five or ten dollars to her sister, who responded by writing, "'Little sister. I am thankful for what you send me.'" And this partial fulfillment of her obligations eased Tina's anguish.

"You Spend What You Earn"

Immigrants communicated their pressures primarily through their actions, through their workaholic lives, not through words. The workaholism is a product of their need to generate more wealth than that required for their own sustenance. It is also the product of U.S. economic realities—the realities of a postindustrial economy that produces more minimally paid than well-paid jobs. As such, people face the task of stretching their meager salaries past self-sustenance—which many native workers cannot achieve at these wage levels—and achieving a surplus to cover debts and family obligations. For many this alone is not disillusioning, since they faced dire economic challenges in their homelands, albeit just to sustain their families. What causes them to despair so immediately upon arrival is the jolt they receive in realizing that "*lo que se gana se gasta*" (you earn [in dollars] and you spend [in dollars]).

Virtually none of my informants, however highly educated, avoided misestimating to some degree the facility of generating surplus income. The miscalculation works this way: A would-be migrant hears he can earn five dollars per hour in the United States. He then translates this five-dollar-an-hour salary into its worth back home where a worker earns five dollars a day. He also subconsciously estimates that his cost of living in the United States will be similar to that at home. Relying on these calculations, a migrant can reasonably assume that he will achieve his goal of a nest egg in a few years. Alfredo's experience illustrates this type of planning, characteristic of what migration scholars label "target earners."

Alfredo, a schoolteacher with a university education in Peru, heard through his friends Berta and Manuel that he could earn $6 per hour on Long Island. "When they told me, 'We're earning $6 per hour. Imagine. Here we generally work twelve hours, fourteen hours, and $6 per hour.' 'Six dollars per hour,' I would say, 'in eight hours that's $48. I will make this in eight hours. I will make more than $60, $70, $80 per day. I'll work seven days a week; I don't care about Sunday, holidays, or anything like that. I will be making at least $400 or $500 per week. After a few weeks, I will have $2,000 or $2,500.'" This estimate, because it does not measure expenses in the host country's terms, dooms the new immigrant to disillusionment upon arrival. Immigrants often refer to this new realization with the saying "You spend what you earn." Migrants from urban, educated backgrounds like Alfredo's are deceived roughly as often as peasants. As I have mentioned, I found that peasants were quite savvy about avoiding migration to cities in their home countries because they understood that this would make them completely dependent on a wage economy with little hope of betterment and with no subsistence agriculture to fall back on. However, they were not necessarily able to apply the same analysis when contemplating the economics of migrating to the United States. "I thought that housing was going to be cheaper and that finding work wasn't going to be so hard," Jesús, a Salvadoran peasant and a key informant, told me when I asked him what he had expected. "But no, here it's papers, permits, and so on. And you find a little bit of work in landscaping but it's only for six months and you have to save up some money to wait until the summer comes [so you can work again]." He too miscalculated the economics and found himself shocked and dismayed by the reality.

The exigencies of earning dollars descend swiftly on newly arrived migrants as they learn the true cost of living in the United States. The stress increases as they also learn that their income must stretch further than subsistence and cover expenses that they did not incur in their homelands and often did not anticipate incurring. Suddenly, as Tina—the spunky woman from Nicaragua—explained to me, you realize that "here you earn in dollars and you buy things in dollars. You have to spend a lot here. Rent is a serious matter here. . . . You can't be without work. Not anyone will tell you to take what you need for yourself; it's easier to find someone who won't tell you that. If you don't work you don't eat. If you're sick or not sick you always have to work. If you get sick it's really hard. It's expensive to have a child here. It's fifty dollars for a [medical] visit, the least would be forty dollars. And if work is slow or if you don't earn enough then you have to find a way to survive. Just for my daughter's care I have to take fifty dollars out of my pocket. Rent is fixed and you have to buy food. When I look around there's always something I need." Tina finds rent payments most irksome because she never paid rent in Nicaragua and she never imagined it would consume a third or more of her income.

When migrants learn that "you spend what you earn," they must face the task of reestimating the time they will need to stay to meet their obligations and, perhaps, their goals. Already feeling dehumanized after their journeys, many migrants are driven to new depths of despair by this realization. Like Don José, they feel deceived and depressed, desirous of returning home. But they cannot return because this would be humiliating (they would be seen as failures at home) and, more important, because they are heavily in debt. It is the fear of humiliation, the burden of their travel debt, and their responsibility to family left behind that figure most prominently among the conditions driving them to stay. Once they make it through the first critical months of adjustments, they are likely to become permanent, albeit undocumented and unintentional, settlers.

"People Change Here"

When I asked individuals about their first impressions of how their lives in the United States differed from their lives at home, I frequently received the response "People change here. They don't act like people do in my country. Here, they're more competitive, egotistical." They offer several reasons for this change, one they confront almost immediately upon arrival. Travelers arrive in the United States exhausted, expecting to find rejuvenation in the sight of familiar faces and a sense of home in friends' and relatives' embraces. Frequently they encounter cold shoulders and individualism instead. They find that the mutuality of immigrant life is shared deprivation more than shared provisioning. When Altagracia was reunited with her family in "Gold Coast," she anticipated hungrily the warmth of her religious, evangelical relatives. In El Salvador, they had often requested assistance from her and now she felt certain she could count on their generosity in return. "'Now it is my turn to receive,'" she told me she was thinking when she saw them. "'Now that I need them they are going to support me.'" But this is not what happened—just the opposite. Altagracia was told by her relatives to leave. "'You have to go elsewhere because, you know, you've got to find work. Food and housing are expensive,' they would say to me bit by bit. I got to see the real world as it is. . . . 'Who' I thought, 'could help me?' They didn't help me. Instead, I got help from people whom I had never even known. I received many favors from them. The law of recompensation exists because although those whom I helped didn't come and help me, there were other people who had such faith in me—so much faith that I was very happy. But this made me think: Why would these people feel so sure of me if they don't even know who I am? . . . I realized that these were good people and I had arrived at the feeling that now there were not good people left. But these people gave me a lot. I, personally, had lost my belief in people, in all people."

Altagracia's experience illustrates both the fiction and the fact of social relations. Much to her surprise, her relatives did not fulfill her expectations for proper treatment of guests or for kinship obligations to reciprocate past favors. She is deeply disillusioned with them, but she is heartened by other unnamed individuals who did come to her aid. Altagracia's story demonstrates that cooperation and mutual assistance *do* occur, but they occur outside home country norms and cannot be assumed.

Regardless of whether they received help in the first, impressionable stage of their lives in the United States, many individuals recall this epoch as formative of their bitter views toward compatriots here. They encounter what they term "egoism" in relatives and neighbors that would have been unimaginable back home. Sister Maria and Roberto Morán employ similar language to contrast the concern and cooperation characteristic of peasant lives in El Salvador with the social disregard and individualism they witness in the United States. "Here things are not like over there," Maria explained. "Over there you eat even if it's only beans with bread. Here you don't. Here whoever has [money] eats and whoever doesn't, can't. You don't know about any groups who will help you or anything. You don't know anything. It's worse living here. Because here everyone lives for himself."

I then asked her why she thinks this happens here and not in El Salvador, and she responded, "Because over there if you don't have anything then you go next door and say, 'Señora So-and-so, don't you have some beans you could give me so I can eat them with tortillas?' But here no. They tell you to go work. This happens even within the same family. I've seen it. They don't help each other because they all work and have their own money and if they give you something they expect you to pay for it. . . . My cousin told me one day, '[Maria], we are not going to be able to help you any more because I had better have some [money] left over for me.' She couldn't [help me anymore] because the expenses were very high and only her husband worked. So she told me, 'Find a way to make your own life.'" Roberto responded to my question about differences between people's behavior in El Salvador and in the United States by voicing an ultimatum. "Here if you don't have work you can't survive. You don't have [money] to pay the rent, to eat. You could die of hunger. Over there, no. If I don't work one week it's the same. I have food to eat. And I don't pay to live. And even without money I am okay but I can't live like that here."

Roberto is a diminutive man in his mid-twenties who worked as a peasant with a rural cooperative sponsored by the Catholic Church in the La Paz Department of El Salvador. He joined their efforts out of his own desire to alleviate human suffering but was forced to flee the country when his organization was targeted as subversive by the government. He describes this action as class repression by the elites against the peasantry; but he has a more difficult time comprehending how it can be that people of his own social class have stopped supporting each other just because they now live in the United States.

Don José has spent much time analyzing the genesis of this apparent change of heart. When he himself arrived in the United States, he could not find a job and became a burden on his brother. Though not rejected by his brother, he felt humiliated by his new status since in El Salvador he had always served as a generous father figure to his siblings. "I don't want to be a burden on anyone," he insisted. "There were eleven of us children in my family and I helped every one of them. . . . I was like a father to [my brother] before. I can't tell you all the things I have done for him; I was just like his father. . . . But [in California] when others were paying rent and food for me I felt bad with each day that came and went. I got sick two times from being without work and thinking that they were supporting me. That's horrible. In El Salvador I know that because people are self-supporting—their own house, their own things, and so on—[then they can help each other out and that's] magnificent! But here everything is money; everything has to be bought. . . . I didn't feel well at all, at all. I felt humiliated, *apenado*. So I said it was better for me to leave and I did."

Unlike some other informants, Don José blames immigrants' retreat from reciprocity on their induction into an economy where everything must be paid for with money. He feels that this is not a change in their temperament, but a change in their own material conditions. A peasant who produced most of his family's needs and who enjoyed few luxuries requiring payment in hard currency, he argues, was freer to help out neighbors in times of need. But monetary demands are different in the United States—particularly the ever-pressing necessity of paying rent, which averages $300 per month for Salvadorans and $425 for South Americans, according to my survey. People react to this reality by scaling back on assistance to others even though they wish to help. During a long conversation, Don José emphatically insisted that "brotherhood among Hispanics has always existed, in El Salvador and in all the countries of the world . . . brotherhood exists. The problem is that [Gold Coast], because it is a city of millionaires, has extremely high rent. So, of course, Hispanics see themselves as obligated not to offer shelter or housing free to anyone who has just arrived and who is unemployed and can't pay rent. [The leaseholder] wants to get people who can pay, who can help pay the rent. So perhaps they deny help to their Hispanic brothers but it is not because they don't want to, but because of circumstances beyond their control. They can't let people in for free when they have to pay more than a thousand dollars for an apartment and they need to have four or five people there who can help them pay the rent. If they let in people for free, who is going to help them make the rent? But if they have a lot of people in the apartment, the building manager will throw them out. So they see themselves obliged, perhaps bothering their conscience, not to help their brothers out. But it is not they are not willing; no, we have the desire because we have the tradition of serving others. I have helped a lot of people . . . in whatever country I'm in I want to help others. But sometimes you can't, you want to but you can't and sometimes someone who can doesn't want to. But we Hispanics, we're like this: we always help each other. But here, there aren't circumstances for doing it. The conditions put us in a position that we can't help others. If you don't have a fixed income—for instance, all the landscapers, all the construction workers who work seasonally don't have work in the winter. They are only able to make it through the winter because of the little savings they have from the working season. But if they start to donate their money to help others, they will have no way to feed themselves. For this reason they have to turn a cold shoulder to their Salvadoran or other Hispanic brothers. Many times they don't collaborate, but it is because of this—they can't help because their circumstances don't allow them."

Don José argues here that reciprocal relations often cannot be sustained given people's pressures to make ends meet. But he bases his argument on the transition migrants undergo from highly self-sufficient peasants to dependent wage earners. Does his reasoning work as well for migrants of urban backgrounds? Informants who had lived in metropolitan areas expressed dismay at how people "change" in the United States too, but they couched their complaints in terms of "competition" and "jealousy," not in the language Don José employs. Juanita's discussion of her uncle's behavior offers a sample. "Here it's competitive, completely competitive," she insisted. "I swear. . . . It's like people are happy when you have problems. I note all of this. I don't know if I'm the only one. I'm going to tell you one story from my own family. I bought myself a small car. I bought it for $350 and I walked to where it was. But I didn't have any papers and since I didn't have papers I called my uncle who has papers and insurance. I asked him to help me. I said, 'Uncle, I bought myself a car.' I called him by phone. 'Oh, good,' he said. 'Now you are going to have to find someone who can get insurance for you.' He didn't want to come and help me. So since I didn't have any way to insure the car I had to give it back."

The universality of my informants' dissatisfaction with their compatriots' demeanor in the United States leads me to conclude, in contrast to Don José, that class background, and even the commodification of social relations resulting from these individuals' greater incorporation into modernity, are insufficient to explain the suspension of home country social rules among them. Both urban and peasant immigrants were innocent of neither the globalization of capitalism nor their dependency on wage income. To a greater or lesser extent, they had been integrated into the world system prior to migration and this had not completely undermined so-called precapitalist social relations based on kinship and mutual trust. Rather, the critical difference to their experience in the United States that so radically affects the quality of their relationships is their mandate to produce a surplus above and beyond that needed to provide for their own needs. It is their transnational obligations that strain their alacrity to engage in mutual assistance with compatriots as they did at home. As I have illustrated above, newly arrived immigrants are burdened with debt and remittance responsibilities which require that they generate more income than that required to meet their own needs. As I shall document later on, they frequently must wring this surplus out of their own deprivation, forgoing everything but an ascetic existence. The fact that most immigrants retain ties to family and friends in their homelands signifies that they are beholden to social networks in two very different countries. Whereas in their premigratory lives, their social networks comprised local and regional ties, now they are stretched to fulfill transnational obligations as well, creating two competing sets of relationships.

Jesús's predicament illustrates this span. About two years after he arrived, Jesús received a letter from his compadre, René Maldonaldo, asking him to finance his own journey. Jesús borrowed money from several friends to send to René. He began the process of repaying the loans while he was working the busy summer season as a landscaper. In September, Jesús's wife called. It was an emergency; his daughter had fallen from a tree and hit her head. She urgently needed medical treatment and there was no money. Could he send some immediately? Jesús was able to assemble the funds only by suspending payment on his debts and hurriedly borrowing more money from other friends. When the end of the landscaping season came, Jesús still owed money to many of his creditors. They became irritated with him because, also unemployed, they needed the money for daily expenses. With no income of his own (undocumented workers do not qualify for unemployment insurance), Jesús could not repay them and his friendships soured as a consequence. The next time he needed to borrow money he encountered few sympathetic ears.

Because immigrants are asked to provide mutual assistance to disparate groups of people in different countries, they may not engage in reciprocal relations in the same way that they did in their homelands. More precisely, while people are called upon and do assist one another quite frequently, they are not always in a position to do so because of demands from home. There is a trade-off; they are simultaneously pulled into and away from relationships with fellow migrants. Other poor communities do not experience this divided attention; they are freer to focus on local relationships alone. This is amply evidenced within the social network literature on poor communities in Latin America (e.g., Lomnitz 1977; Roberts 1973; Brown 1977), in El Salvador (Nieves 1979), and in the United States (e.g., Stack 1974; Horowitz 1983). These authors illustrate how people, women in particular, develop and maintain reciprocal bonds, knitting nuclear and extended families together into networks that exchange many items needed for survival. Items exchanged vary from tangible resources such as money and physical amenities like televisions and clothing to less tangible resources such as child care, emotional support, and information about jobs. The circular exchange of such items functions to distribute wealth quite evenly within the cluster of participating households. Families who acquire resources that they do not wish to share are ostracized by the others. If they choose to withhold distribution of this extra income, they must cut off their networks and they may move out of the community at large. In her research among poor, rural-to-urban migrants in Mexico City, Lomnitz (1977) found that the Latin custom of *compadrazgo*, or fictive kinship, transcended its traditional religious use to include members of these social networks. Normally, compadrazgo links couples through the baptism of their children. A couple chooses another couple to be godparents to their child, and the two couples now are linked as compadres as in the relation between Jesús and René. In Lomnitz's community, "compadre" became a term used among males linked by the networks and not limited to godparent ties. Women could also choose close friends to be "comadres." In this manner compadrazgo was adapted by the migrants to their new urban environments and the exigencies placed on individuals and social groups.

People Do Help Each Other

Compadrazgo has not been extended to friendships and networks among my informants on Long Island. That is, I did not hear friends using the terms "compadre" or "comadre" in casual bantering. I was told that where it is practiced, it has preserved its religious, baptismal function. This does not mean, however, that mutual assistance is nonexistent among these migrants. On the contrary, people help each other frequently. Cooperation *does* occur within households although it does not necessarily involve income sharing or continuous exchange networks. While informants may feel disillusioned with people who do not participate, there is little of the ostracism that Lomnitz observed in her community (1977). Rather, there is an understanding that those who can participate will, and those who do not participate either cannot or are not close associates. For example, within all the housing arrangements I describe in chapter 8 cooking is almost invariably performed by individuals or in small groups of friends or kin. These same groupings buy food together and store it in their rooms or in designated areas of the kitchen. Many individuals write their names with Magic Markers on items stored in collective areas such as the refrigerator and cabinets. These are formal separations of goods. Informally, food is often exchanged among individuals who are not part of the cooking group. For instance, one group may finish cooking and sit down to eat while the next group prepares its food. Ultimately the second group may share some of its food with the first, or the first may leave food for the second. This tends to occur more frequently on Sundays when there is more time to cook and relax. Single men eat out much of the week and cook only on Sundays, when they will often prepare a favorite dish to be shared by everyone. This informal food sharing helps strengthen and solidify social ties to nonrelatives. Some groups, however, never share anything and are most likely to separate. I have noted this most often in households where groups of different nationalities coreside or where there are personality conflicts.

Assistance among coethnics is not limited to people from the same household. Margarita Flores, a Salvadoran mother in her early thirties, for instance, helped out a friend who was injured on the job and could not work for several months. The two met in the United States at a previous job and had been friends for some time before the accident. Margarita's friend later told me that she was able to make ends meet during her recuperation only because her women friends paid her rent and expenses. She considered their help to be a loan, though she did not know if she could repay them even when her disability lawsuit was settled. Margarita, who had been trained as a schoolteacher in El Salvador, also assisted a boarder in her apartment who is illiterate in Spanish. She helped him write letters to his wife and joked to me about her labors, saying, "I guess I had better start charging him for all the time it takes!"

Assistance also flows among neighboring households. When Amalia Sandoval gave birth to a son with heart trouble, her friends who live in the same building donated baby clothes and brought her food. Since she could no longer work at her hotel job, she began to sew clothes for a living. The friends not only ordered clothes from her but also helped to widen her clientele. In another example, Ana Fernández and her common-law husband Jorge Ayala share their telephone with the residents of the apartment next door. Ana and Jorge are a teenage Salvadoran couple with two small children who share their cramped quarters with Jorge's brother and uncle. But the apartment next door holds ten single men who often drop by Ana's house to converse, to use the phone, and so on. Cooperation even exists among people who deny that it does. For instance, as we have seen, Juanita was angry with her uncle when he failed to help her get insurance for her car; she held him up as an example of the competitive lifestyle that so dismayed her in the United States. Yet the same uncle had loaned her the money to come to the United States. He had also taught her how to put advertisements in the *Pennysaver* (a local free paper) to get housecleaning jobs. He made Juanita's transition to life in the United States quite smooth.

While there is ample evidence of mutual assistance among my informants, they feel that this help does not approach the degree of mutual support that they enjoyed in their home countries. There is a good reason for this disparity: at home differences in resources among interconnected households were leveled through continual exchange that strengthened social bonds. That is, the price paid for long-term reciprocity and its insurance against individual disaster was homogeneous social status. Immigrants cannot afford this price. If they followed the rules of balanced or generalized reciprocity as ordained in their home countries, their principal goal of producing a surplus would be defeated; the surplus they produced would have to be redistributed throughout their kinship networks.

As Lomnitz, Stack, and others skillfully illustrate, the centripetal force generated by exchange networks pulls people inward and impedes their escape. Individuals who attempt to extricate themselves from the network are ostracized, particularly if they try to hold onto wealth rather than redistribute it. Migrants undergo two forces simultaneously: centripetal obligations toward relations in the host country and centrifugal obligations toward those in the home country. Since migrants share the compulsion to produce surplus income, they understand that they are unlikely to be completely severed from their friends in the United States if they send home remittances instead of circulating this wealth through their networks here. But the price they pay is that there will not always be someone to help them in times of need. Thus, shortly after arriving in the United States, many people were disappointed by their relatives' behavior. The kind of hospitality and common courtesy they expected was suspended here; they saw people less as a community to rely on than as individuals to compete against for success in the immigrant game. These early experiences served as a solid introduction to the realities they would face daily.

Capitalizing on Greenhorns

There is one more early lesson that immigrants learn as they revise their idealized notions of life in the United States. They learn that their "friends" are capable not only of turning a cold shoulder to them, but also of using them to their own advantage. Many individuals told me that they came to the United States prepared to be exploited by Americans and they often were, but they did not come prepared to be taken advantage of by their own coethnic peers. They told me stories in which they figured as naive newcomers who fell easy prey to older migrants with greater expertise. Typically, this fall from innocence occurred during a time of particular vulnerability: the pursuit of the first job. (Li [1977] has documented this phenomenon among Chinese in Chicago, and Grasmuck and Pessar [1991:185] among Dominicans in New York.) Jaime's example is a good case in point. A baseball jacket manufacturer from Lima, Peru, he arrived on Long Island in 1988 to a royal welcome. His sponsor, a Peruvian immigrant from his Lima barrio, took him in, gave him food, and provided a room for him. The next day, however, the tides turned. Jaime was put to work in his sponsor's construction business laboring fourteen hours per day, six days per week. For his efforts, he was paid $250 but docked $50 each week for the lunches that the sponsor's wife packed for him daily. In addition, he had to pay the sponsor back $200 per month in rent. Jaime remembers these first six months bitterly: "I had to separate me from myself. If I hadn't I would have cried. I had to leave behind my personality—like taking my clothes off and putting new ones on." Jaime says that he was willing to work hard, but not to be exploited, not to lose his dignity. In one short week he descended from boss to laborer, from man to mouse. As soon as he found another opportunity, he left his sponsor and now exclaims proudly, "*Yo bailo con mi propio pañuelo*" (I'm dancing to my own tune now). Determined never to be so humiliated again, particularly at the hands of a compatriot, Jaime in three short years has found a steady, union job working in a nursing home and serves as a manager for an office-cleaning firm at night. He even employs some of his own relatives now. He recently bought a house in Gold Coast and has sublet it to many fellow Peruvians, turning a profit by charging them more in rent than he pays for the mortgage.

   Marco, the Peruvian sociologist, found his first job in construction. He was hired by a fellow Peruvian who held contracts in New York City.

But after several weeks on the job, Marco had not been paid; when he complained to his boss, he was summarily dismissed. Roberto had a similar experience. A Salvadoran peasant and volunteer church worker, Roberto is in his twenties but has a boyish face that exudes innocence. The first job he found was painting houses and doing odd jobs for fourteen hours per day. His boss, a Salvadoran acquaintance of the man who had sponsored Roberto's emigration, refused to pay him after two weeks. Aware that he was being taken advantage of and feeling the pressure to repay his debts, Roberto quit and started a job landscaping. He has kept that job, with no raise, ever since.

First job experiences of many informants mirror the kind of frustration Jaime expresses above. Jaime's and Marco's anguish was exacerbated by their drop in status from owner and organizer to worker. Marco's treatment put him inside a world that he had previously observed as an outsider. An academic and union organizer in his native Peru, Marco only truly experienced blue-collar life once he became a worker in the United States. "I just recently began to understand why it was that workers in my country found it difficult to go to a meeting, a conference. or to read a book," he confessed one day. "Now, somehow I understand their reasons. Why? Because when you do physical work, especially when it's heavy, the person who is not used to this gets tired. He's not going to be ready to study. Being tired makes you go to bed; it's the tiredness. You don't feel pushed to study, especially complex things. I feel this. This is one of my biggest worries—that I am losing my willingness to study, the will to analyze. I am losing my desire to write. . . . When I am doing these jobs I feel strange. It's not that the things are difficult, they are just strange. They aren't undignified." Few Salvadorans feel this same drop in status; most were peasants or workers in their home country who assumed blue-collar jobs such as landscaping and factory work in the United States. But they too feel exploited and disillusioned. What piques their resentment is their exploitation at the hands of peers.

In the rigid class hierarchies of their homelands, migrants were accustomed to patron-client relationships, to being taken advantage of by people of superior class status. Thus, when they arrive in the United States, they accord Americans a similar class deference. When Americans exploit them, they recognize it but do not resent it with the same vehemence as when their compatriot equals take advantage of them. Immigrants are angered when they are exploited by gringos, but they are *embittered* when their own people exploit them. This gives them a strong resolve to learn the ropes as quickly as possible so that they will never be made to feel so vulnerable and humiliated again. "The people who come here change," Sonia insisted. "Before they come here they're naive, fools as we say, but they change once they come to this country. When they come here they become big shots, as if they were children of the wealthy and, maybe, they're really the children of poor folk."

When the innocence of neophyte immigrants is exploited by more ex-perienced coethnics, the newcomers are introduced to the opportunity structure they will face and learn to use to their own ends. They learn that in the land of marvels the pathways to success are fewer than they anticipated; they learn the hard way that one of the best avenues avail-able is utilizing resources within their own community to their advan-tage. Capitalizing on greenhorns is, quite literally, generating capital by paying them less than the value of their labors. There are many forms of expropriating wealth from within the immigrant community, as I will discuss in detail in the coming chapters. But immigrants' critical and disillusioning initiation into the dog-eat-dog world they vividly describe occurs too early for them to comprehend why their friends and family behave so differently here.

Chapter Five

THE CONSTRUCTION OF MARGINALITY

DO NOT LOOK for Noemí Orellana by ringing the bell on the small, two-story clapboard house where she lives in Wyandanch, Long Island. Go down the dusty driveway dotted with glass shards, broken plastic, and bits of car parts to the back of the house where the yard yields to a large car on cinder blocks adorned by greasy tools and hand cloths. Turn right and descend the thick cement steps to the basement door. Knock loudly. This is where Noemí and her year-old daughter live. On a scorching July afternoon the door opens to reveal a stove, several large pots boiling away on the burners, and a small table covered with a plastic tablecloth. It is difficult to see further into the windowless interior. There is a hall light glowing a few feet past the old refrigerator and a flickering television glued to the Spanish-language channel that illuminates through the darkness as best it can. On the right is a door latched tight to a tether on the wall lest it swing open and obstruct the hallway. Inside the door there is a toilet with no seat, a sweaty floor leading to a slim shower. No window, no fan. Next to the bathroom is another room, small and so opaque that only dim outlines of beds and clothes are intelligible. In Noemí's bedroom a twin-size mattress abuts the wall on one side and piles of worldly goods hug the other walls and embrace the small playpen in the middle.

The apartment entombs Noemí; she emerges from the stairwell only rarely during the day—to retrieve her daughter from the driveway or to get into her decrepit Chevrolet Chevette (for which she has no license or insurance) for short junkets nearby. Before she became pregnant, she worked as a maid for an American family in the distant town of Hempstead. After the baby was born, Noemí found a factory job but was laid off several months ago. Now she supports herself and her daughter through splicing together income from several sources. She awakes early, shifting the sleeping baby from the bed to the playpen, and drives a friend with no car to work for a weekly fee. She cooks for her entire household, does the cleaning, and manages affairs while the men who occupy the other bedroom work during the day as landscapers. They pay her rent and additional cash for board. And during the week-ends and evenings she scours among her friends and their acquaintances for clients to buy the Mary Kay cosmetics she stores in a large cardboard box in the hatchback of her car. She does not recreate at the movies or in restaurants but under the shade of the large maple tree beside the driveway. And her big excursions entail going to the grocery store and to the office where she renews her permit to work every six months— although it has been of little use since she got it.

From Noemí's front door, mainstream America cannot be seen. She does not hide from it—indeed she would like to find it—but she only glimpses it at the grocery store or post office, and then only when she leaves Wyandanch. This town, a quintessential Long Island minority pocket, is 85 percent African-American and the rest Latino, mostly Puerto Ricans and Salvadorans like Noemí. Noemí's world, the world in which most of my informants live, has evolved parallel to the world of the larger society, and there are few links between the two. Immigrants yearn for a taste of what they know exists beyond their thresholds and beyond their reach. Time after time my presence would ignite their passions to see the "real" America or, particularly among women who worked as maids or provided child care for middle-class families, to understand "real" Americans' behavior. White and blonde (at least according to them), I looked "real" American to them but, unlike most other "real" Americans they came across, could speak Spanish. Alfredo was particularly keen on deciphering the America of his dreams. As soon as I drew near, he would drill me with so many questions about "real" American life that I could barely get a question of my own in edgewise.

From Alfredo and the others I learned to interpret their yearning for inclusion in the mainstream through their language of exclusion. Alfredo told me one day, for instance, that "for me Americans are non-communicative, but not because they don't want to be communicative, rather because I can't talk to them because I don't speak English. I can't, I can't communicate. And I observe their customs only from very far away. I haven't seen real American family life. I notice that they go to work every morning; they take a train or their cars and they come back at night. But I know nothing more because, frankly, I don't live with Americans. I live with Latins. And these are [Salvadoran] peasants, they're from the countryside, not even people from towns. So I can't tell you what the customs of North Americans are because I haven't gone into their homes. I see you once in a while but you're not going to act [like a "real" American] when you come visit us as you would in your own house. You're not going to act like you do every day."

In this chapter I examine the structural, economic, and demographic conditions of Long Island that created niches of low-wage jobs and attracted immigrants, especially undocumented immigrants, to fill many of them. These people enter a very restricted sector of the local economy, taking jobs that Long Islanders shun and that offer little opportunity for advancement. Immigrants are also shunted into marginal neighborhoods populated almost exclusively by members of poor minority groups. This residential segregation, a topic I will address in depth in chapter 8, exacerbates immigrants' feelings of isolation from the mainstream. Immigrants also suffer as linguistic and cultural outsiders and from skills mismatches. They lack English and other skills and credentials required by jobs in the mainstream, formal economy. Their prospects have been further diminished by IRCA, the Immigration Reform and Control Act of 1986. All of these disadvantages make immigrants an ideal labor source for employers seeking cheap—and often exploitable—workers. Additionally, since immigrants are saddled with the need to produce surplus income, they are less likely than other workers to complain about their working conditions or about abuses such as nonpayment.

The exploitation of immigrant labor is not unique to Long Island nor is it exclusively a contemporary phenomenon. However, the late-twentieth-century economy, with its emphasis on service sector jobs, differs sharply from the economy that immigrants encountered at the turn of the century, when there were far greater opportunities in manufacturing. Many of these migrants were able to rise within industries owing to a constricted labor supply (immigration was severely regulated in the 1920s), an expanding economy, and unionization (e.g., Calavita 1981; Brody 1980). The prospects for such upward mobility are much less bright for today's immigrants because they enter an economy increasingly polarized between high wage earners and low wage earners (Sassen 1988). My informants are quick to recognize that life in the United States, and particularly their ability to produce surplus income, is not as easy as they envisioned. Not surprisingly, most are unaware of the structural economic conditions that impinge on them, but they do understand that their wages will barely cover their basic necessities, let alone stretch to meet remittance, debt, and other obligations. By observing their own community, immigrants learn that those who advance despite the restrictive climate are those who conduct small-scale business catering to coethnics.

Across time larger numbers of immigrants have started up small businesses than the native-born (Waldinger 1986; Waldinger, Aldrich, and Ward 1990; Portes and Bach 1985; Portes and Zhou 1992). As I trace the limitations that drive the groups I studied toward business pursuits, I will be constructing a history familiar to many earlier generations. However, there is one marked distinction between my portrayal and previous descriptions. My informants perceive themselves as exploited by these small-time entrepreneurs; they paint their community in shades of abuse while the greater society is largely exonerated. For them, their past lives were characterized by cooperation, and their lives in the

United States resemble a dog-eat-dog world driven by coethnic exploiters. From an outsider's perspective, this portrayal appears excessive since, as I have already observed, a great deal of mutual assistance occurs among these people. However, *their* perception of their predicament needs to be understood and explained, for it differs strikingly from most portrayals of immigrant populations. I will begin this process by documenting my informants' marginalization and then show how they turn to it as a source of economic opportunities.

WHY LONG ISLAND?

A first step in the process of describing immigrants' marginalization is to explain why they migrate to Long Island. It will become clear that this explication is far from simple; nor does it conform to any one of the models, discussed in chapter 1, that compete to explain the phenomenon of immigration to postindustrial economies. Rather, select elements of these models illuminate the specific case of Long Island. Additionally, the Long Island job market is being impacted by major demographic shifts, a factor that is not addressed in the other models.

For many readers it may seem strange to hear about people migrating to an area popularly stereotyped as the archetypal white, middle-class suburb. Why would they not migrate to the inner city, where presumably they would encounter more job opportunities and acceptance? First, it is key to note that Long Island has received numerous waves of migrants over the past decades; Italians and Puerto Ricans figure prominently among other groups. More recently, however, immigrants have been flowing onto the island in ever-increasing waves. Salvadorans constitute the largest single group in this wave, estimated to number ninety thousand, but Asians, Middle Easterners, and other Latin Americans have also arrived (see table 7.1 below). It may also seem strange that so many immigrants from developing countries come to Long Island. An area where there is a high cost of living, where the median price of a single-family house is over $200,000, would seem to be within the reach only of families with higher-than-average incomes.

Long Island is an expensive area that has a history of thriving off high-technology, defense-related industries demanding an educated, skilled, and well-paid workforce. Why should such an area become a magnet to immigrants? The answer lies in the fact that during the 1980s the Long Island economy produced many thousands of low-wage, dead-end jobs that few natives would take. Natives spurned these jobs either because they had better opportunities available to them, or because the low wages fell short of the cost of living and they left the island to find a

TABLE 5.1
Unemployment Trends: Nassau-Suffolk Area,
1983 to 1988 (annual averages)

| | Nassau/Suffolk | | | | Outside Area | |
	All Workers	Hispanic[a]	Black	White	New York State	U.S.
1983	6.4	4.6	12.3	5.2	8.6	9.6
1985	4.1	5.5	6.8	3.9	6.5	7.2
1986	3.5	4.6	3.9	3.4	6.3	7.0
1988	2.6	4.1	5.3	2.4	4.2	5.5

Sources: New York State Department of Labor, *Annual Labor Reports* (1985, 1987, 1988, 1990); *Statistical Abstract of the United States* (1987, 1988, 1990).
  [a] Persons of Hispanic Origin may be of any race.

more economical place to live. The new jobs were created by three trends: (1) the predominance of defense industries, which spawned peripheral manufacturing industries requiring large quantities of low-cost labor, and which kept Long Island from experiencing the deindustrialization so common elsewhere, (2) a rising demand for services, particularly to households, and (3) a decline in the native-born youth and young worker population that would normally fill the jobs created. In short, a dynamic economy and a tight labor market opened niches for immigrant laborers. The shortage of laborers is reflected in the unemployment rates on the island, which stayed very low through the 1980s, averaging 4 to 4.5 percent during most of the decade (New York State Department of Labor 1988, 1990; see table 5.1).

The Defense Industry Niche

The aircraft and aerospace industry on Long Island was begun in the early 1900s with the establishment of Grumman Aircraft and several other firms (Thruelson 1976). Nurtured by World War II, the Cold War, space exploration in the 1970s, and the military buildup of the 1980s, Long Island's economy was "constructed around a core of Grumman and four other major government contractors (Allied-Signal, Unisys, Harris, and Lockheed) which specialized in technologically sophisticated aerospace weaponry" (Carmean, Romo, and Schwartz n.d.:7). These industries characterized as "core" have engendered an extensive array of "peripheral," dependent firms that supply both manufactured goods and specialty services, such as accounting, management consulting, and lobbying, to the core industries (ibid.:11). The domination of the aerospace industries in Long Island manufacturing—at least until the 1990s recession and the downsizing of the military—is staggering; the Big Five contractors and their trading network account for some 72 percent of the industrial jobs in the region (ibid.:8).[1] The industry spurred a demand for highly trained engineers, managers, and the like, which, in turn, stimulated local institutions of higher education to meet these labor needs by forming training programs. The prospect of high-paying jobs has kept many of the highest-skilled young adult workers from leaving the area despite the spiraling cost of housing, energy, tax, and transportation.[2]

The core industries did not provide direct employment to my informants; rather, many obtained jobs in firms that supply parts to the core. These factories, concentrated in areas like Farmingdale, are basically light manufacturers specializing in plastics and metals. The wages offered in these firms, averaging no more than six dollars per hour (and generally without benefits), pale in comparison with the wages of workers, managers, and engineers in the core industries. The small companies also suffer from the boom-and-bust cycles of major defense contractors. Undocumented immigrants are easy to lay off, and there is a continual supply available when their labor is needed. In addition to the defense-related contractors, there are numerous other light industries on Long Island where immigrants are employed. These include direct-mail marketing, as well as the manufacture of office supplies, condiments, cosmetics, household items, spare car parts, and grocery carts, to name a few. Here too, migrant labor is generally welcome, although the degree to which employers comply with IRCA mandates to verify work authorization varies widely. This has led to a concentration of undocumented immigrants in those firms that are less strict about following the letter of the law.

Not surprisingly, immigrants are one of the populations most affected by downturns in the local and the greater economy. Long Island was able to skirt the deindustrial plague infecting New York City and other major industrial centers during the 1980s, but it was not immune to the late-decade recession and the downsizing of the U.S. military machine in the 1990s. The latter has had very severe repercussions for Long Island; Northrop Grumman (the product of a 1994 merger) will have reduced its workforce to 3,800 by the end of 1995 from a high of 9,170 in early 1994 (*New York Times* September 23, 1994). Both economic downturns have contributed to a much more hostile climate for employment in general, but their impact has been especially severe on my informants, who occupy the lowest and most vulnerable positions. As middle-class families cut back their expenses, they hire fewer house cleaners and landscapers and eat out less often; as the defense contracts dwindle,

Immigrant women at work. Photograph by Susan Calvin

companies scale back orders to peripheral firms. Consequently, the briskest business to be found in the immigrant communities during the hard winter of 1990–1991 was in the food pantries. During those months I often heard people complain, "At least if we lived in El Salvador, Doña Fulana would lend us some beans. No one except the church helps us here."

Domestic Services Niche

The highly paid defense workers, along with other high-income Long Islanders such as business executives who commute into New York City and local government officials, increased the demand for services on the island, especially those of domestic workers such as live-in housekeepers and nannies, landscapers, and house cleaners. The need for these workers has also increased owing to the growth in female labor force participation starting in the 1970s, perhaps best known as the "Zoë Baird phenomenon."[3] Characterized by low salaries and low status, the majority of the service jobs created are filled by new, often undocumented immigrants. Indeed, nearly all of my female informants worked either in factories or in domestic service jobs. There were few other options open to them, and the domestic jobs, while humiliating and confining, hide workers from exposure to the INS. These workers may be poorly remunerated, as are *internas* (live-in domestics), who average $150–$200 per week. Others are relatively well paid: house cleaners, for example, average $8–$10 per hour off the books. But if the cottage industry of house-cleaning is comparatively lucrative, the work is exhausting and potentially hazardous. As a result, women tend to suspend housecleaning when they get pregnant, particularly to avoid working with noxious chemicals. Furthermore, it is difficult to find enough houses to sustain full-time employment; many cleaners work only part-time.

Immigrant men provide outdoor services to the Long Island establishment. They labor as landscapers, painters, construction workers, car washers, and pool maintenance attendants. Their work is highly seasonal, generally from March through early December, and they are paid only for the days they work, not for rainy days, sick days, or holidays in most cases. Wages run between $5 and $8 per hour; men are often asked to work twelve-hour days with few breaks and sometimes without access to sanitary facilities. They are exposed to the elements and they are conspicuous to the INS as they push lawnmowers, tote leaf blowers, and ride atop equipment trucks. The more fortunate have steady jobs, while the less fortunate, and the newly arrived in particular, frequent shape-up points seeking day labor jobs. At these shape-ups, men gather at dawn waiting for employers to offer them a day or two of work. By midmorning the failures remain behind, listless and demoralized, knowing that their chances of landing any work that day are slim. Employers of seasonal laborers, many of them descendants of Italian immigrants who toiled on the North Shore's "Gold Coast" of turn-of-the-century mansions as gardeners and laborers (LaGumina 1988), were stung by the Immigration Reform and Control Act of 1986, which required them to find laborers with work authorization. It was nearly impossible to find native replacements for their undocumented workers; youth and young workers preferred other jobs to the backbreaking work of landscaping. One landscaper told me he spent a thousand dollars on advertising to find workers with the proper documents, but with no success. The native workers took more lucrative, and less grimy, jobs.

Changing Demographics and Labor Niches

The third trend in Long Island's economy is a demographic shift that has affected the labor market. In the 1980s youth and young workers on Long Island had become so scarce that in an expanding economy they could be selective about the employment they accepted, if they chose to seek employment at all. The island's spectacular population growth after World War II, when mass production of housing created such communities as Levittown almost overnight, slowed dramatically in the 1970s and 1980s. Growth for Nassau County stalled in the 1970s, then began

Salvadoran landscaper after beating by his boss.
Photograph by Susan Calvin

declining. Between 1970 and 1980, Nassau County lost 7.5 percent of its population and another 2.6 percent between 1980 and 1990. Suffolk County gained 13.9 percent between 1970 and 1980, but this rate dropped to 2.9 percent between 1980 and 1990. The most dramatic losses were caused by the 1970s and 1980s "baby bust." Between 1970 and 1990, Long Island's youthful population (to age twenty-five) dropped by over 25 percent, from 1,177,512 to 873,132. The most precipitous drop was in teenagers, whose numbers plummeted by 31 percent between 1980 and 1990. The impact on the labor market has been a deficit of young, inexperienced workers who traditionally earn low wages (see table 5.2).

The drop in the island's birthrate is reflected in the area's school-age population. Long Island records reveal that between the school years 1969–1970 and 1988–1989 the total enrolled population for Nassau

TABLE 5.2
Population by Age, 1960 to 1990: Nassau-Suffolk Area
(in thousands)

	1960	1970	1980	1990	Change 1980–1990
< 15 years	667.6	780.2	578.6	500.7	–77.9
15–19	119.3	242.4	260.9	179.0	–81.9
20–24	75.6	155.0	206.5	193.4	–13.1
25–44	591.9	631.0	702.7	835.7	133.0
45–64	374.9	546.6	601.2	576.8	–24.4
65 +	137.7	197.9	256.0	323.6	67.6

Source: U.S. Bureau of the Census, Census of Population and Housing (1960, 1970, 1980, 1990).

Note: Figures rounded, may not add up precisely.

and Suffolk Counties dropped by 38 percent, from 631,219 to 391,067. The decline was more precipitous in Nassau County, down 49 percent, compared to Suffolk's 26 percent. But at the same time Latino students' enrollment climbed 237 percent overall—from 9,274 to 22,016.

Youth and young adults, discouraged by high living costs, were moving to other areas. "The dramatic drop in the pool of teen-age workers and the broadening range of job opportunities now open to women have put severe staffing strains on Island employers in these occupations" (New York State Department of Labor 1990:9). The decline in the number of youth and young adults is due in part to declining birthrates but also to the astronomic increases in the cost of housing and maintaining a family on Long Island in the past decade. For instance, the average selling price for homes on Long Island tripled from $78,290 in 1982 to $224,098 in 1988 (Long Island Almanac 1989). Clearly, the escalating cost of housing has become such a disincentive to staying in the region that "the area's economic growth is being negatively affected by the shortage of affordable housing" (New York State Department of Labor 1988:15). The situation is expected to worsen in the near future: projections indicated that between 1985 and 1995 Long Island would lose 124,400 fifteen- to twenty-four-year-olds and would gain 103,600 persons aged sixty-five and older (New York State Department of Labor 1990:1). By the year 2000 only 17 percent of Long Island's population will be young adults (twenty–thirty-four years of age) (Yago, Wu, and Seifert 1987:1).

Thus, young workers on Long Island have recently faced a more open job market than did preceding generations—particularly the "baby boomers," whose mass in the demographic pyramid created a glut of workers and talent leading to job competition and blocked mobility

(Newman 1988). But the "baby busters" cannot afford to support themselves and their families on Long Island now, unless they are highly trained professionals earning large salaries. As a result, some youth resort to living at home while others leave the area. Their misfortune has been a boon to immigrants, who have eagerly populated the niche forsaken by them, landscaping work being a prime example. There are many other examples in the service sector of the economy, such as restaurant jobs. Bailey (1987:63) indicates that nationally 70 percent of all fast-food workers are between the ages of sixteen and twenty, and 85 percent were younger than twenty-four. But many fast-food establishments on Long Island have experienced difficulty in recruiting employees—any employees—and have resorted to hiring two tiers of workers, one tier to handle the language-intensive work of cashiers and managers, and another tier—mostly immigrant—to handle food production and cleanup.

Immigrant men now also dominate low-rank jobs in ethnic restaurants where young descendants of earlier immigrants once labored as dishwashers, busboys, and cooks' assistants. Immigrants rarely serve as waiters, however. This is an example of how immigrants and native workers complement each other *within* the same industry. The immigrants, primarily Salvadorans, are paid in cash and earnings are widely divergent: dishwashers almost always earn four dollars per hour or less and there are numerous reports of exploitation. One Salvadoran, Benjamín, was paid only thirteen dollars per day for a twelve-hour day and had one day's pay deducted to cover his transportation costs. Needless to say, dishwashing represents the very bottom rung of the male job status hierarchy (owing in part to its association with women's work). Busboys do much better and can clear three hundred dollars in a week, depending on how tips are divided with waiters.

Another niche opened to immigrants, in part by the demographic shifts, is commercial and industrial cleaning. Clubs, offices, conference centers, and banquet halls requiring setup, cleaning, and maintenance labor hire many immigrant men. The hierarchical organization of these establishments tends to comprise more tiers than that in other fields, with the result that some ethnics can rise to the level of managers where they make hiring and other decisions. Both South and Central American men and women are also employed in commercial cleaning. Men will not perform housecleaning or chambermaid tasks, but accept positions as commercial cleaners—probably because the jobs are less visible. Office cleaning offers other advantages to both groups: the jobs require no language skills, are performed at night when there is less likelihood of INS raids, and are relatively unregimented. Cleaners work until the job is finished but are paid an hourly wage based on an estimate of how long the job should take. A few cleaning corporations are owned by Latinos who negotiate contracts with buildings and hire other Latinos as laborers. In some cases, one person is picked to manage the group responsible for cleaning a building or buildings, and this person gains the power to hire and dismiss workers. Jaime, the Peruvian who at home had owned a baseball jacket factory, is a good example of this. As manager of a night cleaning crew, he has been able to hire friends and family. New hires tend to be coethnics, and managers often exact a finder's fee, particularly if they hire those outside their inner circle. Some workers come to these jobs at night after regular employment elsewhere. Working with coethnics helps the manager push the group to finish the work faster so that everyone can return home earlier to sleep before starting the next fourteen-hour day. Occasionally, individuals are contracted to handle small cleanup jobs daily or a few times per week, but their pay tends to be higher, eight dollars per hour in one case and fifteen in another. These jobs are considered good catches because the return on immigrants' time invested is high and the pressure is minimal.

Finally, a discussion of the impact of demographic changes on immigrants' labor market opportunities would not be complete without addressing the escalation of Long Island's senior citizen population. Not only have birthrates declined, but the population on Long Island is rapidly aging. In 1990, 12.4 percent of the island's population was over age sixty-five, up from 9.8 percent in 1980 and 7.8 percent in 1970. Already their numbers are expected to constitute 21.5 percent of Nassau County's population and 16.5 percent of Suffolk County's (Yago, Wu, and Seifert 1987:1). This shift has fueled demand for more age-specific services to seniors such as home care, in addition to the normal domestic services of housecleaning and landscaping. Home care, particularly when it requires not a nursing degree but companionship skills, has attracted many immigrant women away from more grinding occupations such as housecleaning. Juanita has exploited this opportunity niche. A follow-up phone call to her in October 1994 revealed that she works three hours per day providing basic care to an elderly Long Island woman, for which she is paid fifty dollars in cash. This part-time job yields more income to her than her full-time job working the red-eye shift at a nursing home.

WHY IMMIGRANT WORKERS?

An expanding economy on Long Island during the 1980s coupled with a local labor force unable to meet its demands contributed to an attractive employment environment. The growing economy generated two levels of jobs: well-paid professional and low-paid factory and service. This bifurcation conforms in many ways to dual labor market theory and to the Sassen (1988) model for economic restructuring and immigrant labor force integration. Why did immigrant workers fill the gaps rather than other native workers? I argue that in such an economy natives could afford to be selective and preferred the better jobs available—jobs offering higher wages, benefits, and better work conditions—while immigrants could not afford to be choosy and also lacked the skills, know-how, and legal status to be competitive.

There is some evidence that Long Island attracted native and legal immigrant workers from New York City as well as undocumented immigrants (*New York Daily News* November 10, 1989; *Newsday* November 22, 1989), many of whom took more desirable well-paying jobs. Long Island youth and young workers with families found that the high cost of living there precluded their taking low-wage jobs; they could not earn a decent family wage on the five to seven dollars per hour typical of the jobs immigrants take. If they did accept low-wage positions, they preferred higher-status jobs, such as clerking in a video rental store, to factory work. I never observed first-generation immigrants in such stores except in their own neighborhoods; and in most restaurants natives served as waiters while immigrants bused tables and washed dishes. Immigrants, in large part because they maintain their families in the home country where their needs can be met more cheaply than in the United States (Portes and Walton 1981) and because they live more ascetic lives than natives (Piore 1979), are able to survive on a wage others would find insufficient. The median weekly income for immigrants was $250 for South Americans and $229 for the Salvadorans, far lower than the $450.47 average for all Long Island workers (New York State Business Statistics Quarterly Summary 1989). And though immigrant earnings on Long Island are low compared to natives', they often exceed those in other major immigrant-receiving areas such as Texas and California. Several of my informants began their sojourns in the United States in those areas, heard of better opportunities on Long Island, and arrived on the island only to find that just as the wages were higher, so too were the living costs.

When native workers spurned low-wage, dead-end jobs, they opened niches for immigrants to fill—a phenomenon predicted by Roger Waldinger's model, as discussed in chapter 1. My informants flowed into these niches grateful for jobs, particularly since most of them were undocumented and therefore lacked work authorization. This lack of proper work documents, coupled with migrants' deficiency in English and other skills, made them an ideal workforce for the bottom of Long Island's economy. This relationship worked symbiotically until migrants realized that their wages could not cover their obligations and that they enjoyed little likelihood of extricating themselves from their predicament.

THE ROLE OF IRCA IN IMMIGRANTS' MARGINALIZATION

The Immigration Reform and Control Act (IRCA), passed by Congress in 1986, was designed to inhibit illegal immigration into the United States by precluding access to jobs. For the first time in U.S. history, it became illegal for employers to knowingly hire undocumented workers—those who lack legal authorization to work; it had always been illegal for people without the proper authorization to accept employment. IRCA has enjoyed limited success at curbing illegal immigration, but it has effectively placed obstacles in the pathways migrants follow to improve their socioeconomic status. It has created a hostile climate for people to live in, and it has forced many migrants further down the socioeconomic ladder, even into the informal economy.

The genesis of IRCA dates back to the 1970s when illegal immigration over the United States' southern border rose precipitously, causing some to despair over its "uncontrollable borders." During the years preceding IRCA, Congress debated how to curb illegal immigration. The principal method proposed was employer sanctions, penalties imposed on people who knowingly hired unauthorized workers. This became IRCA's centerpiece. Prior to IRCA's enactment and the initiation of sanctions in 1988, only employees, not employers, were legally liable; when caught, they faced fines, incarceration, and deportation proceedings. Through IRCA, lawmakers sought to eradicate this so-called Texas Proviso. IRCA also provided a legalization program for undocumented immigrants who either had worked in agriculture (the SAWS program) or had been residing continuously and without legal status in the United States since before January 1, 1982.

IRCA worked well to instill fear among employers and employees alike; it was much less successful at fulfilling its promise of stemming the tide of illegal immigration. While employer sanctions were implemented in most workplaces, sanctions failed to provide a strong enough deterrent to curtail illegal immigration. Enough employers were willing to hire undocumented workers, despite the sanctions (although enforcement has not been aggressive), to maintain signficant demand. Only in 1987, the first year following the passage of IRCA, did border apprehensions drop significantly while potential immigrants waited to see IRCA's effects. But this drop was short-lived, and apprehensions have risen again to approach the levels of pre-IRCA days. "For those who expected employer sanctions to halt the flow of undocumented immigrants into the United States in the short run, the evidence clearly shows that such sanctions have not yet been successful" (Crane et al. 1990:x). Several factors explain the ineffectiveness of sanctions. First, enforcement has not been pursued rigorously enough to serve as a true deterrent; second, in places like Long Island the demand for inexpensive labor has not been, and is not likely to be, met by native workers or even immigrants with appropriate authorization. Finally, for some employers the benefits of hiring undocumented immigrants and keeping them off the books outweigh even the possible costs of sanctions.

Meanwhile, IRCA stimulated increased discrimination by employers against U.S. citizens and legal permanent residents (LPRs), particularly minorities who looked foreign (US GAO 1990; CHIRLA 1990; NYS IATF 1988). Ultimately, even the government acknowledged that IRCA had resulted in a "widespread pattern of discrimination."[4] Among immigrants in the United States, IRCA created a temporary tranquillity that veiled their inner fears. On May 4, 1988, the day the legalization program ended, Hempstead became a ghost town. Normally teeming with Salvadorans on every corner, the streets were as deserted as if a plague had descended. Word had spread like wildfire in the months before: As soon as the "amnesty" (the legalization program) was over, the INS would descend like cowboys to ferret out all the undocumented, rope them up, and deport them en masse to their countries. This apprehension subsided as the days wore on and the raids never materialized— at least not on a large scale. But the first months following IRCA were marked by a wide range of abuses against employees, particularly minorities and immigrants.[5] Scared employers fired old employees even though those hired before November 6, 1986, were not subject to IRCA— the employ*ers* were not liable, but the employ*ees*, as unauthorized workers, were still deportable.[6] Other employers required that their undocumented employees buy bonds that would compensate the employer for INS fines if the workers were detected (a practice strictly forbidden under IRCA). Many others simply initiated or exacerbated exploitation of their unauthorized workers as a means of squeezing more profit out of them. Workers had to be compliant because if they complained, they would be dismissed. Others stayed because finding work under IRCA became a nightmare. Individuals would spend their days moving from one factory or restaurant to another looking for work, only to be asked if they had papers. Nor were newly legalized immigrants shielded from abuse. Employers sometimes treated newly legalized workers as if they were new employees (Loucky, Hamilton, and Chinchilla 1989:26). That is, employers accepted the new Social Security numbers and other documents that workers obtained under the program but treated the individuals as if they were new hires and denied them all accumulated seniority and benefits.

In short, some employers, conscious that the INS did not have the personnel to enforce sanctions, exploited their employees' vulnerability and fear to pad their profits, largely with impunity. IRCA is one principal factor in the pigeonholing of immigrants into narrow and often exploitive sectors of the U.S. economy. It reduced the number of employers willing to hire or keep workers who lacked proper documents (and in some cases even workers who just looked foreign). This shrank their employment opportunities and escalated competition among immigrants for the remaining jobs. To remedy their predicament, immigrants proceeded to search for (1) access to the required documents (a topic I will address in detail in chapter 7) and (2) new employment avenues, including starting their own informal businesses.

IRCA branded undocumented immigrants not only as illegitimate workers, but also as inferior human beings. For my informants, IRCA resulted in indentured servitude to their employers and a terror of discovery. Tina, the Nicaraguan, said that as an undocumented immigrant, "you are always running the risk of being deported at any moment. It's a risk that you take. There are people who look down on undocumented persons. That is, it's very different for someone who doesn't have their papers. [People who have their papers] treat you like they want to humiliate you because you are illegal, because you don't know English. And you don't always know how to defend yourself." Tina's manager at the bakery where she used to work screamed at her constantly to work harder and longer, even when she was well along in her pregnancy. Tina and her Latino coworkers knew that her actions were a threat; the manager always treated Polish workers much better, giving the Latinos the impression that at any time they might be replaced if they did not obey.

Elena Turcios encountered many stories like Tina's in her job at a Hempstead social service agency. As a church worker in the capital of El Salvador before she came to the United States, Elena acquired social work skills. She fled the country when the government labeled her church work with the poor as "subversive," and when she arrived in the United States she became "illegal." "You have problems if you don't have documents here," she stated. "It has gotten more and more and more difficult to find decent work [since IRCA]. The next problem is the language. If you don't speak any English it is very difficult to find a job that pays you a decent wage. There are a lot of cases of exploitation; people who work in restaurants sometimes find themselves unpaid after two to three weeks and then they are fired. This also happens with people hired to clean buildings and they also are not paid. . . . Only this past

Sunday I was talking to a guy who worked in a restaurant and he hadn't been paid for the last two weeks he worked there. They still haven't paid him. And since employers often pay workers in cash there is no way to prove they haven't been paid." "I wouldn't recommend [being undocumented] to anyone," Raquel, the Colombian woman, told me just after she had received her permanent residency card through IRCA's legalization program. "It feels like everyone is looking for you, that wherever you go they're going to demand to see your papers. I suffered completely." She had been a teacher in Colombia, a secure member of the middle class, before she became an "illegal" immigrant in the United States. Her first employment experience inspired her resolve never to be at the bottom again. She recounted the entire humiliating history during our interview.

"I was completely embittered because I had no work, couldn't go out, and because I knew that I was capable of doing many things [but I was illegal]. I [knew that I] was able to work, to develop my skills in this country. So I went to the church . . . and I met a woman who worked in the church, cleaning rooms. She helped me get a job. . . . At this time I was feeling completely destroyed morally and I thought to myself that this job could be an end to my problems. At least I would be doing something. So we agreed that I would work but the priest told me, 'We can only pay you $3.35 per hour here and you have to finish the entire house in three hours.' I said it was okay and started to work [but it was too much]. . . . Each priest had a double room and there were seven priests. I would come home from the job crying. This was the first time that this had happened in my life. First of all, I felt completely undervalued.

"None of the priests or anyone else there even said hello to me. I felt bad, completely destroyed. When the priest saw that I was doing good work, I asked him if it was possible to get a raise—I was earning only $3.35 per hour and they were taking out taxes. He told me that they couldn't pay any more and that I had to finish the work in three hours. And they increased the work. But I needed to acquire references and I needed to earn money. So I would come home crying and go to sleep crying. [They didn't appreciate me] because they saw that I was only the cleaning woman; I wasn't anyone really. . . . It's a *desprecio* [put down]. No one is interested in your life. The church is a place where they should be interested in people because it's where the priests live. . . . They didn't understand that I had to kill myself [to finish] the work. So I talked to the priest who speaks Spanish and I said to him, 'You preach about justice but you don't practice it.' He knew that I was a person who needed to work, that I wasn't working for charity. I think that it's a rich parish, I don't think that it's poor. . . . But I continued to work in order to get the references that I needed. Of the ten dollars I made there I had to pay two just to have my son watched while I worked." Raquel's words speak not only of the indignity she was subject to as an undocumented, exploited worker, but also of her pent-up frustration—knowing that she is an educated, skilled person but unable to exercise her abilities.

Skills Deficiencies

For Raquel and many others, being undocumented brings on the sensation of living under continual surveillance. But their lack of English makes them feel tongue-tied, stupid, alienated from U.S. culture and its opportunities, and incapable of resolving many problems—even simple things like the need to see a doctor—by themselves. They readily admit that their lack of proficiency in English is the most decisive factor in limiting their employment options and in their cultural isolation from the mainstream. "Even though a lot of Spanish is spoken in my town," Don José explained, "we still need English for the pharmacy, the bank, the supermarket, in the street, and when looking for work." Men feel foolish when they frequent bars and try to speak with U.S. women. Since there are fewer Salvadoran women than men on Long Island, they feel they need to socialize outside their own national group but find their English inhibits them. Women also feel stymied by the language. They often work as domestics in American families' homes where knowledge of English is essential to earning and keeping their jobs. But at the very beginning they feel, like Elena, that their lack of English "is one of the principal obstacles. . . . You feel like—how can I explain it?—like an idiot. You don't know what others are saying, what they are talking about. You feel very insecure."

Language deficiency can also be dangerous, as Luz Aguilar found out. Luz was a university-educated professional in her home country. But the Salvadoran worked as a house cleaner shortly after she migrated; her lack of English caused her to burn herself severely. "When you don't know how to speak [the language], you don't know how to ask for what you want," she recalled. "[Your boss] tells you what to do and you don't understand it. You feel like you are stupid, like you know nothing at all about anything. You don't know the areas, you don't know the system of the buses or anything. It's frightening. Another thing is that since you don't know the language you don't know how to read labels. So you might touch something with your hands that you're not supposed to, like I did once. I once touched Easy-Off cleaner with my hands and I burned my fingers. It happened because I wasn't familiar with this product and I couldn't read the label and my boss didn't tell me that I should use gloves with it. Another thing is ammonia. The label says that you have to dilute it with water but I used it straight and it made me cry. I couldn't even breathe from the strength of the smell. And that was because I didn't know English and I didn't know how to read the labels."

A lack of English proficiency causes inconveniences—for instance, in the attempt to make appointments by phone with secretaries who generally speak only English. At moments like these I would often be asked to serve as interpreter. But English is vital to job mobility in many industries. Alfredo faced this obstacle at his job, where he worked stacking boxes in a factory, when a position cleaning machinery opened up; it paid $7.50 per hour, two dollars more than he was earning. Alfredo applied but, as he says, "everyone who was chosen to learn this job had one month to learn how to operate the machinery. And in one month anyone could learn this—but that is if he could learn in his own language. I couldn't apply or ask for this job because all the people who operate these machines speak English. There isn't one of them who speaks Spanish. This way learning would have been too difficult and so it wasn't possible for me to seek this job." Bilingual workers, many of whom are Puerto Ricans, rise into low managerial positions on factory floors precisely because they can communicate between English-speaking higher management and owners and Spanish-speaking immigrant laborers. Puerto Ricans began migrating to Long Island in significant numbers during World War II to fill jobs in farms and defense industries vacated by men going into the service. By the time other Latino immigrants appeared, Puerto Ricans were more established—the younger generations had acquired English—and this group had begun to move up the queue.

In sum, the lack of legal status and of English-language ability are two of the primary obstacles that new undocumented immigrants face in their quest to access good jobs. Those people who have at least been able to acquire English skills find that more opportunities are available to them. Many of the South Americans, and a few of the Salvadorans, learned English in school in their homelands. This gave them a head start, for they often picked it up more readily than most of my other informants. Literate immigrants can learn English through books and courses, but older Salvadorans of peasant origins and with little education face greater barriers to English acquisition. The majority of Salvadorans are far less educated and skilled in general than the South Americans. According to my survey, Salvadorans averaged 6.4 years of education, while Peruvians averaged 10.4, Colombians 9.0 years, and Ecuadorans 9.7 years (see also tables 1.1 and 1.2).

English competence and education plus work authorization can be translated by a few immigrants who possess all of them into mainstream jobs. Not everyone is successful, however. Patricia and Juanita exemplify the successes. Both are Peruvian and from middle-class families; both, university educated, were professionals in Peru before they emigrated to the United States; both started their sojourns as domestics—humiliating jobs they would never have accepted in their home countries. Patricia was an anthropologist working with peasants in a northern province of Peru. She obtained a legal visa to come to the United States as a tourist and stayed with her aunt in Queens. The aunt helped her find work as a housekeeper for a rich family nearby. Patricia worked with the family for a year, cleaning houses on the side and earning enough to bring her husband, Marco, to the United States. Through personal networks she heard about a counseling job at a Hispanic community center serving Long Island's North Shore. She applied and was hired for the job. In order to obtain this job, she needed a work permit. So she and Marco consulted a Chilean "lawyer" who put a stamp in their passports that resembled the INS's work authorization stamp. Though not authentic, the stamps enabled them to obtain legitimate Social Security cards and licenses (because they were improper, however, these stamps later jeopardized the couple's ability to obtain legal residency). After several months of work, the agency sponsored her for temporary (H-1 visa) and then permanent residency, which she received in 1994.

Juanita, like Patricia, started her immigrant career as a domestic. She cleaned houses, baby-sat both children and dogs (she calls this "baby-perro"), and worked in fast-food restaurants. After three years, she began studying for her license as a practical nurse at the local community college, using her fake Social Security number to register. She had taken ESL classes over several years and could speak passable English. Though Juanita had been a registered nurse in Peru, her license was useless in the United States, and she had to begin the credentialing process over. But her investment has paid off. After obtaining work authorization and a valid Social Security number by applying for political asylum (a process explained in chapter 7), she now (in addition to freelancing elsewhere) works in a nursing home with a regular schedule and expects to receive medical benefits in a few months. Meanwhile, her siblings still toil as housekeepers and cleaners despite having similar educational backgrounds and English skills.

Skills Mismatches

Unlike Juanita, most immigrants find themselves in a world where the skills they *do* possess are virtually worthless. This skills mismatch is felt by peasants and urbanites alike at the beginning of their immigrant experiences, but for different reasons. Like Juanita when she was a new immigrant, professionals who arrive generally lack English as well as the necessary professional licenses and other credentials to practice their professions here. This predicament befell Jaime's brother and sister-in-law when Jaime was finally able to save the money to send for them from Peru. His brother is an architect by trade, and his sister-in-law was a successful dentist in Lima. After discussing their dilemma with many people and realizing that they would have to start over to acquire the credentials they needed, they decided that one would work and support the other's professional pursuits. Jaime's brother began working two jobs, one in a factory and the other as a food stocker in a supermarket, to support his wife while she studied English. After some time, she was able to find a job as a dental assistant with a Peruvian dentist in Queens but not as a dentist herself.

Margarita also found that her studies in El Salvador were of little use to her in the United States. "It's hard," she recalled, "because you have studied to do a job that requires preparation and you come here and do a job that anyone who hasn't studied can do. But academic achievements from my country are worthless here, especially if you're illegal. I would have to start all over again here in order to have a job that isn't in a factory or cleaning houses. My cousin was a deputy, an important job [in El Salvador]. The deputy is a position higher than the mayorship. And when she came here she had to take care of an elderly man and a dog. This was a very different type of job for her and in my country she had up to five bodyguards who looked after her. Imagine coming here to do such a lowly job, given her background! She had been a law student." Margarita cleaned houses shortly after she arrived in the early 1980s. She now works in a factory earning six dollars per hour and seems resigned to life as a factory worker. She is not too disappointed, perhaps because the immigrants' experience functions as a leveler to the lowest point on the hierarchy: "Here we are all equal," she explains, "We all do just about the same work even though we've been trained for something [else]. In our own country, we were teachers, secretaries, or whatever; here we're nobody." She says that in her country the educated feel superior to others, but here everyone is homogenized "because we don't know the language." Manuel expresses the same sentiment this way: "The fact that you pick up a broom and start sweeping makes you feel like friends [with everyone else]." But Manuel feels more embittered. Over time his own loss of status has sunk in. In Peru he worked in an office handling telegrams. It was an "honorable job," he laments. "Here my job needs only brute force. . . . It's a manual, routine job." He regrets having left the job in Peru, which was "decent, easier, and less demanding."

Peasants also feel a skills mismatch, but theirs is caused primarily by migration from country to city. Santos, the peasant from Morazán Department in El Salvador, arrived in the United States and spent several months looking for work, but found only occasional day jobs. "When I first got here, everything was very hard for me," he recalled. "Everything, everything that I knew how to do was useless to me here—how to work the land, harvest corn, plant beans, and so on. Here they were of no use to me at all." Santos's statement helps illustrate what Portes and Rumbaut (1990:155) call the "social distance" experienced by migrants. This is a measure of their culture shock and helps prognosticate their ability to cope with all the changes. Social distance is lower for those from urban backgrounds; similarly, the higher the educational level and class status of an immigrant, the lower the "social distance" will be. Peasants who migrate from rural villages, where formal education and training are rare, experience considerable social distance when they arrive in the United States and find themselves in urban and suburban environments where education is key to class mobility. Social distance—as a measure of integration into modernity—is a proxy for human capital. As I have noted previously, Central and South American immigrants differ enormously in terms of human capital variables such as class background. What I have observed is that migrants with the greatest human capital fall furthest in status in the United States. The fall impels them to recoup social status through business ventures faster and more frequently than peasant migrants, although these ventures are not necessarily successful.

STRUGGLING UP FROM THE MARGINS

When my informants reached Long Island, they found themselves on the fringes of U.S. society and at the bottom of the Long Island economy. Learning that you "earn in dollars and pay in dollars," they realized that five dollars per hour would barely permit them to survive on Long Island, let alone pay back their debts, send remittances home, and save up a nest egg. Furthermore, even five-dollar-an-hour jobs do not fall from heaven like manna; there is always someone eager to take any job. "One person told me in a conversation that here people begged you to come and work," Manuel reflected, reminiscing about the misconceptions he had held of life in the United States before he emigrated from Peru. "They told me that they invited you to their house to ask you to work, so that they would have you with them. But, with all the people who have come from Central America and so on, there's a lot more competition than I imagined." Manuel learned quickly that he might find work, but not necessarily stable work. "More than anything else, there is no security in your job. Work is not guaranteed," he explained.

"But what kind of job did you expect to get here?" I asked him.

"Anything,' he responded, "but I wanted a stable job. Because here you have to pay rent, eat, send money home to the family, and you get a tremendous surprise when one day you work and the next day there is no work. Right there everything practically ends. You don't get any benefits and you begin to despair here. You look for work and during this time you have to spend the money you had saved up. And if you don't get money, you look *afligido* [anguished]. Whatever you have you have to spend on basic things—to eat, to pay the rent, and you are desperate because you don't have anything to send home."

The feeling of failure nipping his heels spurred Manuel, much as it does many other immigrants, into adopting strategies for increasing income and decreasing expenses in order to meet short- and long-term goals. The tactics immigrants employ to increase their income are varied, ranging from standard approaches, like working more jobs or hours, to more extreme methods such as get-rich-quick schemes. People often switch from strategy to strategy, or—like Noemí, introduced at the beginning of this chapter—they juggle several at the same time. As they experiment they learn valuable lessons about which tactics work and for what reasons; they are acquiring "immigrant capital." Alfredo's early experiences in the United States illustrate how the burden of paying back one's travel debt spurs initiation into these income-enhancing tactics. When Alfredo arrived from Peru in August 1989, his friends Berta and Manuel took him door-to-door looking for work. After a month of searching, Alfredo landed a job ironing sweaters, at a piece rate of $1.20 per dozen. At first he managed to iron only two and a half dozen an hour for $3.00. Then his friends started asking him to repay the money they had loaned him for his trip. Pressured, he started to sign up for overtime, working an extended shift of twelve hours from eight in the morning to eight at night. He shared a room with these friends, sleeping on the floor, but they worked the evening shift and would wake him up when they arrived home at around one in the morning. Before the first month was over, he was so haggard and discouraged, he told me, he would have gone back to Peru except that he had fulfilled none of his goals. One of his principal goals was to save some capital with which he could resurrect the jewelry business he left behind when he migrated. With free time only on the weekends, he found it difficult to make the business contacts in the New York jewelry industry that would enable him to find a job there and negotiate contracts he could take home. Finally, he coaxed an American acquaintance to introduce him to some jewelry makers in New York City, but after several attempts they told him there were no openings for him. He continued to pursue this avenue, but to no avail, even one year later.

After a couple of months at the sweater factory Alfredo was shifted to an hourly wage of $4.25, and his hours per day were increased to fourteen. Despite a seventy-hour work week, he grossed only $300 weekly and netted less than $250. This was not enough; he later told me that he wanted to return home, but "I don't even have enough to pay my ticket out of this situation!" Fortunately, an opening appeared at the factory where his friends worked, and Alfredo jumped at the opportunity. The pay was better, $5.50 per hour, and after six months they offered insurance and other benefits—something the sweater factory did not. Still, after paying rent of $150 per month, $300 per month in remittances, and $100 in phone calls home, plus his transportation and food costs, he could not get ahead. Incapable of saving even a few dollars, let alone the $5,000 he wanted to return to Peru with, he began to shift strategies. First, he started to talk about obtaining a loan to start up a business buying and selling used cars. "You can't get ahead here with a factory job," he insisted to me. "The only people who make money are the ones with their own businesses. I want to start my own business because this is the only way I can get the capital I need to go back to Peru." But with no Social Security card he knew he could not get access to banks, and there was no one who would lend him the money, so Alfredo put the idea aside; fortunately, he landed a second job three nights a week for $5 per hour. "I didn't sleep, I didn't sleep at all," he told me. "This was the only way to pay off my [travel] debt."

When other strategies do not yield the desired results, immigrants often dream up get-rich-quick schemes, the most popular of which is the accident-related lawsuit. Almost everyone has heard a tale of an immigrant who won a large accident settlement and returned home to live like a king. Moreover, the Spanish-language media bombards its captive audience with advertisements from ambulance-chasing attorneys goading immigrants to sue for any wrong they may have suffered. This insistence is not unwarranted; throughout Latin America people are enculturated to the idea that they have little if any legal recourse when wronged, particularly by the state, and must capitulate to fate unless they seek personal revenge. Thus, the ads selectively acculturate immigrants to a different system. One illustrative instance occurred after an August 28, 1991, subway derailment in New York City, which killed 5 and injured 171. Radio announcements on Spanish stations specifically implored victims to call a certain law firm. At least one lawsuit was filed the day after the crash. Such ambulance chasing does not teach immigrants legal principles as much as it merely entices them to take advantage of the system. Tina's friend Rafael Ramírez actually filed a case with one of these attorneys. Originally from a middle-class family in Callao, Peru, Rafael stowed away on a ship bound for New York. He hid in a closet for thirty days, eating little and drinking only water. When he emerged his

legs would not bend and he had lost a lot of weight, but he was determined to make good. After several years doing odd construction jobs,
he was injured at work, and five years later he was awarded a $40,000
settlement. Rafael decided it was time to return to Peru where his wife
and family were waiting for him. When he arrived, however, he realized
that he had grown accustomed to the hectic New York lifestyle. "I spent
the first month drinking beers with everyone I knew. But I got bored. I
had bought a house and furniture for it and everything, but I knew that
I could no longer stay. So my wife and I decided to come back to the
United States and we snuck over the border."

Work Breeds Isolation

The strategies most regularly used to boost income, increasing working
hours or taking on additional jobs, have the unpleasant effect of further
isolating immigrants from one another. Sonia, the peasant woman from
eastern El Salvador, expressed her isolation this way. "[In El Salvador]
you don't live very far away from your relatives. Rather, you build your
house very close to your relatives. . . . Here, no; even if you want to be
together you can't. Because there are people who in our country were
from the same town and who lived closely together—even sharing the
same patio—but here they don't have time to visit each other because of
their jobs. Days, months, and years pass by and you can't get together
with other people because of your work. For example, here I don't see
my cousin each week. There, you visit every couple of days. . . . When I
was working I wouldn't see my brothers even though I lived in the same
apartment with them. We would run into each other sometimes, or I
would see them only when they were asleep. When I was asleep they
would come home because they worked at night. They would see me
but I wouldn't see them because I was asleep! We didn't even say hello
and we lived together in the same apartment!" For Sonia, the exigencies
of work precluded socializing even with her close family, limiting the
kind of interchange they were accustomed to back home. Even holidays,
when one might expect immigrants to be free, tend to be workdays. One
Fourth of July I tried to see Juanita and her toddler son. I called a week
beforehand and learned that she would be available Sunday morning.
On Friday evening I called to confirm this plan and was told that she was
working. I called again on Saturday and stopped by. She was out working, and it was the same story on Sunday. Capitalizing on Long Islanders' desire to take the weekend off she was working their shifts; meanwhile her sisters also worked constantly, serving food at holiday parties
thrown by the families for whom they normally cleaned houses. The
Fourth of July was a bonanza of extra income but no day of rest.

Indeed, I found that the only day to expect to find immigrants at home was Sunday. These days were anything but relaxing, however, as the shopping and wash had to be done. But by late afternoon, pots of boiling soup and beans and rice would signal the onset of social time. Women gathered in the kitchen preparing the food and exchanging the week's small talk; men lounged on their beds or on couches drinking beers and watching sporting events. Often, men's social time actually started on Saturday night, and by Sunday morning the living area would be strewn with Budweiser bottles. These few moments of relaxation provided a respite from the psychological and physical stress of the week; they also were the forum for exchanging information about jobs and used cars, baby-sitters and locations of cheap goods. In sum, though they lament the changes they endure in the United States and often long to return home and reclaim a more relaxed lifestyle, immigrants adapt and, like Rafael, find that this acculturation contributes to their inability to feel at home even when they are "at home" in their country. Unwittingly they have become settlers.

The strategies immigrants employ to lighten their expense burdens are varied and too numerous to mention in detail here. Overall, they prove less useful to immigrants than strategies that increase income because there is little fat to slice off to begin with. Like Noemí, immigrants tend to live minimalist lives and endure conditions that most people strive to avoid. They occupy overcrowded and substandard housing, with little or no privacy, where hygiene is difficult to maintain. Children scurry across floors where the linoleum has peeled away and on grass strewn with debris. Deprivation is highly visible in their housing because rent is the single greatest expense they incur and it is the easiest to manipulate, as I will discuss fully in chapter 8. Rarely is money squandered on entertainment; videos are swapped, not rented, and few people ever go to the movies since there are none in Spanish on the island. A case of beer, a birthday celebration, or an afternoon at the beach suffices. People eat well by their standards, however—much better than they did in their homelands. Meat is coveted and immigrants can be seen in supermarket aisles pushing shopping carts laden heavily with packages of beef and chicken. But they economize by preparing at home the food they take to work. Landscapers learn quickly that a sandwich and a soda purchased at the deli with the boss easily consumes one hour's pay. They reduce expenditures on clothing by obtaining much of it from charities, although immigrants always have a change or two of "Sunday" clothes that are store-bought and much more presentable.

There are dozens of other methods people employ, not only to make ends meet, but to conserve income for repaying debts and making remittance payments. Only in rare cases do the strategies listed above, both for augmenting income and for capping outlays, prove sufficient to enable immigrants to save their nest egg. One of Roberto's roommates, Amilcar Sorto, a landscaper, was lucky. He returned to El Salvador after only five years with $5,000 in his pocket. With his remittances he had bought his family a piece of land. They had been landless before but now had their own soil to till. All of Amilcar's roommates remarked upon his departure that he had been extremely ascetic, never wasting a penny on entertainment or unnecessary expenses like a new change of clothes. But he is the exception, not the rule, and he recently returned to the United States—an indication that Salvadorans are adopting a circular migratory pattern highly characteristic of Mexican and many Caribbean migrants. Most of my informants show modest improvements in their lives over the years I have known them, but few would be the subjects of a Horatio Alger story. Some buy old cars and move into their own apartments; but they cannot afford to insure the cars or to live alone.

Further, immigrant lives are buffeted by forces that lie far outside their control, like the worldwide recession and the downfall of the Long Island defense industry. Their budgets have little fat, and what little is there is trimmed by bouts of unemployment and remittance demands from home. For example, according to my ESL survey, the median monthly income of Salvadoran and South American immigrants on Long Island is $1,000. But they spend between $300 and $425 for rent and send home $200–$300. This leaves them $275–$500 to cover food, clothing, child care, transportation, health care, communications, and all other expenses for the month. These immigrants also enjoy little or no government safety net to fall back on; they sail when the winds whistle, and they stagnate when the winds whisper. Immigrants rarely attribute their fortunes to outside forces, however. What they most frequently mention as the principal obstacle to their own success in the United States is *not* their lack of skills or papers, nor structural barriers like racial discrimination or licensing processes, nor even the state of the economy; what they blame most is themselves as a group for having saturated the market with cheap immigrant labor. Everything has changed "because of the increase in the Latino population," explained Don José, a commonly heard lament. "When I came there were fewer Hispanics but more arrive every day because [Gold Coast] has the reputation of having work. That's why people come here. Also, many Hispanics who live in Hempstead come here, people from Flushing [Queens] come here and others from many other cities nearby come here. This place has been a central location for finding jobs and therefore many have come here looking for work. So now it's full of people. Those who lived in Hempstead have come here and those who live close by too. So now people don't find work. Now, instead, you find that there is an absence of work but it's because of the influx of people from other cities who have come here. Last year there wasn't the same number of persons here in [this town] and you felt that there was more work. But this year I thought that there would be a lot of work, that there would be more work than workers, and there are many people out of work. Many complain that they have no jobs. Why? Because too many have come."

Detecting an attitude evocative of Foster's (1965) much criticized "image of the limited good," I asked him for a clarification. "You're saying that you blame the Salvadorans for coming in such large numbers?"

"It's not that I blame them," he responded "but rather—imagine that here there are two thousand jobs and four thousand people come. Then two thousand have to be without jobs. No new jobs have been created; the same jobs are here and have not increased. There has been only an increase in the number of people looking for jobs and, therefore, you feel that there is no work. It's because there has not been an increase in the number of jobs."

The fact that Don José is an educated businessman underscores the pervasiveness of this conviction, transmitted by peasant and middle-class immigrants alike. Only occasionally would individuals blame U.S. actors for their fate, and the informants doing so were invariably university-educated South Americans like Marco and Patricia, Alfredo, Berta and Manuel. The belief that immigrants bring on their own demise also fuels, and perhaps instigates, their perception that "people in the United States change," become more competitive and less reciprocating than at home. "Now things are very difficult because of the large quantity of people who are arriving or who have already come," Eugenia Fuentes insisted. She is a Salvadoran living in Gold Coast who has been in the United States nearly ten years. Trained as a schoolteacher in her homeland, Eugenia has found employment only as a cleaning woman and baby-sitter. She knows the housecleaning cottage industry well. "Many offer their labor very cheaply. So the women [employers] take advantage of that. They go around looking for who will work for the least. . . . The [immigrant] women offer their services through the *Pennysaver*, not personally. They advertise how much they want to make for so many hours, trying to undercut the rest of us." She is particularly exasperated by newcomers who will bid two to three dollars per hour less than experienced house cleaners.

How, then, do some immigrants realize the American dream? When I asked Alfredo this question, he replied, "Who are the ones who get ahead? The ones who, by luck, know [English] very well. They have a lot of help to fulfill themselves. But he who doesn't speak the language is lost. It's like he was dumb [unable to speak]. The deaf cannot speak—they don't know anything. The rest are workers like us who are des-esperados. Like me, I have been here almost nine months and I can say that I don't have even one cent saved up here. Contrarily, I am in debt. I never thought I would become indebted here in the United States. But my friends and I have because we have taken out loans. That's because lately we have had some economic problems. You know that [Manuel and Berta] didn't work for awhile and therefore we have had to borrow money. Just as one time they helped me out economically I now am trying to help them out. But I didn't have any money on hand and had to borrow it." Alfredo knows that English opens doors, as do other skills and proper work authorization—although work permits are most useful to people who also have skills. Sometimes these immigrants are able to access mainstream jobs, as Patricia and Juanita did; more often, they merely garner better-paying or more secure jobs within the lower tiers of the employment structure.

From Worker to Entrepreneur

An earlier quotation of Alfredo's offers an alternative—and, I would argue, truer—vision of who gets ahead: "You can't get ahead here with a factory job. The only people who make money are the ones with their own businesses. I want to start my own business because this is the only way I can get the capital I need to go back to Peru." Within a certain stratum of my informants, the idea of starting up their own business became a passion, for precisely Alfredo's reason. He learned within days of arrival that his careful nest egg calculation, the expectation that he would save several thousand dollars in the space of a few months, was pie in the sky. He discarded the idea of mastering English because he worked double shifts that left no time for ESL classes. Instead, he concluded that a business would be the only avenue to his success in the United States. He, Manuel, and Berta schemed for weeks, darting between different possibilities and settling ultimately on starting a Peruvian restaurant. "All we need is some start-up capital," they insisted, hoping that I could loan them the cash (I politely refused) because they knew that as undocumented immigrants they would never get a bank loan. The difficulty of securing capital is indeed a major obstacle in a population where I never observed rotating credit associations, institutions traditionally linked to the rapid ascension of immigrants to entrepreneurship (e.g., Light 1972; Hendricks 1974; Lomnitz 1977; Bonnett 1981). Juanita informed me that a Peruvian friend had obtained the financing to buy a used car through a coethnic credit association, but this is the only instance I heard of during more than three years of fieldwork.

Marco and Patricia were smitten with the same obsession to become their own bosses. In the wake of the anguish and humiliation they experienced as greenhorns, it took them quite some time to turn their lives around; Marco's self-esteem plunged and grew worse in the winter of 1990 when he spent three months without work. Finally, when Patricia landed her job in the community center, Marco found work cleaning offices. He later started a second job driving an ambulette during the day. Patricia would often help Marco clean the offices so that they could finish the work in half the time. Their day would start at 7:00 in the morning and end, with luck, at midnight or 1:00 A.M. when they would return home.

While it is true that their jobs generated greater income, they also began to allow themselves more material comforts. They forsook the small bedroom they shared in a Peruvian's apartment and now rent a two-bedroom apartment themselves, occasionally subletting one of the bedrooms to defray costs. Their first year was very difficult, and, as Marco says, "poverty is the condition that makes you think of grandeur. Going without things is poverty and this condition makes your imagination livelier and livelier." Discouraged that their fourteen-hour workdays barely paid the bills, the couple aspired to leave wage labor jobs behind and form a small business. Marco discussed with a coworker the idea of starting a cleaning company. They readily admitted that the idea of going into any business, let alone industrial cleaning, would never have crossed their minds in their native Peru.

But their tenure in the United States has taught them that the people who get ahead are concentrated in business. Marco pursued the idea of a small business with a vengeance, gathering clients and hiring other workers to do the actual cleaning.[7] He hoped that this way he could guarantee an income and free himself to return to studying for a graduate degree. Rather than just talking about their idea, Marco and Patricia consulted several people and then sent away for an employer's identification number from New York State. By coaxing a friend into co-signing their loan, they were able to lease a van to carry cleaning equipment. They found few clients, however, and, unable to negotiate large cleaning jobs, they had to scuttle their business idea within several months. They converted the van for passenger transporting, but the jobs Marco obtained never justified his car loan. Ultimately the van was stolen, and Marco found hourly work for a lawyer. Though their business failed, it was in one sense a successful venture, for its conception arose from a desire to recoup personal dignity, not just generate income. "In economic terms, maybe you rise to a better social class here," he began. "But in terms of social structure, of social relations, you are on the bottom level. In economic terms, [immigrants] are better off here than in their own country. . . . But, in general, we Hispanics are nobodies, nothing. In my own country [I] was a good person, a professional person, [I] was a sociologist, [I] was a director and had even published some things. I wrote in newspapers. I was *someone*—someone whom you could greet, someone whom you could respect and who could respect others. I was known. Here I am anonymous in a way. Why? Because where I live people don't know me. . . . I could be walking in Manhattan and be hit by a gunshot and it would be as if nothing happened. He died and that's it. There is the sensation—and I tell you this because I have talked and interviewed others who have felt the same sensation. They hadn't finished their studies [in their own countries] but at least over there they were studying. Here no. They know about philosophy, electricity, physics. But here they don't have the need to know who are the scientists in NASA, what is happening in Europe. . . . In their countries, they were people with substance but here, no. They are workers; they go to their jobs and come back, go and come back. But, nevertheless, they search for the way to make themselves feel like someone. And they will feel this amongst the few friends they have, in the little indirect family they have. . . . They will feel their presence there. But the truth is that during the week, during most days, they feel like they aren't worth anything. It's even worse when you are undocumented. Here, in the United States, you have a price . . . if you are undocumented you are assigned one price; if you are professional you get another price. . . . Here you feel like you are nobody."

Marco and Patricia resorted to business not out of any cultural predisposition but as a strategy to accumulate capital and to recoup their dignity. Ironically, it is precisely their *temporary* goals that propelled them to employ strategies which would deepen their commitment to the United States. Their van lease alone signified a six-year commitment. The demise of their business cost them much time and money, linking them more inextricably to the United States despite their stated desire to return to Peru. Already in their mid-thirties, they will probably have to begin their family in the country they had expected would be a much more temporary home. In short, no matter which way they turn, Marco and Patricia are not likely to return to Peru soon. Nor will other "failures."

Salvadorans, too, are conscious of the opportunities afforded merchants and owners of small businesses in their communities. These people hold some of the highest social positions. But when the idea of starting a business came up in my conversations with peasant Salvadorans, their responses resembled Jesús's: "How could I go into business in the United States if I can't even read or write? In my own country I could set up a business without being literate with no problem but here it would be impossible. What I want to do is start one up when I return." Tina is similarly discouraged by the idea of going into business in the United States. She used to sell fruits and vegetables in Managua, Nicaragua, and dreams of going back home with enough money to buy a stand or begin another type of business. But when asked if she would consider such a move in the United States, she responded, "No. Here there are too many regulations and problems you can get into here. I'd rather go home and do it." Tina's comment highlights how intimidating the legal morass looks to an undocumented immigrant who never had to battle with permits and taxes before. A more experienced home country merchant like Jaime or Alfredo is already accustomed to state regulations and merely expects to encounter a different set of rules in the United States. For them the mere existence of the regulations need not dash their hopes of becoming entrepreneurs; the key is gaining access to the necessary information.

Immigrants range widely in the level of interest they have in forming businesses in the United States. This range serves to illustrate the class cleavages in the undocumented immigrant community on Long Island and the effects of these cleavages. Middle-class immigrants, stymied by low salaries, undignified jobs, and living conditions they would never stand for in their home countries, are eager to pursue enterprise and see it as their salvation. People from more modest backgrounds look homeward when they dream of exercising their entrepreneurial aspirations. But regardless of class, all immigrants recognize shortly after arrival that they will have a much harder time meeting their objectives than they had imagined. They live in restricted spheres, segregated from a mainstream of which they have little concept. Modest success is broadcast through wearing gold chains and new clothes, but more substantial success remains elusive.

There are many ethnographies of people who live in desperate, restricted spheres not terribly unlike those endured by undocumented immigrants on Long Island. In the work of Oscar Lewis the description of such so-called cultures of poverty marked by social pathologies reached a wide popular audience. More recently, Philippe Bourgois (1993) and Joan Moore (1991) have linked structural exclusion of Latino populations from mainstream society to their development of "cultures of resistance." In these subcultures mainstream institutions such as school and the church are supplanted by institutions within the culture of resistance, such as drug dealing, violence, gangs, and prostitution. My informants, by and large, do not turn to the illicit economy as a result of their social isolation, nor do they evidence a Lewisonian culture of poverty. On the contrary, they exhibit the "right" values of hard work, personal sacrifice, and entrepreneurship. Yet despite their refusal to succumb to the darker temptations of modern America (although I worry that the second generation will), most of my informants are not economically mobile. At best most rise merely from penniless greenhorn to working poor, and that *is* an accomplishment. But it is not the American dream. A select few do rise further, perhaps eclipsing the dream. How they accomplish this, and at what cost, is the subject of chapter 6.

Chapter Six

MAKING MONEY OFF THE MARGINS

A TAXI RIDE in upper Manhattan taught me much about the opportunity structure immigrants face in the inner city. My experience of a more informal taxi service on Long Island taught me much about the different opportunity structure immigrants face in New York's suburbs. The first incident occurred one day when I was in a hurry and hailed a gypsy cab on 168th Street. The cab was promptly stopped by the TLC, the taxi police, because they realized that the cab, which was supposed to pick up only passengers who called ahead, had picked up someone curbside.[1] When the cabdriver returned with his one-hundred-dollar ticket in hand, he complained loudly, "I told them that they have two choices. Either they leave me alone to make a *decent* living for my family by driving this cab ten or twelve hours a day, or they pick me up for selling crack [cocaine] on the street corner. I don't have any other options." Within a few weeks of this event, I sat down one day to have lunch with Alonso Quintanilla, a Salvadoran from Santa Tecla, a suburb of the capital city, whom I had known for years; I had served as an interpreter during his immigration hearings. Over the years, Alonso has become a manager at a huge Long Island industrial laundry. He began working there mixing dirty sheets and chemical cleaners in huge vats with long poles, the brew dousing his arms and clothes. Now we sat in a *pupusería* (Salvadoran restaurant) where he proudly told me of buying an aged Chevrolet. This car had proven to be a valuable investment in more ways than one. "Originally, I bought it to provide my coworkers with rides to work," he said. "They would pay me twenty dollars per week per person. Then somebody rammed the car and crushed the trunk. Their insurance paid me two thousand dollars for the damage, more than I paid for the car!" As we continued chatting, Alonso spilled out his hopes for buying a house that year with these windfall profits.

Immigrants, no matter where, spy opportunities and seize them. Many face few choices for enriching themselves, especially in an age in which the historical bridges to immigrant prosperity—solid, well-paying manufacturing jobs and an expanding economy—are singed, if not burned completely, even for native youth. Some grasp opportunities in the illicit economy, forsaking a life of hard work with dubious rewards within the legitimate economy. Jamaican, Dominican, and Colombian cocaine rings are infamous, while Chinese immigrants direct the heroin trade and traffic in smuggled human cargo for thirty thousand dollars a head. But the world of Latino immigrants on Long Island that I came to know lacks even these illicit links to mainstream society. As described in the past chapter and covered further in chapter 8, their isolation is so thorough that most of my informants have little comprehension of the mainstream and demonstrate a pervasive resignation to their exclusion.

But it is precisely because of their isolation from the mainstream that immigrants have come to recognize that their own ethnic community offers opportunities for a few to achieve the American dream. That is, immigrants' very separation has created a fertile climate for the germination and ripening of parallel institutions within the immigrant sphere: legal, housing, transportation, communication, and other systems which meet the immigrants' needs that have not been met by the greater society's institutions. Within these parallel institutions immigrants have nurtured opportunities for the success that they find ever more elusive in the mainstream. It is here that people with very few skills seek their American dream, but they must pursue it by standing on the shoulders of their compatriots. In the pages and chapters to come, I describe the myriad ways that immigrants have transformed vacuums left by the larger society into business opportunities. Because they fill vacuums, they operate parallel to the greater society's institutions but are also dependent on those institutions. Most but not all such activities operate outside state regulation—that is, they are part of an informal economy. Immigrants are drawn into the informal sector because within it they can provide cheaper services and products to consumers by skirting state regulations. To the hard-pressed immigrant consumer, this sector offers important savings and fuels the further development of such parallel enterprises.

By concentrating on the evolution of a parallel economy based largely on informal activities, I do not mean to imply that there are no established and law-abiding Latino-owned businesses. Indeed, in most of Long Island's communities where there is a Latino population, one finds at least a small grocery store known as a *bodega*, a restaurant, and possibly a multiple-service agency (described below). In these communities the rest of the local businesses are owned by non-Latinos and do not specifically cater to a Latino clientele. The exception to this rule on the island is Hempstead. Hempstead, located in central Nassau County, is the hub of the Salvadoran community as well as of Latino-owned businesses. As a community that hosts an association of Hispanic businesses and a few Spanish-language newspapers, as well as several dozen Latino businesses, Hempstead serves the second most concentrated Latino population on the island (after Brentwood). Regardless of its Latino entrepreneurial strength, however, Hempstead is still predominated politically and numerically by African Americans. According to 1990 census figures, 59 percent of its inhabitants are black and only 18.5 percent Latino. Furthermore, the ethnic sector is a small employer; most Latino residents work for local factories and in landscaping. In other towns where there are sizable Latino populations, such as Glen Cove, Brentwood, Freeport, Huntington Station, and Wyandanch, Latinos are visible but very much a minority (see table 8.1 below). In short, while some areas—Hempstead in particular—are experiencing a rapid influx of Latino residents, they have yet to generate ethnic-owned businesses that can account for the significant proportion (a third or more) of Latino employment that would qualify them as "ethnic enclave[s]" (Portes and Zhou 1992).[2]

My research further reveals that those Latino-owned businesses which have been established are being undercut consistently by less formal entrepreneurial activities. As I have demonstrated, these latter efforts arise from immigrants' recognition that their low-paying jobs will never permit them to achieve the success they desire. So individuals like Alfredo, quoted in the previous chapter, turn to business—generally not just any business, but business that addresses needs within the immigrant population itself. The pursuit of these activities, sometimes to lower one's costs and sometimes to increase income as well, is often so informal and hidden as to go unnoticed. One such example discussed below is child care. In other cases that I will describe here and particularly in chapters 7 and 8, entire industries have arisen and thrive on the periphery of their counterparts in the mainstream world.

MULTIPURPOSE AGENCIES

The multipurpose agency—generally a small office housing travel, insurance, remittance, and legal services—is perhaps the most formalized parallel institution in the Long Island immigrant community. But its success has spawned more informal competitors, a phenomenon that underscores the difficulty of generating a full-blown ethnic enclave within capital-scarce and economically depressed areas. The multipurpose agency is ubiquitous and prominent; most towns with several hundred Latinos have one. Generally they are owned and operated by educated, middle-class Latinos from South America or the Caribbean. I know of only a couple owned by Salvadorans. Most agencies resemble the one to which I accompanied Jesús when he needed to settle a car insurance accident claim. The office was located on a main thoroughfare in Bay Shore next to a bodega. On the windows was a jumble of neon letters advertising cheap trips to the Caribbean and Central America. Beneath these homemade displays, the telltale insignia of multiple insurance companies had been pasted. And on the door, the bold letters beneath the company's name read: "Notary Public," "Translations," "Remittances to Anywhere in the World," and "Real Estate Broker," all in Spanish. After we entered, the cooled air rushed around us as we walked past desks covered with travel brochures and file folders spilling insurance documents from their berths. One employee was busily assisting an immigrant with the paperwork for sending remittances and a letter home. As Jesús and I were attended to by a Dominican employee, several men entered the store and asked if the office handled workers' compensation claims. It did not, they were told. During the resurrection of Jesús's file, I chatted with the employee about her homeland and migration experience. Born in the highlands of the Dominican Republic, she had emigrated as a teenager and gone to high school in Bay Shore before coming to work at the agency. Exercising her bilingual skills and gaining office experience, she saw this job as a springboard to a position in a U.S. corporation.

Multipurpose agencies exploit the difference between immigrant and U.S. culture regarding legal issues. For example, often the agencies advertise the services of *notarios*, a term that translates to "notary public" in English but signifies someone who holds a position comparable to a lawyer's in Latin America. The appropriation of the prestige attributed to the notario in Latin culture provides a curtain of credibility to the agency. Thus, the office carries a certain formal, professional air that is found in few other institutions within the immigrant sector. The employees also capitalize on this aura, dressing stylishly and speaking smoothly like good bureaucrats from home. They form an interface between the immigrant and the mainstream worlds, handling such matters as insurance and travel arrangements, which many immigrants find too intimidating to handle on their own. The agencies provide services in their language and can translate the incomprehensible deluge of correspondence in English that descends on someone after an accident. Some of these agencies are reputed to be the local links to the travel agencies that orchestrate much of the illegal migratory flow to the United States, as I discussed in chapter 3. This is only hearsay; I have no direct evidence of collaboration outside what my informants have told me secondhand.

The multipurpose agencies that I witnessed operate largely within the formal economy, paying taxes and upholding labor laws among their employees. Although they may finagle by not charging taxes on translated documents, they operate close to the law. They also pay rent and must compensate their employees; these disbursements preclude their offering rock-bottom prices on their services to clients. Consequently, various forms of more informal enterprises have arisen to compete with the formal agencies. Itinerant translators and self-professed "lawyers"

A multiservice agency and restaurant in downtown Hempstead.
Photograph by Susan Calvin

travel from town to town like nineteenth-century quacks selling home-made remedies. As I will develop further in the next chapter, they attempt to fill a vacuum for legal services that arose out of the exorbitant fees charged by true lawyers and even the less exorbitant fees charged by agencies—whose employees generally lack authority to practice law anyway. Similarly, the real estate side of the multiservice agency, as we will see in chapter 8, has been undermined by cunning slum landlords who do not charge a finder's fee as the agencies do.

The remittance services of the agency have also been under attack. The threat comes, in part, from companies that have specialized in remittances, like Urgente Express and Gigante Express, which have their own offices or permit remittances to be sent directly to post office boxes and to be processed out of town. But a greater threat is posed by people who, like Carlos García's brother, have become personal couriers. Carlos's family was driven from their land in the Chalatenango Department of northern El Salvador. They stayed in the capital and set up a store, but it was bombed during the civil war. Afterward, they fled to the United States. Carlos's brother was one of the first in his family to come, and he was able to obtain his permanent residency through IRCA's legalization program. Now he makes his living by delivering monies and goods directly to the families of clients. He specializes in traveling to Chalatenango Department while other such couriers have carved their turf out of other departments and even towns within departments. I accompanied Jesús and Roberto when they sent Christmas packages to their families via another courier. Both agreed that this method far surpassed the remittance agency because it was cheaper and more personalized. The couriers seal their transactions with handshakes, not receipts. They also carry back any reverse flow of goods. There are many items that are unavailable in the United States and flow into the country this way, particularly local medicines and foods. Several of my informants waited weeks to receive salves or pills from home instead of seeking costly medical care and prescription drugs here.

The personal couriers' greatest asset is their *confianza* with clients at both poles of the transnational circuit. This confianza is being threatened by increasing *ladronismo*, or delinquency, all over El Salvador since the end of the civil war. The large remittance agencies as well as some couriers publicize the names of people receiving gifts either by radio shows, such as in the large city of San Miguel, or by asking people who are picking up their remittances to inform neighbors that they, too, have a package awaiting them. Information is not confidential. An American photographer told me that she obtained a monthly list of recipient families and the amounts sent to them without their knowledge or permission. Carmen lived in San Miguel until late 1989 when guerrillas launched an offensive and the city was besieged for a week; she reports that there are many thieves who exploit the publicity and ambush people who have received monies. Her concern is echoed among other Salvadoran informants; they hold that unemployed ex-soldiers and ex-guerrillas have kept their weapons and use them to rob and otherwise terrorize people. Most targeted are the recipients of remittances.

In short, the growth of immigrant communities propagates a variety of innovative solutions to people's needs, strategies that compete with one another in price, convenience, and security. Thus, the multipurpose agency diversifies its income-producing activities as a survival strategy. It seeks to profit from immigrants' isolation from the mainstream, but to do so the agency must practice in the formal economy. As a result, such businesses, with one foot in the immigrant world and one in the mainstream, are vulnerable to the encroachments of less formal enterprises. This is what has occurred in the remittance business wherein a parallel, informal courier system has evolved that operates an alternative transnational supply system running from home country to host country. The couriers undercut both the formal multipurpose and remittance agencies and the U.S. government's postal service, which is the least efficient means to remit money. Though I cannot estimate their percentage of the $400–$700 million in remittances believed to enter El Salvador from the United States alone (Funkhouser 1991; *New York Times* March 11, 1992), my observations lead me to believe that the personal courier business is expanding rapidly. The construction and expansion of this courier system provides better and often cheaper services than the mainstream society's institution, the postal service. But the two parallel institutions also function symbiotically. Many immigrants buy U.S. postal service money orders, which, remitted through couriers or formal *envíos* (remittance agencies), are cashed in the home country. This method ensures that the cash reaches the intended beneficiaries. In short, the institutions generally serve different clienteles but occasionally complement one another as a result of immigrant initiatives.

FOOD SERVICE AND RESTAURANTS

Converting immigrants' desire for ethnic foods into small-scale enterprise has proven lucrative for a few people, women in particular. Doña Felicidad Campos's example is the most spectacular. Having grown up poor in El Salvador, she married a man who ran a small grocery store. They had nine children, and she was pregnant with the tenth when they separated. In 1961 she moved her family to San Salvador and bought a restaurant. In 1967 the business burned; in despair but not defeat, Doña Felicidad told a friend about her bad luck. The friend encouraged Felicidad to apply for a resident visa to come to the United States, telling her that the embassy was recruiting seamstresses. Felicidad, who had experience sewing for her children, collected the requisite reference letters, applied at the embassy, and after three months was issued an immigrant visa. She left all her children with her mother and traveled to Long Island where her friend had already established herself. The friend arranged for Felicidad to work as a live-in housekeeper for a family in Nassau County, earning thirty-five dollars per week. Doña Felicidad arrived on Long Island when there were few other Salvadorans there; the only services geared to the Latino community were dominated by Cubans and Puerto Ricans. She began working several jobs, cooking Salvadoran food in her kitchen and selling it on the side to coworkers. Ultimately, she saved enough money to send for her children and start a restaurant. She now owns two pupuserías; her children run the restaurants, but it is she who carries the honored title of "Doña."

Doña Felicidad was able to transform her informal income-enhancing activity into a full-blown business not unlike the one she had had to leave behind in El Salvador. Most food entrepreneurs do not operate on such a large scale. Doña Teresa Bonilla, in contrast, prepares breakfast, lunch, and dinner in her apartment in Gold Coast. Men who live in her neighborhood frequent her kitchen, where the table is draped in a red-

and-white checkered oilcloth adorned with plastic salt and pepper shakers and a small bowl of chili sauce. She arises before dawn to hand-pat the morning's tortillas, much as she did back home in El Salvador. And for four dollars she will pack each man a lunch to take with him. In an even less formal atmosphere than Teresa's, numerous other women prepare such time-consuming Salvadoran specialties as *pupusas* (a type of tortilla filled with cheese or meat) and *tamales* for sale from their homes. I had breakfast recently with Yolanda and Edgar in Gold Coast. Yolanda delicately placed a silver foil–wrapped package on my plate. Inside was a tamal, a cornmeal-and-meat mixture wrapped in banana leaves and steam-cooked. She had bought them that morning in a nearby town from a friend. In other parts of Long Island, there are vans that reconnoiter immigrant neighborhoods vending pupusas and tamales by the hundreds. At a dollar or two apiece, the foodstuffs do not necessarily earn much profit. What the homegrown industry offers—particularly to women—is a source of income with flexible hours that permits them to tend their children at the same time. This is especially crucial when they drop out of the labor force, even temporarily, in the later stages of pregnancy.

While Salvadorans and a smattering of South Americans have been able to establish food-marketing establishments on the island, the small bodega has been dominated by Dominican immigrants in much the same way that they have come to predominate in New York City, supplanting Puerto Ricans. They appear to have accomplished this by accessing the business relationships already established by their compatriots in the city.

TRANSPORTATION

Transportation on Long Island can be frustrating, particularly if the notorious Long Island Expressway is jammed during rush hour, as typically happens. But having to do without a car is crippling. This is largely due to a poor transportation infrastructure that was designed to emphasize the building of roads and highways to New York City, with little attention given to mass transportation on the island itself (Zschock 1969). Consequently, a vehicle is a necessity, but the expense of owning and maintaining a car is prohibitive for many of my informants. Immigrants have developed a variety of strategies to address this unavoidable dilemma. A few make transportation not only available, but profitable as well.

To lessen transportation expenses, immigrants often walk as much as they can. For instance, they walk to the supermarkets on weekends and call taxis to take them home with their groceries. They also walk over to friends' homes as often as possible, even in the driving rain. Salvadorans, much more than other Latino immigrants, are highly visible as pedestrians, and their visibility has been one of the main reasons for community resentment toward them (see Mahler 1994). Townsfolk in places like Gold Coast are frequently heard denigrating the Salvadorans for their obtrusive public presence. They are particularly critical of landscape laborers who appear unkempt and slovenly, walking home in clothes covered in sweat and dust from their day's efforts. The Salvadorans would prefer not to walk, but few can afford a car; many, lacking legal papers, cannot obtain licenses or, because they are illiterate, cannot take the permit exams. Thus, when the distance to be traveled exceeds a mile or two, some immigrants resort to bicycles. During warm months, bicycling landscapers can be observed along the roads throughout the North Shore. Likewise, Alfredo pedaled to his factory job even though he worked the graveyard shift and the roads he had to negotiate at night were unlit and dangerous. Other people take what limited public transportation is available; in the mornings and afternoons bus stops become meccas for immigrants and other low-income residents.

Walking and biking are considered very dangerous in many communities where immigrants live since these forms of transportation leave immigrants vulnerable to assaults and robberies. Still, they continue to take the risks because they cannot afford taxis or private cars. For months after her baby's birth, Tina would bundle up the child and push her stroller through the early morning darkness on the way to the sitter's house. Although she was fearful of the neighborhood, Tina's meager salary would not cover both a ride to work and her daughter's child care.

Deterred by astronomical insurance rates, frustrated that no adequate transportation alternatives exist, but driven by the association of cars to social status and to pure need, many immigrants try to buy a car as soon as possible. Car ownership brings expenses and requirements that the aspiring owner may not be able to meet in conventional ways. Thus, on Long Island as well as in New York City there are many ways to buy used cars for relatively inexpensive prices, five hundred dollars or less. Licensing and insurance represent major hurdles but not impossible obstacles. As I have indicated, there are legal and literacy barriers to obtaining a driver's license. Among other requisites, the New York State Department of Motor Vehicles (DMV) demands work authorization and a valid visa stamped in one's passport—something very few undocumented immigrants have. But the rules are applied with varying degrees of stringency, and immigrants quickly learn which are the least rigorous offices and apply there. Salvadoran Ernesto Reyes obtained his license before restrictions on converting international licenses into New York State licenses went into effect in the late 1980s, but when his brother-in-law arrived, his application was rejected at the Hempstead DMV and several others. Then Ernesto drove him to Virginia where, with a friend's address, they were able to get a license processed in one day.

Ernesto chose to skirt the New York State licensing impediments; many other immigrants pay to have someone else deal with the problem. In New York everything has a price and with money everything is obtainable. During my field research, forty employees of the DMV were indicted for selling at least seven hundred driver's licenses and other DMV documents to undocumented immigrants (*New York Times* December 19, 1991). My informants, none of whom admitted to having purchased a license themselves, indicated that they knew of others who paid approximately three hundred dollars to obtain a valid license fraudulently through immigrant service brokers. Insurance, a major expense to a car owner—particularly in the case of the many immigrants who are young, unmarried males—is also dealt with flexibly. Individuals who cannot afford the high premiums operate cars without insurance or "borrow" insurance cards from friends. Similar techniques are employed to dodge car registration and other legal requirements. Berta, the Peruvian schoolteacher, registered only one of the two used cars she owned. She took one license plate from the registered car and made two copies of it on cardboard. Then she affixed one real plate and one facsimile to each car and operated both without incident for over six months.

Of course, not all immigrants drive uninsured cars, drive without licenses, or fail to register their cars. Some immigrants are merely innocent of U.S. rules and regulations; others become unwitting victims. In Wyandanch one day, a Salvadoran stole a car and offered rides to the supermarket to two other Salvadorans. En route home, the car was in an accident and the driver fled, leaving the passengers in the hands of police. Unaware that the car had been stolen, the two were booked as accessories to grand theft and became entangled in many months of legal difficulties. To be sure, bending the rules can have dire consequences, but the need for transportation makes shortcuts a necessary risk.

The acquisition of vehicles by immigrants has given rise to a car repair industry parallel to that catering to mainstream Long Islanders. Because immigrants generally can afford only well-worn cars, they spend an inordinate amount of free time repairing them. The "shops" they patronize typically look like Salvadoran Don Federico Chávez's yard. Vidal, an undocumented Guatemalan in his twenties, lives there and has gained a reputation as an expert mechanic. He always has various projects sitting on cinder blocks in the yard and driveway. Several hulks have not moved in months, including one of Berta's cars. One day I arrived to find Don Federico and Vidal hoisting a transmission with a makeshift pulley tied to the shady oak tree out front. Just as the baby was being lowered into its cradle, the car slipped off its blocks and the transmission crashed against the body. Both men, greasy beads of sweat running down their chests, shouted obscenities and then collapsed. Vidal has contacts at all the local shops and parts dealerships who help him obtain the materials he needs at a discount. He also knows where to buy inspection stickers for fifty dollars from local garages when his best efforts fail to get a car past emissions tests. That is, Vidal's business—and many others like his—operates just a level deeper in the local informal economy than other businesses run by Americans. They function symbiotically, prospering from the grinding local poverty.

But the most popular means of reducing the expense of owning a car is to use the vehicle itself as a moneymaking venture. Providing rides to immigrants who lack their own transportation not only compensates for the expenses of owning and operating a car, but can also produce extra income. Alonso, whose example I used at the beginning of this chapter, transports six coworkers, each of whom pays twenty dollars per week for the service. Since he paid only a few hundred dollars for the car, he has rapidly been able to make back his investment and then some. He feels he is providing a service at a fair price and therefore is not exploiting anyone. Occasionally but not frequently, friends or family members will offer rides without exacting a fare. Otherwise, the passenger's phrase "*Cuánto me gana?*" (literally, "How much will you make off of me?") is the standard formula for transactions. During my research, I frequently offered rides to informants, finding that this helped cement relationships and provided optimal times to chat. Invariably, though I never charged them, my passengers would ask, "Cuánto me gana?" as if I drove a taxi.

This expression piqued my interest because I was accustomed to hearing the phrase "Cuánto le debo?" (How much do I owe you?) or "Cuánto es?" (How much is it?) following these types of transactions. In El Salvador, I was told that "Cuánto me gana?" is an antiquated phrase used in the past primarily by people in the countryside. I observed its use only once when a peasant woman claimed to have been overcharged by the driver. This left me with the distinct impression that the use of "Cuánto me gana?" carries the connotation of profiteerism. At a minimum, implicit in the language of "Cuánto me gana?" is the understanding that this is a *service* to be paid for, a market exchange, not a reciprocal exchange. Immigrants must seek rides to the supermarket, to the laundromat, to the baby-sitter, to work, and so on. The layout of suburban Long Island, with its vast tracts of residential housing and commercial centers concentrated miles away, exacerbates the need for constant transportation. For many immigrants, the lack of a car is a continual reminder of their dependence and inferior status. And, while owning a car provides status much as it does in their home countries, immigrants like Tina argue that private automobiles on Long Island are primarily a necessity. "What's difficult here is that a car is not a luxury, it's a necessity. That's complicated because you have to go around to find who can take you to the laundry, to the store. Even though you can buy things nearby, what happens is that your money doesn't go very far. Generally, things here are much more expensive than in [the big supermarkets]. But when you are by yourself then you always have to be bothering other people. But you have to adapt yourself to what it's like; you have to buy things expensive. It's very rare that someone would do a favor for you without you saying that you will pay them for it. If you don't say that you will pay so much to take you to the laundromat, then it's difficult to find someone willing to do it. There was only one person who never asked to be paid [*ni me cobró ni un cinco*] but the rest have always taken my money to go to the laundry or shopping."

One of the problems that arise in the wake of acquiring a car, however, is the difficulty of imagining life without one. Immigrants frequently remark about how much easier and cheaper the purchase of a used car is in the United States than in their home countries. At the same time, they realize that they would probably not be able to afford any type of vehicle if they returned home. This realization weighs heavily on them; although by itself it is not enough to convince them to stay, their acculturation to life with a car and the prestige it bestows makes the thought of returning to life on foot less appealing. A car is a powerful fetish; as I have mentioned, it provides the preferred backdrop to a photograph sent home—a message that the American dream has been achieved. But those who successfully operate their cars as businesses know that they would find this more difficult in El Salvador and other countries where vehicles were frequently stolen or destroyed in the war.

It was in studying how immigrants took the burden of transportation and made it into an income-producing edge over other immigrants that I began to comprehend the importance of parallel institutions to immigrant socioeconomic mobility. The first time I gave an informant a ride that ended with her saying, "Cuánto me gana?" I did not understand its significance. The phrase puzzled me enough that I pursued it even though it deviated my research from its original path. It is a pivotal phrase because it not only communicates the rider's recognition that a trip is a service which must be compensated for, it also conveys the rider's sensation of being taken advantage of. It communicates the transformation of relationships that immigrants experience in the United States, a qualitative shift from reciprocity to commodification born out of the necessity to produce surplus income.

COMMUNICATIONS

The desire to communicate homeward to loved ones is universal among my informants; it has also become fertile ground for enterprising individuals to reap enormous profits. Although some correspondence is conducted through letters sent via remittance agencies and couriers, most immigrants—at least during the early stages following migration when family has been left behind—conduct much of their communication by phone. For people who are illiterate the phone is the most convenient and private method to maintain family ties. "Writing" home for them entails pressing a literate friend or relative into the service of writing letters for them. In this way privacy is lost. But calling is extremely expensive unless done through alternative means. Those people who dare install a telephone in their residences generally regret it shortly thereafter since easy access often leads to abuse—both by people in the United States and by those left at home. In several of the homes where my informants live, telephone bills exceed several hundred dollars per month. Billing housemates can be very difficult, if not impossible, because users can deny making the calls. And once a number is established and communicated to family in the home country, collect calls become a problem. A telephone also invites neighbors who do not have one to drop by and ask to use the phone. Thus, telephones are frequently installed in bedrooms and are locked up when the owner is away from the apartment. Sometimes the telephone company is asked to block all collect calls and all but local outgoing calls. Despite such methods, bills tend to get out of hand with the result that service is cut. A nine-hundred-dollar phone bill went unpaid in Jesús's house, so the telephone company cut off service. At Don Federico's, a similar problem has prohibited him from installing a new phone for several years. "Maybe if I could talk to the phone company in English, I could resolve this problem," he said. "But I can't so we still don't have a phone."

Because phones are such an integral part of life in the United States, and because so many immigrants lacked regular access to them, their feelings of isolation were heightened. In this country, people need phones to obtain jobs and information. For those with no access to private phones, public phones provide a recourse. Expensive and impersonal, these phones consume what may strike an observer as a surprising amount of immigrants' money. A simple ten-minute local conversation costs $1.00 in contrast to the $0.10 it costs a caller with a private phone. Long-distance calls require deft fingers to insert the dozens of quarters required for a three-minute call, and operators interrupt conversations to press the caller to insert more coins. One day I watched Jesús make such a call to his wife who was waiting at a convent in El Salvador to receive the call at a preordained time. When he finished, he was beaming: "I only spent $6.25!"

Fortunately for immigrants concerned about conserving resources, a parallel communications industry has sprung up in immigrant communities. People obtain *claves*, which are access codes, often stolen from calling cards, to make long-distance calls. This racket emanates from New York City but has a devoted following among Long Islanders. Berta, Manuel, and Alfredo traveled to upper Manhattan every two weeks where they contacted their *clavero* at the bus station. At ten dollars per call, the clavero types in an access code on a public telephone, then enters the telephone number, being careful not to let the caller see the code. The caller is permitted to speak up to one-half hour while the clavero moves his next client to an adjacent public phone. Claveros and others obtain calling codes by "surfing" callers who are using their calling cards at public phones in areas such as train stations and, in my case, the INS building in Manhattan. Standing at an adjacent phone or some distance away, the surfers memorize numbers as they are entered on the keypads and then use them or sell them to claveros. My code was stolen at the Federal Building in New York City during a visit to the INS, and, in less than a day, over two thousand dollars' worth of calls to countries ranging from Ecuador and the Dominican Republic to Algeria had been made before a computer program recognized the high usage and blocked access. The credit card calling scam is estimated to have cost legitimate phone companies and consumers some $4 billion (*New York Times* November 20, 1992). It has grown to nationwide proportions and is widely used among immigrants, who save tremendous amounts of cash, albeit illegally. Claveros have even learned to glean codes from cellular phones (*New York Times* April 7, 1992).

While my informants on Long Island use the clavero communications industry, though not universally, they did not conceive of it nor do they control it. But there is another, small-time, alternative that I have seen exercised only on Long Island. It also involves public phones. A small hole is bored on the left side of the phone in a very particular position. Then, a large paper clip must be straightened and inserted into the hole as far as it will go. When positioned correctly, the paper clip triggers some internal mechanism that keeps coins from falling into the cash box and permits them to cascade down the change chute instead. One public phone near my apartment in Gold Coast had been doctored in this way, and Juanita and a Mexican friend took me there one night to show me the trick. They inserted $6.25 in quarters and dialed overseas. When the first three minutes were up, the quarters were released and the operator requested additional payment. Juanita's friend deftly inserted the same quarters into the slot and spoke for another five minutes, when the procedure was repeated again. She talked for twenty minutes and paid nothing.

The latter technique illustrates how some strategies function solely to lower costs to immigrants. Other techniques, the ones that become most popular, go beyond cutting costs to generate income. Thus, claveros not only make free telephone calls, but they generate an income far superior to that they would likely make in the legitimate economy as factory workers or landscapers. They risk being caught and incarcerated for this line of business, but they risk never meeting their goals if they pursue a straight and narrow trajectory in the mainstream economy. Perhaps because of the danger of the enterprise, the clavero industry in New York has been partially replaced by formal phone-calling locales. In these places, immigrants may place calls in private booths for as little as $0.25 per minute.

Child Care

Not all immigrant-initiated parallel institutions are illegal and hugely lucrative like the clavero industry. Some arise merely as adaptive and flexible means for meeting immigrants' needs. The need for child care is shaped by immigrants' life cycles. Although most of my informants were unattached when they arrived or joined spouses here but left their children at home, within several years of immigration many had had children born in the United States. I watched this process intimately even after my formal fieldwork was finished when I went through pregnancy, childbirth, and child care with six of my informants. Women tend to find employment more readily than men; sometimes they earn more money than men, particularly if they work as house cleaners. But most drop out of the job market toward the end of their pregnancies. They must reevaluate their new status as mothers and determine what type of employment they can sustain while juggling the care for their babies. The worst times are when the children get sick, because undocumented immigrants generally lack job security and benefits; they risk losing their jobs if they are absent for any reason. As in mainstream society, there is among immigrants no magical recipe for balancing work and family. Each individual or family handles the dilemma differently.

When Yolanda became pregnant she was working as a housekeeper and child care provider for a middle-class American family in Gold Coast. As the pregnancy progressed, Yolanda could no longer hide it and finally confided her secret to her boss. The decision was made that she would stop working when she was in her eighth month, and Yolanda helped search for a replacement. Yolanda was unemployed for several months around the time of her son's birth; her husband, Edgar, worked in the pool maintenance industry and was also unemployed during those winter months. They exhausted their resources and borrowed money from family members to cover expenses. Yolanda knew she had to find work as soon as possible. Fortunately, her mother was employed as a housekeeper for a woman who fell in love with the infant and volunteered to let Yolanda's mother care for the baby while still fulfilling her functions. This arrangement put Yolanda's mind at ease. She did not want a stranger to take care of her newborn; she had had to entrust her older son to a neighbor in El Salvador when she emigrated, and she always regretted abandoning her son in order to take care of someone else's child in the United States. While relaxing in the park one Sunday, she lamented how her "working life has been turned completely upside down. In my house in El Salvador I had someone who took care of my son. Here I have come to do the same job but for someone else's child. And I abandoned my own son in the hands of someone else and I would get word that he wasn't doing well, that they would leave him by himself. Here, the child I took care of I would never leave alone and this is what the person who took care of my son was supposed to do. But what happened is that when I would call a neighbor to get my son so I could speak to him, they'd tell me that there was no one at home except my son who was locked in. The woman who was supposed to be taking care of him was out shopping. And I'd say to myself, 'Why doesn't she wait until he is in school to go to the store?' There is a lot of conflict in that neighborhood and I'd fear that when there would be [political] demonstrations, they could start fires and my child would be locked in the house! What you do is come here, abandoning your own children, so that you can try to provide a better future for your children. You don't take care of your own here; you take care of others' children. It's really hard, it costs you a lot and you suffer a lot for this."

Another Salvadoran couple resolved their child care needs by working opposite shifts. Living *acompañados*, or in common-law marriage, Jorge and Ana have two children, a boy and a girl. Jorge is from a large Salvadoran family in Polorós and would like to have many children; Ana grew up poor in San Salvador after her mother abandoned her. She wants to work hard and better her children's lives as well as her own. At age twenty-one, she desires no more children. Ana cleans houses and does odd jobs; Jorge works as a busboy in a restaurant near Gold Coast where they live. He is gone at night and cares for the children by day; Ana keeps house and tends the children when Jorge is gone. He does not like the fact that Ana works, and he gets angry when she is not home in time for him to go to his soccer games in the afternoons before work. But he concedes that with their family they need more than one income, particularly because he hopes to take them all back to live in his hometown within a few years. Ana winks at me when Jorge talks of his dream; she does not want to return.

Juanita got pregnant after a short relationship with an Egyptian man she met at an ESL class. In part because she had previously been a nun, her out-of-wedlock pregnancy embarrassed her and she kept it secret until as late as possible. She stopped working her housecleaning jobs when she was eight months pregnant. At this point Juanita's small frame sagged under the weight of what appeared to be a huge sack, prohibiting her from moving comfortably, let alone working. Her son was born several weeks overdue and by cesarean section, which led to a long recovery time. During the two months she was unable to work, Juanita's sisters supported her, but Juanita, who had scraped together the money for her sisters' passages to the United States and had gotten them housecleaning jobs, was determined to be on her own as soon as possible. When her son was a month old, she put him in the care of two undocumented Cuban women who ran a makeshift child care business out of their apartment. Juanita paid them $80 per week for five days' care, days that often started at 7:00 A.M. and ended more than twelve hours later. The $80 was more than Juanita had been prepared to pay; a friend of hers, also Peruvian, paid a Puerto Rican woman only $50 to care for her son, but that woman would not accept any more children. Still, the $80 was little compared to the $300 or more Juanita garnered cleaning houses each week before she obtained her nurse's license.

Juanita is more fortunate than many immigrant women. I have spoken with women who earn factory wages of $200 or less and pay $70 per week in child care. Tina started working two jobs when her daughter was only a few weeks old, to make sure that the child "doesn't go without anything she wants." But this work schedule required Tina to leave the child with a baby-sitter from six in the morning until nine at night, five or six days a week. The baby-sitter, a Dominican woman, took very good care of the baby and charged very modestly for the service, only $50 per week. Still, Tina's jobs paid her only around $250, and the baby-sitting expense represented her most significant cost after housing.

When I speak with women about finding baby-sitters, all agree that they would rather care for their children themselves, that no one can give the same care as the mother. Overcrowding, cost, and limited availability of formal day care centers obliges most working mothers to send children to coethnic, often coimmigrant, caregivers. Even when the centers offer a sliding fee scale or free care to U.S.-born children of poor immigrants, the structured schedule for dropping off and picking up children precludes their use. Immigrant schedules like Juanita's are so unconventional and changeable that many women workers prefer the flexibility offered by coethnics even when it is costly. Alternatively, a woman may decide to become a baby-sitter after she has had a second child and the return on her wage labor is diminished by the added child care costs. This happened to Ernesto's sister-in-law; through baby-sitting she now earns an income while taking care of her own children.

For women who can stay at home, the decision to do so often means sacrifices in other areas, particularly with remittances. Eugenia told me that when her first daughter was born she stopped remitting to her family in El Salvador. She was able to work only part-time cleaning houses and needed that income to support her family. A few women are able to conduct some sort of business out of their homes that can supplement their husband's or relatives' income. For instance, Amalia sews clothes and cares for her young son at home. Several other women sell Mary Kay cosmetics and other products through their friendship networks—a structure that enables a woman to earn an income but with greater flexibility than most jobs. Whether they stay home or continue to work, these women want a U.S. education and future opportunities for their children. Some women do send their children back to the home country after they are born. There the children can be cared for more cost-effectively while the women dedicate themselves to making money; the children can be brought back to the United States once they are of school age. Migrants are very aware of the costs of raising a family in the United States, and though they would like to keep their families together, they realize that in doing so they limit their earning power while increasing their expenses. Sonia worked hard during her first years in the United States and saved some money. But it evaporated once she started having children. "I worked and I saved money before my children were born," she assured me. "But the money I had saved I used during the two years after my children were born when I wasn't working. All my money has gone, rapidly! It's like I never did anything."

In summary, parents respond to childbearing and its responsibilities in many different ways. In most cases, children are eagerly welcomed into the world, but parents are apprehensive about how much more expensive it is in the United States to raise them than in their home countries. A simple doctor's visit costs fifty dollars, one-third to one-fifth of a woman's typical income, not including the value of her lost work time. The exigencies of generating an income lead women down pathways of entrepreneurship that they had not developed, perhaps not even considered, until postpartum. Caring for other women's children or devising methods of producing income from the home are approaches women, in particular, develop to meet their needs when they lack other alternatives. But these strategies are not as lucrative as other income-generating immigrant tactics. A woman is lucky to hold her ground economically, and many slide downward.

INFORMATION ASSISTANCE

Juanita's aunt, Adelina Jiménez, was one of the first Peruvians in Gold Coast. She arrived in the late 1970s because her husband had lost his construction contract in Honduras and the family needed to find a place to live. They did not want to return to Peru because they had sold their home to move to Honduras. Low on money, Adelina set out for the United States by herself. She was able to get a visa because her husband is a professional. When Adelina arrived in New York, she headed directly for Jackson Heights, Queens, where she already had some friends living. This section of Queens has been a South American enclave for several decades, and Adelina hoped to find a job there quickly. But when she arrived, she found no work anywhere. After asking around for a number of weeks, she was directed to Gold Coast. Suitcase in hand, she took the Long Island Railroad, stepped off the train, and, to her despair, found no one who spoke Spanish.

By chance, Adelina ran into an older Cuban who took her under his wing—for a price. He found her a room and a job in one of the nearby factories. Such jobs were plentiful then, and the Cuban earned fifty dollars to recruit new workers. No one asked Adelina for papers, so she started working. Over the next years she obtained her legal residency through her job and sponsored her husband and sons. Much of Adelina's success can be traced back to the seasoned immigrant whom she paid to secure employment for her. Adelina learned through this experience what many of my informants learn over the course of their sojourns in the United States: that there is money to be made off of need. Felicidad, the restaurant owner, was also assisted by a Cuban who had been living on Long Island for several years and who had gained sufficient "immigrant capital"—that is, learned how the system worked—to sell his knowledge. He also charged to find newcomers room, board, and a job, as well as for mailing their letters and handling remittances. Another such seasoned immigrant was Pedro Dueño, one of the volunteers at the legal clinic I directed on Saturdays. Pedro used to excuse himself from the clinic early, explaining that he had clients whom he needed to take to different factories. A Puerto Rican, he had emigrated to the Brentwood area of Long Island following World War II at a time of a severe labor shortage. Officially retired, he now occupies his time "assisting" newcomers and pocketing some extra money on the side.

Occasionally, multiple-service centers and informal job placement agencies assist in locating jobs for clients, but most people find employment through their peers and relatives. This information travels most widely on Sundays when people socialize, and it is not always sold, though a person who has been helped is beholden to his sponsor, much as he would be in the home country. Those people who have little luck using these informal channels are the ones who end up lining the streets at the shape-ups or, in the case of women, taking out ads in the *Pennysaver*, advertising their services at cheaper than the going rate. I have never met anyone who actually made a living by serving as an informal information agency, but these activities can be used to supplement a regular income. And it is the generation of *surplus* income that divides those who are getting ahead from those who merely tread water.

ENTERTAINMENT

Although I have elaborated on the isolated lives of my informants, emphasizing their frugality and therefore minimal expenditures on entertainment, I do not mean to suggest that there is no entertainment at all. Soccer leagues are very popular, for instance. But there is also some evidence of profiteering through entertainment. One of the leaders of the Salvadoran community on Long Island has made his fortune by bringing music groups from Central America to play in local nightclubs. On a less formal scale, in Gold Coast rumors abounded that one section of town had become a red-light district with several Salvadoran prostitutes. Gambling was also a part of this entertainment underground; for instance, Eugenia's husband ran a poker joint out of their apartment. I always visited her by day when only she and her two daughters were there. But the starkness of the apartment—bare floors and no living room furniture save a television and a large table surrounded by chairs— had always led me to wonder whether her husband was just extremely frugal or whether something else was going on. One day, upset with her husband for womanizing and for not supporting the girls, Eugenia confirmed rumors that the apartment became a gambling parlor by night. She said that the gamblers often ended the sessions only at daylight and that the noise had led to frequent complaints from the neighbors. "I never see any of the profits he makes," she said. "But I know he makes a lot of money because the men tell me so."

This small-scale illicit "business" appears to provide a forum for male activities, a practice customary in Central America. It generates incalculable profits, but these sums do not approach those generated within the illicit industries, especially drugs, orchestrated by other infamous immigrant populations. In this sense, it is representative of the level of development of the parallel and the informal economy among immigrants on Long Island.

As I will continue to document in the remaining chapters, innovation is the child of necessity and immigrants prove masters of innovation (see also Stepick 1991). The obstacles of IRCA, and of deficits in language and education, have stimulated entrepreneurship, albeit on a very small scale. Immigrants learn through experience that tactics employed by other immigrants may help them reduce costs and even progress toward their goals. Through immigrant parallel institutions there is the possibility of modest mobility; that is, immigrants are not a homogeneous mass of poor workers. But this mobility, this edging toward the American dream, comes at a cost. Many of those who do achieve a modicum of success are condemned by the others as exploiters of their own people. Migrants' disappointments are voiced in the language of coethnic jealousy and bitterness, not in the vocabularies of exclusion, prejudice, or social justice. On these terms, success is bittersweet.

Chapter Seven

LUCRATIVE, LIMINAL LAW

ROBERTO left El Salvador seeking refuge; what he found was a trap. Active in a church group that ran an agricultural cooperative in El Salvador, Roberto fled the country when several of the group's members were killed and the priest was threatened. He, like so many of his compatriots, entered the United States with strong qualifications for political asylum. But within two months of his arrival in the United States, Roberto found himself jobless, homeless, and pursued by the INS who wanted to deport him. He understood little about how he got into this predicament; all he had done, he thought, was to apply for a permit to work. The letter he received from the INS, however, stated that his political asylum application had been denied. Within the same envelope was another document which stated that deportation proceedings were to be carried out against him. Roberto swore that he had never applied for political asylum, only for work authorization with an attorney who was a friend of a friend. Little did he know that the attorney would promise a work permit and then fill out an application for political asylum, using only Roberto's name and birth date. The rest of the information on the papers was fabricated; Roberto was never told a thing. As I explained earlier, INS regulations allow asylum applicants with bona fide claims to receive work authorization while their cases are pending (although this benefit has not always been conferred). Roberto's lawyer knew this and filed an asylum application for Roberto without properly informing him.

When Roberto was called to the INS, he obediently showed up for his *cita*, expecting to receive his work permit. But the INS examiner asked him questions about his life in El Salvador, and when his answers did not match the answers on the asylum application the die was cast—his application was denied. What Roberto also did not know was that 97 percent of Salvadorans' applications[1] were denied at that time; he was simply the latest victim to have been tricked into paying $350 for what he hoped would be a work permit.

Unfortunately, Roberto's story is not unique. Hundreds, if not thousands, of Salvadorans and other undocumented immigrants have been victimized in much the same way on Long Island. The chief engineer of their plight is the Immigration Reform and Control Act of 1986. As explained earlier, IRCA was passed as an effort to curb undocumented

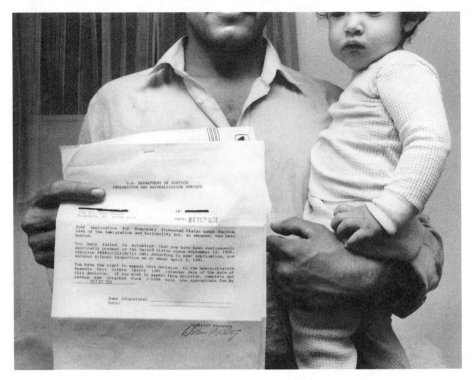

Immigration denial and family devastation. Photograph by Susan Calvin

immigration by restricting labor markets to U.S. citizens, legal permanent residents (LPRs), and other properly authorized workers. While it
has failed to fulfill its purpose (Crane et al. 1990), it has driven immigrants away from the mainstream economy toward the periphery. Some
immigrants have reacted to this marginalization by developing institutions parallel to those in the mainstream. This chapter is devoted to one
such institution, the ballooning informal legal industry, which offers
cheap services but is often little interested in the welfare of its clientele.
Needless to say, the spawning of a pseudo–legal industry was not intended by lawmakers who voted for the legislation in the waning days of
1986.

Most of my informants were unaware of IRCA prior to emigrating, even
though most of them arrived after it was enacted. It proved no deterrent
to them either because they knew nothing about it, because they were
fleeing persecution, or because their dreams overshadowed the information they had about the reality of life in the United States. Because most
did not qualify for the legalization program under IRCA, the law's em-

TABLE 7.1
Long Island Immigrants Who Applied for
Legalization under IRCA

Country of Origin	Number of Applicants
El Salvador	4,013
Colombia	848
Mexico	664
Guatemala	548
Dominican Republic	219
Nicaragua	22
Haiti	640
Poland	430
Jamaica	403
Pakistan	338
India	241
Iran	172
Korea	137
All others	3,432

Source: Immigration and Naturalization Service,
Statistics Branch.

ployer sanctions applied to anyone who hired them.[2] Of the estimated 500,000 (1990 census figures) to 1,000,000 (scholars' estimates) Salvadorans who reside in the United States today, only 143,150 qualified for legalization, and only approximately 100,000 have acquired legal status through other channels. Only 4,000 Salvadorans from Long Island were legalized. But for the estimated 90,000 Salvadorans and an unknown number of other Latinos on Long Island who remain undocumented, IRCA proved devastating (see table 7.1).

IRCA AND THE SCRAMBLE FOR DOCUMENTS

What IRCA did masterfully effect was the innovation of a wealth of ways to overcome its restrictions. Much of this energy was invested in the genesis of a market in documents because IRCA placed a premium on documentation of one's right to work. IRCA turned every employer and virtually every government official into a surrogate INS officer. Employers must fill out an employment authorization verification, or I-9, form for each new hire. The I-9 requires both proof of identity (e.g., a photo driver's license) and proof of work authorization (e.g., a Social Security card); U.S. passports and green cards are proof of both. Although they are supposed to ask for this documentation following an offer of employment, employers generally ask for such papers prior to the offer.

This makes perfect business sense, since an employer does not wish to expend time and energy interviewing unemployable people. But the effect is discriminatory. After IRCA was passed, many aspects of employment and employer-employee relations became increasingly suspicion-laden and even hostile, as my own experience bears out. An immigrant from the Dominican Republic and I were having dinner at a local fast-food restaurant on Long Island. He approached the manager, a U.S. citizen, to ask about a job and was immediately greeted with, "Do you have legal papers?" We were both rather taken aback by her boldness when she added, "We have to be careful, you know." I then inquired whether she would have asked me the same question, and when she said that that would not have been necessary (presumably because I do not look foreign), I reminded her that IRCA requires employers to verify work authorization only *after* an offer of employment.

Furthermore, although employers were not required under IRCA to validate the documents presented to them, the law made many so fearful of an INS investigation that they became overly selective in the types of documents they accepted. For instance, some began requiring U.S. passports; others asked for green cards but accepted only the newest cards and rejected older styles. Citizens and legal residents are not unscathed by these requirements. Puerto Ricans born on the island, in particular, often found that they had to wait a month or more to get their birth certificates from there.[3] Since IRCA gives the prospective employee a mere three days to provide the documentation to employers (twenty-one additional days are available in special cases), many citizens and legal permanent residents, among others, have lost job opportunities because of IRCA. Those so affected tend to be in most need of steady employment.

IRCA's implementation led to a mad scramble among citizens, legal immigrants, and the undocumented alike to find, through lawful or fraudulent means, the requisite papers. One government agency, the Department of Motor Vehicles (DMV), was deluged with people seeking identification cards as well as licenses to use in filling out their proof of work authorization (the I-9 form). The DMV clamped down on issuing the cards by refusing to issue New York State licenses to people holding international licenses and by requiring immigrants to hold valid visas in order to use their passports as identification. This precipitated hostility among DMV employees toward immigrants, a hostility that I witnessed several times. The worst incident took place when I accompanied Salvadoran Don José to the DMV to exchange his valid driver's license and identification card from California for a New York State license. When José moved to New York, his California license was still valid, but local police stopped him several times and threatened to ticket him if he did not obtain a New York license. He then went to the DMV in Hempstead, Long Island, and was denied a license even though the normal exchange requires proof of residence in New York and nothing else. He asked me to accompany him on the second try. When we reached the window, the clerk demanded to see a valid passport, which we provided, and then demanded to see a valid tourist visa stamped inside, which the Salvadoran did not have. I insisted that this was unnecessary since he had a California license and New York sustains reciprocity with other states. She threw us out.

Patricia told me of another incident, which occurred in the Jamaica, Queens, office. A Peruvian friend of hers who is undocumented had obtained a driver's permit through a Long Island office on the eastern end of the island, one of the less strict offices. She had also passed her road test and was bringing the information in to the DMV to obtain a license. When she reached the window, the clerk asked her for her documents, and she reached into her wallet for the permit. As she did so, the clerk noticed what looked like a fake Social Security card and snatched the wallet away. She took the card and the permit papers into an office behind the counter. The Peruvian woman, fearful that the INS would be called in, ran out of the office, went home, and moved out within hours. She was afraid that the information on her driver's permit would lead the INS to her home.

The enactment of employer sanctions was not the only facet of IRCA that led to a scramble for papers; the legalization process did too. Applicants were required to prove that they had entered the United States prior to January 1, 1982, and had resided continuously since then, or that they had performed agricultural labor under the Seasonal Agricultural Workers (SAWs) regulations. For undocumented immigrants who had become seasoned veterans at avoiding a paper trail, the legalization documentation requirements seemed insurmountable. Consequently, some people who qualified were unable to gather the proof and either did not apply at all or had their applications denied. Other enterprising individuals saw the legalization program as an opportunity not to be missed—even though they did not qualify officially. This is because legalization left gaping holes for fraud. Some three million people applied and their applications could not be carefully scrutinized for falsified and counterfeit proof. Consequently, even the INS admits that fraud raged rampant, particularly within the SAWs program (Crane et al. 1990; *New York Times* November 12, 1989). The most common type was the filing of false legalization applications by people who did not truly qualify under IRCA. Since so many undocumented immigrants did not arrive before the IRCA qualifying cutoff date of January 1, 1982, and others never worked in agriculture so as to qualify for the SAWs program but wanted to get work papers or permanent residency, they tended to jump at any chance offered. This is precisely what Jaime did. He falsified an application for SAWs that was not detected by the INS and was able to obtain his permanent resident card after a few years. With his "legal" papers, he found a well-paying job in a unionized nursing home and later petitioned for his wife to get her papers as well.

. Immigrants excluded by the legalization program, much less generous than other countries' similar programs, were enticed into fraud by the hope of securing legal papers; but most would not have been able to succeed in their mission had it not been for the overabundance of pseudo-legal offices and assistants that materialized quickly after IRCA's passage. In some cases, aspiring applicants knowingly sought services from these offices, but innocents were drawn to slaughter as well. A case in point is that of an Uruguayan man with whom I spoke at CARECEN on a Saturday. He paid a pastoral counseling center in Queens to file a seasonal agricultural worker case to which he was not entitled, although the priest there told him he was. When I discussed the matter with him, he was shocked. "Since he was a priest," he said, "I never thought he might deceive me." Many others were misled by advertisements in Spanish newspapers, even years after the legalization program formally ended, that exhorted their readers to apply and claimed that there were new opportunities for "amnesty."[4] One principal informant, Isabel Zapata, a Peruvian woman from Lima, responded to these advertisements and paid over a thousand dollars to an agency that falsified all the information on her legalization claim. They arranged for her to leave Long Island and fly to Las Vegas to have her interview. Although she was informed that the agency's practices were fraudulent, she responded tearfully, "My mother is eighty years old and all I want to do is to see her once more before I die. If I don't do this, I will never get my papers and I won't be able to go home to see her. I don't know what to do." As fate would have it, the interview was scheduled for the end of March 1991, the due date for the baby she was carrying. She had to choose between the best interests of her old and her new family. She did not make the trip. The $1,500 she lost on the contract was her entire savings, and she had very little left to provide for her newborn child. But Isabel's loss contributed to the hefty profits made by IRCA opportunists.

Even many of the immigrants who truly qualified for legalization, and became temporary and then permanent residents, never escaped the documentation ordeal. This is because IRCA's two-edged sword divided families into documented and undocumented members. It also divided them between the employed and the unemployed, and it created artificial distinctions between the lucky "haves" and the not-so-lucky "have nots." Thus, while one or two members of a family might overcome IRCA, the rest were still shackled by it. The Bustamantes are a good example. The father came to the United States first, in the early 1980s, when the fighting in El Salvador was fierce. He spent several years working incessantly, earning enough money to send for his wife. She arrived in the mid-1980s and found work as a domestic. Together they saved the thousands needed to bring their children over the border with a trusted coyote. The family was reunited in early 1986; IRCA was passed later that year, and only the father qualified for legalization.[5] He applied and received work authorization, but his wife had entered the country after the cutoff date, as had the children. Lacking papers, the wife lost her job, and the large family was forced to subsist on one paycheck. They had to invite boarders to live in their apartment. The entire family moved into one room, and the children had nowhere to study quietly.

From these few examples it is readily apparent that IRCA has had an enormous impact. Relations between employers and employees have been strained, families have been stressed, and many people have been made to feel illegitimate. The strongest feeling inspired by IRCA among many of my informants is that of living amid spies. Under IRCA, Juanita explained, "I know that at any moment, say on my job, [the INS] could grab me and then I'd have to pay a [bond] of three thousand dollars. . . . So I have to work hard, hard, hard to earn money so that if I have to go I will take some money back with me to my country. . . . A legal person doesn't have to do that; he doesn't have to think about anything because if he loses his job he can find another because he has papers. But with me, no." Government agencies like the DMV become another loop of the spy ring whose officials serve as police, restricting their every movement.

THE RISE OF A NEW LEGAL(?) INDUSTRY

The enormous demand for documents spawned by IRCA was not met by a void. Virtually overnight, organizations both new and old jumped onto the IRCA bandwagon to supply the necessary paperwork to the millions of undocumented immigrants who ultimately applied for legalization under IRCA. IRCA was, and continues to be, a bonanza to many people. Naturally, licensed attorneys were eager to cash in on the windfall. But their fees—generally five hundred dollars or more to handle a single legalization case—were prohibitive to many immigrants. In anticipation of this and recognizing the enormous demand for legal services during the one-year legalization period, the U.S. government authorized nonprofit, voluntary agencies (volags) to process applications as well. The Catholic Church became the largest volag, but many organizations, some of which had served immigrants for years and some of which instantly appeared, applied for volag status and handled applications.

Further, fly-by-night offices popped up spontaneously, particularly in immigrant neighborhoods. Often resembling the familiar multiservice agencies and advertising as "notarios," these opportunistic outfits were popular among immigrants because their offices were conveniently located in their neighborhoods and because they were open evenings and weekends. Also, the staff could speak their clients' languages and comprehend their cultures. In the neighborhood where I was living during the early phase of the legalization program, Washington Heights in upper Manhattan—a heavily Dominican neighborhood—a brownstone turned into one such office. Dr. López's office (he liked to be referred to as "Doctor") was three stories high and always packed with applicants who spilled out onto the steps. Outside, large white signs with blue and red letters (the colors of the Dominican flag) flashed promises of speedy service and results. Gesturing toward large, steel filing cabinets lining the walls, Dr. López confided to me that he had handled over two thousand cases in only four months. Within a few more months, however, the López empire had crashed. Clients, infuriated with delays and errors in their paperwork, denounced the agency and took their business elsewhere. Dr. López was believed to have fled back home to the Dominican Republic, carrying an unknown quantity of "retirement" cash with him. The López enterprise exemplifies the homespun opportunism that had sprung up across the country even before IRCA (e.g., Chavez 1992:169–71; *New York Times* July 21, 1991; February 19, 1992). Indeed, there is evidence that shysters have preyed upon undocumented immigrants for decades (e.g., Nelson 1975). But while many legalization qualifiers fell into less than reputable hands like Dr. López's, few channels existed through which they could seek remuneration, and they had to find assistance elsewhere.

Those undocumented immigrants who did not qualify for legalization became a vast market for even more unscrupulous operators seeking to profit from their desperation to obtain work authorization. A veritable industry arose to provide the desired services and to reap untold profits. An infrastructure to this industry existed prior to IRCA, but IRCA ushered in an era of windfall opportunities that drew a whole host of new players into the immigrant document market—some state-sanctioned, others more shadowy operators. The principal branches of the post-IRCA industry are a market in counterfeit papers and the political asylum trap (my term), although there are other avenues people have pursued such as marriages for convenience. The latter, often called "green card marriages" since the immigrant spouse marries with the sole purpose of obtaining legal status through the marriage, have become much more difficult since 1986. In that year, in tandem with IRCA, Congress passed the Marriage Fraud Act, which established large fines for people engaging in such marriages and required spouses to prove the validity of their marriage for two years before a permanent green card could be issued. My informants spoke frequently about marrying for a green card, only to be discouraged after I explained the changes in the law. Raquel and Pablo actually divorced each other in the early 1980s and then each married a U.S. citizen. But there were complications with their paperwork for residency. Fortunately for them, they qualified for legalization, and after obtaining their green cards that way, they remarried.

More important than the green card marriage escape route (which is actually an old technique) is the explosion in the market for fraudulent documents that IRCA has caused. Many of those who could not avail themselves of the legalization program, or could find no other means to obtain legal status (such as being a relative of a U.S. citizen or LPR who could petition for them legally), buy fake documents and present them to their employers. Among undocumented immigrants arriving in the United States, a common rite of passage is for their sponsors to buy them a set of bogus papers—a card and green card. Manuel and Berta were escorted by their sponsor, one of their compadres from Trujillo, Peru, to Manhattan within a day of their arrival in the United States. There each was supplied with a counterfeit Social Security card and green card for sixty dollars. Their compadre had even told them to bring photographs of a certain size with them from Peru that could be laminated onto the green card. The cards proved to be of poor quality. The Social Security card was visibly off-color and had no serial number on the back. The green card was a facsimile of a true green card—that is, the document manufactured until the late 1970s, which had a green face and wavy lines through the photograph. The production of this type of card has been discontinued, at least in part because it was so easily counterfeited. New "green" cards are multicolored and bear holograms of the letters "INS"; they are designed to be foolproof (although they have not proven to be so), and the INS now requires that holders of the outdated green cards replace them with the newer cards.

People who fabricate or even carry fake Social Security cards or other U.S. government–issued documents face federal felony charges. But the IRCA-driven need for such documents outweighs the risks, particularly for those people who sell them. I found that the document-manufacturing industry mirrored the immigrant world in general. Informal entrepreneurs were always arising, searching for cheaper and less-complicated solutions to the document obstacles faced by the undocumented. The production of work authorization letters is a case in point. A low-technology method employed by a few of my informants was to photocopy valid INS work authorization letters issued to political asylum applicants (a now-abandoned format) and blot out the legitimate bearer's name. They then photocopied the form and wrote their own names in the blank space. This technique was facilitated by the New York district office of the INS, where sloppy documentation methods at the time included the use of these photocopied forms. The forms became almost illegible after multiple photocopyings. Not only did the official work authorization forms look plainly unofficial, particularly to employers, their shoddy manufacture invited abuse by others desperate for work authorization.

Generally, however, fake documents (known as *chuecos* among immigrants) are purchased from local brokers accessed through friends and family. A few days after I began research in Wyandanch, for instance, two Salvadorans were arrested for selling counterfeit Social Security and green cards. Neighbors claimed that they had operated a printing press in their basement apartment, but later evidence showed that they merely obtained blank cards from a supplier in California and personalized them locally for a fee. The California link has also been documented elsewhere (*New York Times* February 19, 1992). I have seen counterfeit Temporary Resident Cards too, the type of card issued to approved legalization applicants. These cards were perfect—in one sense, too perfect. The only flaw I noted was that the typewriter used to fill in the bearer's information before it is photographed was *superior* to the one used by the INS. These cards were so authentic-looking that, rumor has it, they were good enough for use in obtaining legitimate Social Security cards and even for travel abroad. Another extraordinary scheme is the procurement of Puerto Rican birth certificates that are used to obtain U.S. passports and other necessary documents. In one such case, a Chilean acquired the documents of a deceased Puerto Rican and then requested a passport in the Puerto Rican's name. The Chilean traveled back and forth between the United States and Chile for some ten years this way without being caught. His only problem was the likelihood that this deception would reach the attention of the INS if he filed for legalization.

Chuecos make a good business for vendors (up to three hundred dollars for the temporary resident cards described above), but they are neither foolproof nor always helpful, depending on employers' policies.

Some employers may try to comply with IRCA's employer sanctions but find them too complicated to follow to the letter. Others—like the fast-food outlet mentioned above—are very strict. I returned there several weeks after that incident, providing a ride for Salvadoran Fermín Romero so that he could apply for a job. He had heard that they were hiring and asked me to speak to the manager on his behalf. When I complied, the manager immediately requested I-9 documentation, which Fermín supplied. But he possessed only a fake green card, one of the old style, and the manager rejected it forthwith, dismissing us with "Come back when you get better papers."

Many employers, landscapers in particular, prefer to hire workers off the books in order to avoid paying Social Security and other payroll taxes. Immigrants who obtained legitimate documents found that these employers refused to accept them. Still other landscapers sympathize with the undocumented. I have overheard several landscapers laud their laborers. One told me, "The Salvadorans are really good workers. They are here because they have had to leave their country. They need a break and they really work hard and I think that we should help them." But this employer lives in a town where the mayor, among others, has tried a variety of tricks to get the Salvadorans to leave. These tactics include having the local police report to the INS the license plate numbers of landscapers who appear to hire undocumented workers. In one case, the INS impounded a landscaper's truck and he was forced to pay eight thousand dollars in fines. Thus, despite open empathy for their workers, these employers cannot afford to advocate for their cause: "It's too much of a risk for us to hire workers without papers because we may lose our trucks. It's not worth it to us to take such risks because it can cost us thousands of dollars," one told me. Another lamented, "They don't go after the construction people. They don't go into the restaurants or into the supermarkets. They only go after us landscapers. Why?"

Using fraudulent documents can lead to other serious problems. Perhaps the most damaging is the possibility of being jailed and prosecuted for carrying a document like a chueco Social Security card. Several of my informants have had this experience. Vidal, the Guatemalan mechanic, was arrested by police in a sweep of a Suffolk County laundromat that had a reputation for being a drug market. They found no drugs on him but did find counterfeit Social Security and green cards. He was jailed on two counts of possession of counterfeit documents and went through numerous court hearings before he was released several weeks later. Similarly, Jesús was in the back seat of a car when the police were conducting a sting operation. Although he was guilty of no crime, Jesús and the entire carload were searched, and a variety of chuecos were found.

Several of the men were jailed and held for weeks because they could not make bail. Needless to say, these incidents were disastrous, not only because of the legal entanglements but also because of the time and income the men lost while incarcerated.

Another tactic used to overcome IRCA's work authorization requirements is to employ relatives' or friends' documents when the I-9 form must be filled out. Although this might seem an unlikely strategy, since a job candidate must produce an identity document, I know of several cases in which cousins who look somewhat alike have secured jobs in this way. One has legal papers, which she lends, often for a price, to her cousin or friend, who uses them only to fill out the I-9. Eugenia lent a cousin her work authorization card when her second child was born and she knew she could not work full-time. The cousin presented the card to a factory in Gold Coast and secured employment, but under Eugenia's name. Eugenia came to me one day concerned about this situation because she thought her cousin was having too few taxes deducted. Eugenia needed a clean tax record: her husband, a legalization beneficiary, had petitioned for her to receive her green card and she had to present proof of payment of taxes at the U.S. embassy when she was called for her interview. Her favor to her cousin turned into a predicament for Eugenia. The phony paper trail could also complicate her cousin's life later on if she ever has the chance to regularize her own status.

The Benefits of Looking the Other Way

If all else fails, as it often does, an undocumented immigrant can skirt IRCA by finding a job where the employer does not require documentation. This is the shadowy world of the underground economy. Thirty-seven percent of the people who filled out my survey in ESL classes had not been required to show their papers when they were hired; of these, 39 percent were actually authorized to work. This indicates that there is a demand for laborers who will work off the books, regardless of their immigration status. Immigrants describe employers who do not ask for documentation of work authorization with the phrase "*Echan mirada gorda*" (They look the other way). Other employers request documentation but pay little attention to its authenticity. This way they will appear to have complied with IRCA in case of an INS inverstigation. As Alfredo explained to me, such employers "know that [the documents] are fraudulent but they act as if they are legal. I think that in this industrial society here on the island or wherever [employers] try to get the most out of immigrants' work possible. Thus, even though the laws prohibit giving work to people who don't have permits, they have to take advantage of it [the labor] because it's a good way to earn good profits. There is good profit where the salaries paid are minimum—the lowest. And they aren't going to have problems with insurance or payment for accident claims or payments for social benefits. Also, the state knows that people who are illegal and working in factories are paying taxes. They don't say anything because they need the money. That's why they are tolerant and don't do anything against the illegal people."

There are many benefits to be reaped by "looking the other way," despite the threat of employer sanctions. Employers such as the landscapers mentioned above who keep their employees off the books save thousands of dollars in taxes and other employer deductions, such as Social Security co-payments, unemployment insurance, and so on. Money saved this way enhances the company's profits and offsets the risks of employer sanctions. It is the employers who benefit the most; meanwhile, the employees endure low wages and the lack of medical insurance and other benefits, and they are afraid to report abuses.

Some employees also glean profits by exploiting IRCA's restrictions on undocumented workers. Altagracia described to me how people position themselves as gatekeepers to jobs and, for a price, will waive document requirements. She encountered this phenomenon when applying for a housekeeper's job at a club in Gold Coast. A Peruvian had worked his way up to manager and used his status to his advantage against the Salvadoran woman. "The first thing they ask you for is papers," Altagracia told me. "'Do you have a green card?' . . . 'No, I don't have one,' I said. 'Do you have a passport?' 'No, neither.' 'Work permit?' 'No.' 'Okay, you know what, I will get you a card, a fake card. Give me three hundred dollars and you can stay here and work.'" Altagracia added that the scheme continued because the manager would soon fire the undocumented worker, claiming that everyone was in jeopardy if the boss found out "illegals" were working there. And, she added, "you couldn't do anything about it because you were illegal, so I decided not to apply."

Altagracia's example illustrates once again how immigrants feel pitted against each other in the restricted sphere of their undocumented lives. But I also found that it was in the depths of the marginal economy that a few informants, frustrated by IRCA's caste system, would actually blame mainstream forces and players for their exploitation and inability to meet their goals. These commentaries were launched almost invariably by South Americans; Salvadorans would complain about other Hispanics, particularly Puerto Ricans, and also Italian landscapers and African Americans—all of whom they did not consider to be "legitimate" Americans. The South Americans perceived a mainstream enemy because their home country middle-class status was shattered when they fell from grace to become blue-collar workers.[6] For instance, when I asked my interviewees, "What do Americans think about immigrants?" Berta and Alfredo responded in angry tones:

> BERTA: I don't know what they think about us. But I think that whatever you feel, we are your slaves. We are the force behind all the machinery in this country. If we weren't here, the machines wouldn't run. . . . You have your machines and we are the labor force. Without the hands, the machines wouldn't run. . . . If immigration wanted to clean up all of these people who are not legal, they would have done it a long time ago. But they know that these people are here and that every day more enter; there is nothing else to say except that they [the INS] don't choose to see them. They let them stay so that they work. Because if there were people from this country who would work in the different jobs that we do, then there wouldn't be work for us. Everywhere we would go looking [for work] they would say that there was none. But if you are fired from one job, you go somewhere else and you get a job. . . . But there is a lot of exploitation because you have to produce or you are let go. I would say that we, people without documents, are the ones who produce the most, and I am referring to the blacks. I see the blacks as being very slow, very *haraganes* [lazy]. And they have a lot of privileges we don't have because if they miss one day, the next day they come and they have their jobs. But if we miss or are late or leave without calling first, the boss will call us and tell us that they don't need us here. But, nevertheless, those who were born here have more rights to exercise. If they are thrown out, they give them layoffs and still pay them, all the things that we can't get.

> ALFREDO: For me, to the North American the immigrant represents a new slavery. It's a modern slavery. The Hispanics work like burros. The Salvadoran, Peruvian, Honduran, Guatemalan man works hard and he works much harder than the blacks from here. He works twice or three times as hard. The Puerto Rican is very relaxed. He doesn't work like he should. He believes that he is a citizen and feels comforted by this. He knows that if he is kicked out of his job, he can collect and doesn't have a problem. This is what has happened with several Puerto Ricans. They've been kicked out and they've collected and they've gone to work in other places. They collect and work in the other place. I say [immigrants form] a modern slavery because there is no *azote*, no whipping or anything of this type, but, nevertheless, the American takes advantage of the immigrants' need to get ahead. I know that he is getting rich. He, himself, knows. The American State knows that now most factories live off the work provided by Hispanics. How? Because you know that the United States is a country where everything is computerized and they know that

in such and such a place such and such a thing exists. Everything is planned. And they know that now by firing, by taking out the Hispanics, the factories would be left with very few laborers. And what's happening—the Americans are accustomed to this. Now, in the factories you don't find whites; there are very few. And sometimes they aren't even North Americans. They're Poles, Dutch, Irish, Argentines—people from other countries. There are very few Americans, at least from all of what I have seen.

Alfredo sees his labor as contributing sweat equity to the wealth accumulated by North Americans and not to his own. What the undocumented worker is to his or her employer, Alfredo confided in me one day, is nothing more than a "necessary evil." "They put up with us because they need our labor. But if they had a way to replace us they would do it." While he treads water faster and faster, the U.S. citizens advance. But as he has also witnessed, immigrants find a myriad of methods by which to advance as well, even though they are prohibited from using many of those enjoyed by Americans.

THE TRAP OF POLITICAL ASYLUM

In addition to the legalization program of IRCA and the methods cited so far to overcome employer sanctions, the 1980s witnessed the arrival of another scramble for documentation—the political asylum trap. During that decade, the number of foreigners applying for political asylum in the United States rose precipitously, from 26,512 in 1980 to 101,679 in 1989 (Immigration and Naturalization Service 1991). The vast majority of the new asylum applicants during the late 1980s were from El Salvador and other Central American countries; 86 percent of all applicants in 1989 were Central Americans. Yet people from these countries, with the exception of Nicaraguans, have had an extremely poor chance of being granted asylum (see table 7.2). Nicaraguans benefited from a more lenient policy initiated in the mid-1980s during the tenure of the Sandinista government, a regime that the U.S. government did not support. In contrast to those of the Nicaraguans, nearly all Salvadoran applications were denied until very recently.

One would expect that the low approval rates would discourage applicants, and this is precisely what happened until IRCA was passed. Afterward, the number of applications skyrocketed even though denial rates remained abominable. What can explain the seeming contradiction? The answer is contained in the story of Roberto that began this chapter. He applied for asylum believing that he had merely applied for work authorization—hoping that he could meet IRCA's requirements this way and

TABLE 7.2

Approval Rates for Asylum Cases Filed with INS District Directors

Country	6/83–9/90 Cumulative	FY 1987	FY 1988	FY 1989	FY 1990
TOTAL[a]	23.4%	54.0%	39.1%	18.0%	14.7%
El Salvador	2.6	3.6	2.7	2.3	2.5
Honduras	2.0	4.9	7.4	1.3	1.1
Guatemala	1.8	3.8	5.0	1.9	1.4
Nicaragua	25.2	83.9[c]	53.1	25.6	16.2
USSR	76.7	NL[b]	NL	81.6	82.4
Romania	68.2	59.7	82.9	90.9	54.9
Iran	61.0	67.4	75.0	57.4	42.7
Czechoslovakia	42.7	39.3	44.8	56.6	21.3
Ethiopia	45.6	47.3	77.0	65.8	59.2
China	64.9	63.6	69.7	80.9	91.9
Syria	44.4	83.9	65.7	58.3	68.4
South Africa	38.0	NL	NL	42.4	27.6
Poland	33.6	47.4	53.7	29.2	4.2
Afghanistan	36.7	26.2	39.5	29.6	38.8
Somalia	45.9	36.8	67.9	65.3	86.5
Vietnam	33.9	66.7	80.0	63.6	45.0
Hungary	26.7	20.0	28.9	28.4	9.0
Uganda	25.7	4.2	51.7	28.0	13.3
Philippines	15.4	2.2	10.0	7.3	4.8
Pakistan	16.0	16.1	57.8	51.8	36.3
Cuba	17.3	38.9	31.9	29.0	29.0
Yugoslavia	11.3	30.8	9.2	4.9	8.3
Lebanon	11.9	26.4	36.6	31.8	32.5
Sri Lanka	5.3	NL	NL	4.3	24.0
Haiti	1.9	0.0	31.5	3.5	0.5

Source: Refugee Reports (December 18, 1987; December 16, 1988; December 29, 1989; December 21, 1990).

Note: Beginning in May 1983, the INS has kept asylum statistics by numbers of cases. One application may include more than one individual. This table includes only asylum applications filed with district directors (affirmative asylum petitions) and does not include those filed with immigration judges because the judges, do not keep approval/denial statistics.

[a] Total includes all nationalities, not just those listed.

[b] NL means this country was not listed for this year.

[c] The INS claims that this figure does not include "substantial numbers of drafted denials" that were not completed prior to the end of the fiscal year.

get a job. His mistake, his naïveté, is shared by many other immigrants, Salvadorans in particular. They fall into what I refer to as the political asylum trap. They are tricked because political asylum is advertised—over the radio and across friends' lips—as a sure way to obtain work authorization. The catch is that applicants are told they are applying for *permisos* (work authorization), not political asylum, because many, if not most, would not knowingly apply for political asylum. This is not because they have no claim for asylum, but because they fear that if they apply for asylum, their government will deem them subversives and persecute those family members who remain in their home country.

Asylum as a Convention

Before I explain how the asylum trap is set, let me provide an overview of asylum history, theory, and practice. Simply, asylum is the provision of humanitarian relief to persecuted populations. Internationally, asylum has a long history of use for moral or humanitarian reasons but a short history as a legal concept (Silk 1986). Before 1968 the United States had no formal legislation providing for asylum/refugee status, but in that year the country acceded to the 1967 United Nations Protocol Relating to the Status of Refugees, which defines a refugee as any person who,

> owing to a well-founded fear of being persecuted for reasons of race, religion, nationality, membership of a particular social group or political opinion, is outside the country of his nationality and is unable or, owing to such fear, is unwilling to avail himself of the protection of that country.

During the years before this formal codification of refugee policy, congressional acts or attorney general decrees permitted over one million refugees to be admitted into the United States between 1946 and 1968. In the 1960s and 1970s hundreds of thousands of Cubans and Southeast Asians fleeing Communism were also admitted. During the 1970s, however, a growing concern that politics overshadowed humanitarian concerns in the granting of refugee status—that is, "for each statistic of welcome, there is another of exclusion" (Loescher and Scanlan 1986:209)—led to the passage of the Refugee Act of 1980. The act adopted a definition of *refugee* almost identical to that of the 1967 protocol. It was enacted to bring U.S. laws into conformity with international law. Under the 1980 act, political asylum (hereafter referred to as "asylum" or "political asylum") is virtually equivalent to refugee status except that whereas refugees are processed outside the United States and then admitted into the country, applicants for asylum must apply for it from within the United States. Rights and privileges are similar once a person has been granted refugee or asylum status. The adoption of the Refugee Act promised that the new procedures would provide for unbiased case-by-case assessment of individual claims for refugee and asylum status. But this is not what happened.

Much to the dismay of many immigrant advocates, scholars, and others, the 1980 Refugee Act continued the tradition of favoring Eastern

European and other applicants fleeing Communist countries or countries unfriendly to the United States, a product of the Cold War (see table 7.2; also Loescher and Scanlan 1986; Weiss Fagen 1988). This bias was perpetuated in part by restrictions on access to refugee visas, primarily through geographic ceilings. For fiscal year (FY) 1991, the ceilings were divided as follows: 50,000 for the Soviet Union, 52,000 for Southeast Asia, 4,900 for Africa, 5,000 for Eastern Europe, 6,000 for the Near East and South Asia, and 3,100 for the Caribbean and Latin America. It is impossible to overlook how tiny the availability for Latin American applicants is—it has consistently been the lowest for the past decade—and even these slots have been filled almost exclusively by Cubans (Weiss Fagen 1988:61). For the decade after the 1980 act was signed, twelve countries, the "big twelve," procured nearly all of the refugee visas available in every year, leaving people from other countries with little incentive to apply for refugee status from their homelands. The twelve were the Soviet Union, Vietnam, Laos, Iran, Poland, Cambodia, Romania, Cuba, Afghanistan, Ethiopia, Czechoslovakia, and Hungary. In FY 1988, these twelve countries received 75,089 of 75,754 visas issued (Robinson 1989:4). Robinson argues that the predominance of the "big twelve" creates an imbalance wherein "persons of other nationalities must rely more heavily on the individual merits of their case" (ibid.:5).

In short, a person from a nonfavored nation needs to submit a much stronger case for persecution than a person from the "big twelve" in order to be considered for refugee status.[7] Otherwise the government treats the applicant as an economic, not political, refugee, and her case is denied. Instead of facing these odds, and fearful that seeking refuge in the U.S. embassy might link them to embassy employees who have been known to assist repressive governments, Salvadorans and others merely fled their countries and entered the United States. Although most of my Salvadoran informants experienced persecution in their homeland as described in chapter 2, they did not come with the intention of filing for asylum in order to obtain work authorization. (This premeditated strategy has been suggested for members of certain immigrant groups.)[8] Subsequently many of these Salvadoran migrants have applied, generally to stall a deportation process or to obtain work authorization because of IRCA regulations. Among the latter, some applied intentionally, and others, like Roberto, were tricked.

Setting the Trap

Suppose an undocumented Central American such as Roberto enters the United States illegally after fleeing the civil war at home. Though political forces drove him from his homeland, he could not apply for refugee status in his country because the United States would likely deny his application and he would have exposed himself to political retribution. Instead, he escaped. At this point in the story, one of two possible scenarios is played out. The first is set in motion if the immigrant is detained by the INS; the second occurs when the immigrant has no INS record and voluntarily initiates a request for asylum. If immigrants are caught entering the United States (or even much later), deportation proceedings are initiated; undocumented immigrants may then file an application for political asylum at their court hearings. An application with a prima facie claim of persecution will stay deportation and qualify the applicant for work authorization while the claim is adjudicated (as I will explain below). This scenario illustrates what is called a "defensive" asylum application since people apply for asylum not only to assert their claim but also in order to keep from being deported. Defensive cases are heard as requests for relief from deportation and within a legal court presided over by INS judges. (Their formal title is Executive Office of Immigration Review [EOIR] judges.)

The number of undocumented immigrants who are detained by the INS does not vary enough over the past decade to explain the meteoric rise in asylum applications, however. Most of these applicants appear to have been lured into an asylum trap with promises of permisos, of work authorizations. Let us return to the immigrant story left off above and pursue the second scenario. If the immigrant is not detained by the INS and reaches his destination without incident, he still needs to find a job to support himself. When he applies for jobs, however, employers ask to see his work authorization in order to comply with IRCA, and he has none. From his friends he finds out that he can get a permiso by visiting a "lawyer." Out of desperation, he borrows several hundred dollars for the fee and provides some basic information to the lawyer. The lawyer tells him to expect to wait several months for his permiso. What he does not tell the immigrant is that the papers are an application for political asylum, which, if deemed nonfrivolous, will likely provide him with temporary work authorization while his asylum case is pending. The applicant, like Roberto, thinks he is buying one type of service and, as I will explain below, would probably *not* apply for asylum if he knew the true purpose of the papers he signed.

The asylum applicant may ultimately receive a permiso, but he generally will have his case denied and he will then be placed in deportation proceedings. Thus, the asylum trap is a double-edged sword. According to pre-1995 INS regulations, a person filing a "nonfrivolous" application for asylum should be granted work authorization within ninety days of submitting the application. Although frequently misunderstood, this regulation became the linchpin of the asylum "industry." This loophole was effectively closed on January 1, 1995, when new INS regulations went into effect. Under the new regulations, asylum applicants may not even request work authorization for six months after filing their application. The INS expects to process all applications within this time period, approving work authorization only for individuals with well-supported claims. An asylum application, when it leads to the granting of work authorization, proves to be the gateway to obtaining the bona fide documents undocumented immigrants need to overcome IRCA's employer sanctions: Social Security cards, licenses, and other identification documents.

The INS masterfully limited the use of political asylum as an avenue to obtaining legitimate documents during most of the 1980s by declaring Central Americans' asylum applications frivolous (with the notable exception of Nicaraguans in the late 1980s because of cool U.S. relations with the Sandinista government then in power). The "frivolous" label is supposed to be reserved for applications deemed grossly unfounded, such as an application stating, "I came here to work." Once the application is judged frivolous, the INS denies work authorization to the applicant. But to do so on the massive scale that resulted in a 97 percent denial rate for Salvadorans required a campaign of discrediting applicants by nationality. The INS commissioner under former president Reagan, Alan C. Nelson, chided asylum seekers who filed asylum claims as "queue jumpers" (Simcox 1988:54) and declared that "this willful manipulation of America's generosity must and will stop" (*New York Times* February 21, 1989).

As a direct result of the high denial rate for Salvadoran asylum applicants and the difficulty in obtaining work authorization for their clients as their applications were processed, few lawyers or community-based organizations with the immigrants' best interests at heart would recommend that their clients apply for asylum. CARECEN, the Central American Refugee Center located in Hempstead, Long Island, where I helped run a legal clinic on Saturdays, carefully screened immigrants seeking their assistance. Only those people whose stories included direct, personal persecution fitting one of the narrow legal grounds for asylum and therefore least likely to have their case summarily denied were accepted as clients. Others, even friends or relatives of the persecuted, were turned away as too risky.

Although well-intentioned organizations discouraged immigrants from applying for asylum, there has been no shortage of less conscientious operators ready and willing to file applications for a price. In dozens of conversations I heard from individuals who purchased these services only to receive nothing at all for their money—or, worse, deportation letters when their applications were denied; most of the victims were not correctly informed about what was being done on their behalf. For fees ranging from a low of $350 to a high of thousands of dollars, a wide variety of characters lure despondent immigrants into their webs by promising work authorization cards in a matter of weeks. They then proceed to fill out affirmative asylum applications using only basic demographic information provided by the client. Answers to sensitive questions, such as "Why did you leave your country?" are often fabricated. These applications also tend to be full of grammatical and spelling errors. But these flaws are minor in comparison to the damage done to the unsuspecting applicant. The contrived answers often so taint asylum cases that immigrants are guaranteed not only that their applications will be rejected as frivolous (after which they will most likely face deportation proceedings), but also that their cherished hope of obtaining work authorization—the very purpose of the whole ordeal—will be lost. The unscrupulous attorney or "friend" does not care; he or she has been paid and escapes unscathed. The client learns only much later the trick that has been played on him. This is the fate that befell Roberto, whose story opened this chapter.

The following—an excerpt from an asylum application filled out by one of these brokers and presented to counselors at CARECEN—exemplifies the asylum trap. The errors are in the original:

Q26: Why did you obtain a United States visa?
A: I don't have visa, I come ilegal.
Q31: What do you think would happen to you if you returned?
A: I go back I might get killd and also there is no job for me to do there and I need to work to suppot mysalf.
Q32: When you left your home country, to what country did you intend to go?
A: To come to the United States toying to get a job.
Q35: Have you taken any action that you believe will result in persecution in your home country?
A: [Box checked] No.
Q37: If you base your claim on current conditions in your country, do these conditions affect your freedom more than the rest of that country's population?
A: [Box checked] No.
Q38: Have you, or any member of your immediate family, ever been mistreated by the authorities of your home country/country of nationality?
A: [Box checked] No.
Q40: Why did you continue traveling to the United States?
A: Because I think maybe in NY will be a better place for me to get a job.
Q41: Did you apply for asylum in any other country?
A: There is no asylum in Matamoros or Los Angeles.

For an asylum adjudicator reading this application, the filer's claim is indeed frivolous. There is no evidence of mistreatment or persecution.

Furthermore, the individual's stated intent is to obtain work—seeming to prove the government's assumption that the applicant is nothing more than an economic immigrant. Not surprisingly, this application was denied; based on the information written on the form, the denial was valid. Once the client was interviewed at CARECEN, it was established that he had a much stronger claim to asylum than that communicated in his application. However, the shoddy application crippled his credibility if he pursued his case further. He represented yet another victim of the asylum trap.

Many Groups Profit

Some of the authors of applications like the one cited above sit in offices of licensed attorneys. They practice law under these attorneys' auspices although the authors have no formal legal training. There are many shady characters exploiting the IRCA-generated document market for their personal profit on Long Island. One of the most famous persons fitting this description is Oswaldo Buenaventura. An immigrant himself (from Ecuador, I believe), Oswaldo has been in the United States for years and operates very efficiently through immigrant networks. He claims to have a "friend" inside the INS who can obtain information for him, and him alone. Outside of this, he is very secretive about his methods. During several days of phone calls, for instance, I was unable to secure personal documents from him for an immigrant who had once been his client. Even after a signed attorney representation document was delivered, Oswaldo would not turn over the documents. He refused to give them to the client, either, until she paid him several hundred dollars. Holding papers for ransom is but one of his many specialties.

A few of the less ethical players in the asylum drama were licensed attorneys. Some of these even had the audacity to publicize their efforts over the airwaves and on special "ask the lawyer" call-in programs. More abundant were the less well-known but highly effective people who worked the streets and buildings in immigrant neighborhoods. One informant told me that he applied for a permiso through someone who came to his building and for $350 prepared the paperwork right there in a few minutes. Only later did the client learn he had been *estafado*, swindled. "Doña Marta" is known for running a work authorization "business" out of a van that she drives from community to community seeking Salvadoran prey. This saga is repeated daily despite the best efforts of community members to inform possible applicants about the traps. A newly arrived immigrant is too desperate to find work, and—like would-be immigrants whose returning compatriots try to tell them the harsh truth—the newcomer does not want to hear the bad news. Rather, he interprets such information as a trick designed to bar him from an opportunity enjoyed by the others. Only after he has fallen for the ruse and paid a dear price for it does he learn the lesson. Meanwhile, others come and fall prey too.

Gilberto, a Salvadoran peasant and also godfather to the Salvadorans in one North Shore Long Island town, brought yet another scam to my attention. He told me that some Salvadorans in the area were selling letters as if they were work authorization documents. These turned out to be form letters from a legitimate community organization in New York City that represents Central Americans in asylum proceedings. On the top was an individual's name, and written below was a brief statement indicating that the individual had a bona fide claim to asylum and might be represented by the office listed above. In no way was it work authorization, nor could it protect an individual against the INS. Regardless of this, photocopies of the letter were being sold locally for ninety dollars.

Finally, my favorite examples of how IRCA has created unparalleled opportunities for swindles are two pastors who operated for several years in Suffolk County. One ran a storefront operation in Central Islip, and the other worked out of his evangelical church in Brentwood. I had encountered disgruntled clients of theirs many times at my Saturday clinic by the time Brígida appeared. She told me that she had gone to Reverend García's office several months earlier when the INS raided her factory and initiated deportation proceedings against her and several others. He promised to represent all thirteen of them in deportation court for $360 apiece, and he further promised to obtain work authorizations for them. Brígida paid the money and provided answers to a few questions he asked; he then sent her away, saying, "Call me when you get your appointment from La Migra and I will meet you in court." When Brígida's court date arrived, she called the reverend but was told that he was unavailable. She called back a few days later and was told that he was traveling in El Salvador. Brígida had to go to her appointment alone; so did the others, and no one received work authorization. I accompanied Brígida to the reverend's office to obtain her file in order to ascertain whether an asylum application had been filed on her behalf to halt the deportation process. I found an application in the folder, the quality of which mirrored the one quoted above, but with no indication that it had even been mailed. Needless to say, Brígida and her friends took their business elsewhere. Similar stories abound regarding the other reverend as well. Several unhappy clients were particularly dismayed at being taken advantage of by a man, purportedly, of the cloth.

Deportation hearings rarely proceed without an attorney present. This makes them a source of bread and butter for the parallel legal system. More scrupulous attorneys generate the vast proportion of their fees by filing for work visas for qualified clients. These procedures are complicated and often take many years—not attractive to those seeking quick profits. Such opportunists prefer asylum applications, which can be prepared rapidly and yet generate a good income. When an affirmative asylum application is denied and the applicant is placed in deportation proceedings, it often happens that the denial letter and the Order to Show Cause (the paper initiating the deportation proceedings) arrive in the same envelope. Thus, even if his client is not granted asylum the first time (the likely outcome, given the poor quality of the workmanship and the history of nationality-based denials), savvy operators do not lose. They can explain to their clients that this is commonplace, that a few more papers must be filed, for an additional fee, and all will be corrected. This method works if clients at least obtain a permiso; my experience with hundreds of clients over several years has taught me that their key objective is the permiso, which allows them to access legitimate documents and go on with their lives in peace. IRCA's employer sanctions provisions and the demands upon people to produce surplus income drive them into this corner. Since most plan to return home someday, they do not always fret about the deportation process and some never show up for their appointments in court.

The Fear of Asylum

Lastly, it is important to note that while IRCA has resulted in immigrants' seeking work authorization regardless of the costs, my informants did not arrive with plans to apply for asylum in order to obtain work authorization or public benefits such as welfare, which are available to those granted asylum or refugee status. Quite the contrary—Salvadorans emphatically did *not* want to apply for asylum even though most had legitimate claims. When the word "asylum" was even mentioned, Salvadorans' first reaction was to say that they would never apply for asylum. There are three reasons for such a reaction. First, an asylum application during the civil war (and even afterward, since the situation there has remained politically tense) is believed to label an individual as partisan with one bando, one side of the civil war, or the other. Salvadorans' fear of this label is almost reflexive. Most survived the war by establishing and maintaining the appearance of neutrality. It is very difficult for them to overcome the fear of taking a partisan stand, and most, in point of fact, did not voluntarily favor either side. Second, they believe that any information they provide to the U.S. government can end up in the wrong hands in El Salvador. They fear that this could lead to attacks on their families. These are not unfounded fears. Some notable cases of deported Salvadorans, Santana Chirino Amaya in particular, have established that information gathered in the United States has resulted in persecution and deaths in the home country. (Amaya was deported to El Salvador from the United States and was killed there by government forces.) Third, Salvadorans believe that if they apply for asylum they will be deemed unpatriotic and even subversive; therefore, they will never be able to return to their country. While untrue, this is a very widespread myth that I have heard over and over again. Salvadorans by and large expressed the desire to return when the situation there "normalizes." They did not want to jeopardize this dream.

There are other, perhaps less fully articulated, fears which Salvadorans share about asylum that also act as disincentives to their participation. It might be helpful to imagine what applying for asylum is like for a foreigner, unfamiliar with the U.S. institutions and laws. Imagine, for instance, what courage it must take for individuals to offer incriminating information to the INS when they live in fear of it and constantly seek to avoid contact with it. To defend their right to asylum they must appear at a hearing—walk into the very jaws of the institution and sit before a judge and an INS attorney. Hearings (for defensive applications) generally are not comfortable environments; even for an applicant who has been coached by a sensitive attorney, the experience can be confusing at best and terrifying at worst. Judges tower over petitioners, voicing noticeably crisp commands but in an unintelligible tongue. The forum is public; there is no privacy for the applicant divulging personal testimony, and even the court interpreter is a complete stranger.[9] Furthermore, hearings are often plagued by delays. This means that people prepare themselves for the ordeal only to arrive at the INS and find that the hearing has been postponed to another date. This costs an applicant a day's wages—sometimes it has cost individuals their jobs since they cannot necessarily admit to their bosses that they are undocumented and must go to the INS for hearings. The appearance fee for a private attorney can also cost the applicant one hundred dollars or more. In short, the process can instill fear and drain the pocketbook.

The asylum trap was a disaster waiting to happen long before it actually came to public attention. Much of the blame lies with the inequitable application of the Refugee Act of 1980. If the act had brought the United States into compliance with international law, if there had not been several international crises in the Western Hemisphere that spurred the outmigration of hundreds of thousands of individuals right after its enactment (e.g., the Cuban Mariel boatlift), and if IRCA had not been passed at the height of these migrations, then the asylum trap might never have formed. But this was not the case. Civil wars in Central America uprooted masses who became migrants, throngs of people who were either so afraid to apply for refugee status in their homelands or so resigned to being denied legal entry into the United States that they crossed borders despite the dangers. They came seeking safe haven, albeit not on paper, and they were treated as outlaws. When IRCA was passed, panic hit the streets and it fostered unbridled opportunities for profiteering off the illegals' plight. The trap was set, and it snared thousands—millions in legal fees. And even immigrants' advocates—those who diligently worked to eliminate the inequities facing asylum seekers—inadvertently helped to expand the trap and inflate its profits.

THE ABC FACTOR

The use, and abuse, of asylum to overcome IRCA's hurdles turned into an epidemic when work permits became virtually guaranteed to applicants regardless of the merits of their asylum claims in the early 1990s. This practice did not come about because of any generosity or foolishness on the INS's part; it was the unintended consequence of settling litigation against the INS's prejudicial, Cold War–biased record on granting asylum. On December 19, 1990, the INS and several legal advocates for Central Americans arrived at a settlement of a five-year lawsuit against the government, *American Baptist Churches v. Thornburgh* (hereafter "ABC"). The essence of the class-action suit was the claim that the government had not "decided on the granting of political asylum in a neutral, non-political manner, as required by law [under the 1980 Refugee Act]" (*New York Times* December 20, 1990). The agreement stipulated that the INS offer de novo asylum hearings under new and fairer regulations to all Salvadorans and Guatemalans whose previous applications had been denied (98 percent of Guatemalans' applications were denied in the 1980s). Those who failed to file for asylum because they felt they could never win, or for any other reason, were also given an opportunity to apply under the new regulations. It is unclear why the government decided to settle and avoid a trial. However, one of the attorneys who negotiated the settlement suggested to me that the U.S. government sought to save face internationally. That is, the publicity of a trial would have shown how the U.S. government systematically and prejudicially denied refugee status to some groups while it criticized other states for similar policies. The accord, then, would avoid further international embarrassment.[10]

Under the ABC agreement, the INS set up a new, specially trained corps of asylum adjudicators. Several offices were opened in different parts of the country, but, with only 150 adjudicators, they were immediately overloaded with so much work that they could never hope to catch up. The new adjudicators could not summarily dismiss most applications as frivolous, as the previous policy had allowed. As a result of these changes, the approval rates for Salvadoran asylum applicants rose to over 25 percent within a year, and 15 percent of Guatemalan applicants were approved (*Refugee Reports* December 30, 1991). But given the scrutiny that each application had to be given, their processing was time-consuming, and responses could not be generated within the ninety-day period stipulated by INS regulations (sixty days for asylum applicants included in the ABC agreement) during which work authorization could be denied. This meant that if applicants could prove that ninety days had elapsed since the INS received their applications, they could demand their permisos on the ninety-first day. This is precisely the strategy followed by the attorney I worked with between October 1991 and May 1992. He had been a staff attorney at CARECEN and, though in private practice now, charges nominal fees compared to those of other private attorneys. By accompanying clients to demand permisos on the ninety-first day, he quickly built an impressive reputation among undocumented immigrants on Long Island.

The beauty of the post-ABC era to immigrants, until the 1995 changes, was that the INS became so swamped—over 250,000 applications were pending nationwide in April 1993 (*New York Times* April 25, 1993)—that anyone, with or without a valid asylum claim, could obtain a permiso by hiring a persistent advocate. Before ABC, the ease of procuring work permits varied by INS district; Southern California and Florida were noted as easier places to get them while New York was particularly difficult. But the ABC loophole evened out much of the disparity. Additionally, the asylum backlog became so severe that applicants could expect to wait up to several years just to see one of the adjudicators; even after their cases are denied at this first stage, several levels of appeals may be filed that prolong applicants' right to stay and work in the United States for years more.

This crisis arose out of attempts to better the system. It has received much negative press recently, however, because of certain notorious applicants: Mohammed Salameh, who was convicted of the bombing of the World Trade Center in February 1993; and Mir Aimal Kansi, who shot and killed two CIA agents a few weeks before. It is also the loophole that Juanita and her siblings used to obtain their work permits, though they were never persecuted in their homeland, Peru. This situation was not intended by the authors of the ABC settlement. They were concerned about eliminating an injustice, not opening the floodgates to people outside the class-action suit and to people interested in committing fraud. But this is precisely what happened, and it is why news reports claim that the "public" is outraged about the asylum system. It is also a principal reason behind the alteration of INS regulations regarding the granting of work authorization discussed earlier. The INS has also added many new asylum adjudicators. Its philosophy has become essentially "last in, first out," in order to close the asylum loophole.

Temporary Protected Status

The ABC settlement coincided with the granting of "Temporary Protected Status" (TPS) to Salvadorans, a program legislated in the Immigration Act of 1990 after nearly a decade of lobbying efforts by many groups on behalf of the Salvadorans. TPS originally provided for eighteen months of protection against deportation for Salvadorans resident in the United States as of September 19, 1990. It was extended three times, relabeled DED, Deferred Enforced Departure, and will expire on September 30, 1995, despite unstable conditions in El Salvador. Applicants for TPS/DED had to provide proof that they qualified and pay initial and renewal fees (amounting to several hundreds of dollars per person). Nationwide some 187,000 Salvadorans applied; the number of applicants on Long Island is unknown because the INS does not break down this information (INS, personal communication). However, CARECEN alone processed over 8,500 TPS cases on Long Island. Though this is a large number, it is nowhere near their estimates of the full undocumented Salvadoran population (90,000). Some people who qualified did not apply, expressing fear that the INS was trying to trick them into giving incriminating information to the government; others lacked the fees or required documents; still others came too late to qualify, as did René, Jesús's compadre who arrived only days after the cutoff. Much like the IRCA legalization program, ABC became a windfall for both legitimate and shyster members of the legal industry. The attorney I worked for charged only thirty dollars to prepare TPS renewals; others charged whatever the market would bear. All TPS participants face deportation proceedings when the program expires, at which point they can either resurrect old asylum applications or file new ones if they have no other means of becoming legal residents. This prospect ensures hefty future profits to the immigrants' representatives.

In summary, IRCA has had an enormous impact on the immigrant community of Long Island. For some, it was a blessing that offered an escape out of lawlessness and the stigma of being illegal. "I always think about the people in this country who don't have any papers," Raquel told me. "When you've had the experience yourself, you know how others feel. I think that it's worse than being poor. Because it's something that keeps you from getting ahead. Many people want to do something but they can't because this problem stops you." Many others found that IRCA drove them further into the isolated, parallel world inhabited by undocumented workers. They had to invest hard-earned money in acquiring documents through fraud or try to skirt IRCA by finding or creating jobs in the informal economy, particularly in the immigrant opportunity structure. IRCA set them back, but it did not send them home. Even among those who did acquire work authorization, even legal permanent residency, few found greater socioeconomic success when the legal barriers fell. For many of my informants, particularly those from El Salvador with little education, the American dream has proven elusive. While Juanita took her permiso and nurse's training and parlayed them into a nine-dollar-an-hour job in a nursing home, Roberto toils at the same landscaping job he has held since arriving in the United States. He has never had a raise, though he now has legal papers. Noemí cannot even find steady work, despite a high school education, office experience in El Salvador, and a work permit.

But there are some people who have definitely found riches in the post-IRCA era. IRCA has created a giant windfall for legitimate, honest immigration law practitioners who have assisted people in their legalization, asylum, and other immigration claims. The attorney I worked with started his office with no employees in January of 1991. He barely generated enough income to pay the rent. Now, he has over a dozen employees and a cash flow of thousands of dollars per week. His success is the direct result of securing tangible benefits for his clients; many other, less reputable practitioners have bled their compatriots dry. And through this practice they have been able to amass the capital to build more legitimate, yet still exploitive, businesses in their own communities. They start up multiservice agencies or shops or restaurants that cater to these communities' needs. In short, traps as well as trappers existed prior to IRCA, but IRCA created an environment in which they could thrive. That they have thrived, largely with impunity, is due to the fact that organizations which might hunt them down and prosecute them are too busy cleaning up the mess that they leave behind.

Chapter Eight

THE ENCARGADO INDUSTRY

BRÍGIDA is a dynamic woman in her forties whose explosive energy has never failed her. She is from El Salvador where she supported her family by selling food at a local market until her sister's husband was murdered and Brígida fled to the United States. She found work in Suffolk County at a cosmetics factory almost immediately after arrival and has continued to work there since. From Monday to Saturday her days are dedicated to factory work beginning at 7:00 A.M. and ending at 4:30 P.M. She takes the bus to work, and when she returns, she works another shift, from 5:00 P.M. to 9:30 P.M. at a local delicatessen. On Sunday afternoons she also works at the deli. When I commented on her schedule, she brushed off my admiration with "I've worked this way all my life." Brígida's work ethic does not emanate primarily from a desire to succeed in the United States; rather, her first concern has been the reunification of her family, and this has required an enormous investment of money. As discussed in chapter 3, over the past years she has brought each of her three teenage children to the United States illegally (but safely) by purchasing visas for them on the black market at three thousand dollars each. The last child was detained by the INS at the airport and returned to El Salvador. Brígida lost her investment and had to finance a new visa for an additional three thousand dollars. Brígida brought her business acumen with her, although she has not put it to use in marketing; she is a master of the "*encargado*" system, a method of profiteering off the narrow affordable housing market on Long Island.

Not long after arriving in the United States, Brígida learned to use the encargado system to her advantage. While she worked hard to generate the money she needed to reunite her family, she was able to invest these surplus earnings by becoming an *encargada*, a sublessor. She rented a two-bedroom apartment for $750 (plus utilities). She then sublet both bedrooms for $300 each, so that she herself paid only $150 per month. When the rent was raised to $800, she added another person. Brígida now rents a house for $1,000. She lives there with her three children and a married couple who sublet a bedroom. When I visited them one day, Brígida was orchestrating the renovation of the basement. Several single beds were lifted into the cellar, and Brígida proudly announced that renting a number of beds would substantially lower her rent burden. She is so buoyant that she convinces her listeners that this is not exploitive but merely a very clever means of improving her financial situation. Her most recent endeavor is to find a way to buy the house she is renting. As she figures, why pay so much rent and gain no equity? One try at financing a mortgage failed because she had no money for a down payment, but she still keeps her hopes up.

Brígida's experience exemplifies a phenomenon so ubiquitous on Long Island that no immigrant I have ever spoken with has escaped it entirely: the construction of a housing rental market parallel and marginal to the mainstream market. Albeit the product of forces within the larger market, as I will discuss in detail shortly, this parallel market is controlled by a small echelon of immigrants for their own gain. I call this the "encargado system" because those immigrants who are in charge and who profit from it are referred to by their tenants as the "*encargados.*" Underlying and nourishing the encargado system are the extraordinary cost of housing on Long Island and the practice of residential segregation. The system evolved from a universal need among immigrants to reduce the cost of their housing—some $300 to $425 per month (see table 1.2) and usually the largest item in their budgets—primarily through different strategies of overcrowding and even homelessness.

LONG ISLAND HOUSING: SCARCE, EXPENSIVE, AND SEGREGATED

Newly arrived immigrants encounter one of the most expensive and restricted housing markets in the country. Constructed for middle-class-to-affluent white homeowners, Long Island's residential neighborhoods consist predominantly of single-family homes, and only 18 percent of the housing stock is rental units (*Newsday* May 19, 1991). In 1991, the average price of a house in Nassau County was $202,660, in Suffolk County $163,633 (*New York Times* December 21, 1991); apartment rents rose from a median of $314 per month in Nassau County ($297 in Suffolk) in 1980 to $678 in 1990 ($696 in Suffolk) (*Newsday* May 19, 1991). During the 1980s, Long Island faced such a critical shortage of affordable housing, particularly for young families, that an estimated 90,000 illegal apartments were carved out of single-family homes through the conversion of basements, attics, and the like into rentable space (*New York Times* April 14, 1991; *Newsday* December 8, 1989). The illegal market represents one-third of the entire rental market, according to conservative estimates (*New York Times* February 15, 1994), and urban planners forecast that the island will need to build some 100,000 units of affordable housing by the end of the decade to meet demand (*New York Times* December 21, 1991). As I have mentioned, the lack of affordable housing has been cited as a principal cause of the loss of youthful Long Islanders; their numbers have declined by 150,000 between 1980 and 1990.

These aggregate figures do not adequately express the rental market faced by blacks and Latinos on Long Island who for decades have been subject to systematic segregation. A 1991 *Miami Herald* investigation ranked Long Island as the fifteenth most segregated metropolitan area in the United States out of 318 studied (*Newsday* May 18, 1992). Segregation is most extreme for African-American Long Islanders: two-thirds of Long Island neighborhoods are less than 1 percent black, and one-half have no blacks at all. The average white resident of Nassau County lives in a census tract where only 8 percent of the neighbors are black or Latino (*New York Times* March 17, 1994). Towns experiencing white flight, such as Freeport and Uniondale in Nassau County, found their populations replaced by blacks and Latinos. Indeed, as I shall discuss shortly, Latino immigrants tend to find their housing options restricted largely to communities with significant minority populations.

The living situation my informants found themselves in shocked them for two principal reasons: (1) either the practice of paying rent was new to them or the amount they needed to pay on Long Island far surpassed what they had paid at home; and (2) they found themselves severely isolated from mainstream America, the "real America," in their words, that they only glimpsed at work or from the confines of public transportation. As I shall explain, the latter complaint is most common among middle-class and urban immigrants. The former, however, is ubiquitous. Rents are most shocking to people who were completely unaccustomed to the practice of paying rent. Most Salvadorans of rural origins lived in their own small homes, though these were sometimes no more than single-room adobe huts. Among urban dwellers, many paid rent or mortgages, but the amounts were relatively modest compared to their salaries. They never dreamed that an apartment in the United States would cost seven or more times the minimum salaries in their countries. When these people envisioned their expenses in the United States, they never factored in the true cost of housing.

The miscalculation immigrants make about their projected earnings versus expenses is quickly recognized and corrected once they arrive. But the pressure of housing costs, in particular, weighs heavily on everyone. They realize immediately that they can afford neither their own apartment nor even their own room. Don José explained it to me, saying, "What you think is that life here is different, that you are going to live well here, in peace. . . . Here rents are expensive, everything is expensive. Of course, if you earn in dollars you spend dollars too. So you don't save what you thought you would. I had made a plan like this: If I earn three hundred dollars then I will spend so much and save so much. So after so much time I will have saved so much money. You think that you can save. But it's not so. Here you come to find out that your expenses are two or three times what you thought they'd be. This is the great disillusionment that you carry with you. You think that if you earn a good salary you will be happy but it's not true. You can earn what they told you that you would earn, but they never tell you how much your expenses will be, especially rent. No one tells you about this. They only tell you what they earn, not what they spend. That's the problem. So when you start to see how much you spend, you begin to feel deceived."

If immigrants merely conformed to neoclassical economic rules, they would flow out of areas that they could not afford to live in. But immigrants, particularly the undocumented, are very dependent upon finding jobs, and the labor market they face, as discussed previously, is so constricted that they do not enjoy the same flexibility as natives enjoy. As a result, they leave areas such as Houston, Texas, where housing is cheap and abundant but jobs are scarce, and head for areas offering employment, despite the costs.[1] They resort to the only other technique available to them: finding ways to minimize their housing expenditures by living in overcrowded, substandard housing in the least expensive neighborhoods.

In contrast to the universality of disillusionment over the high cost of housing, the sting of social isolation from the American mainstream was felt principally by the South Americans and urban Salvadorans. The rural Salvadorans had been exposed to few, if any, media images of the United States because their illiteracy precluded reading newspapers and the areas they lived in lacked televisions and movie theaters. These individuals grew up largely in isolation from their greater society and from the world at large. The ideas about the United States that migrated with them were fashioned by word of mouth. But Salvadorans and South Americans who lived in cities prior to emigration carried with them a knowledge of mainstream America that they had gained by watching television and movies. They expressed their sense of being excluded from the mainstream, or of being privy to it only as servants to middle-class families. I recall having a lengthy conversation with Alfredo about his feelings of isolation while we sat in the room that he shared with three others. Roaches crawled in and out of food containers that sat piled on the floor in the narrow spaces between beds. No one dared put the food in the kitchen lest it be appropriated by one of the other ten housemates. The only "adornment" on the wall consisted of a taped-on television antenna wire, to which scores of roaches had stuck and died. Alfredo joked with me cynically about how he endured worse living conditions in the United States than he ever had in Peru. "I would never have lived like this in my country," he said. "But here I have no choice in order to take care of my family there and save money so I can go home someday." The irony silenced us. Alfredo lived on the furthest margins of America in order to prevent his family from slipping out of the middle class and into the margins of Peru. "That's why I never send home pictures of the way I live," he concluded and then switched the topic of conversation.

The Genesis of Exclusion

The construction of Long Island as a sea of white, middle-class bedroom communities dotted by a smattering of "minority pockets" dates back primarily to the great post–World War II suburbanization of the island. Although blacks and Latinos settled on the island prior to the 1940s, it was the G.I. Bill that stimulated many veterans to seek suburban housing. Federal housing subsidies promoted white flight to the suburbs, especially to planned, mass-produced communities like Levittown, by making it cheaper for a family to own a home on the island than to rent in the inner city (Jackson 1985). However, blacks were expressly excluded from Levittown and other subdivisions by restrictive covenants which stated in 1947 that "no dwelling shall be used or occupied by members of other than the Caucasian race, but the employment and maintenance of other than Caucasian domestic servants shall be permitted" (*New York Times* June 28, 1992).[2] Consequently, black veterans and their families headed for towns where there were few restrictions, places such as Wyandanch and North Amityville in Suffolk County. Puerto Ricans, drawn to the island by labor contracts in farming and defense manufacturing industries, settled primarily around the Brentwood–Central Islip area—a stone's throw from the other towns, and another "minority pocket" today.

Racial covenants have not been the only tactic employed in the effort to segregate minorities from the white population on Long Island. Other effective techniques are blockbusting and racial steering, practices still widespread today but much more difficult to document than covenants. Best detailed in the extraordinary book *American Apartheid* (Massey and Denton 1993), blockbusting and racial steering are practiced by real estate agents who artificially segregate neighborhoods. In blockbusting, agents buy a home, rent or sell it to an African-American or Latino family, and then "scare" white families into believing that the neighborhood is turning over. This tactic yields quick sales and high profits. In racial steering, agents show properties only to a renter/buyer whose race matches that of the owner/landlord, such that neighborhoods are kept from becoming racially mixed. The extreme segregation of people of color on Long Island suggests that such practices have occurred and do occur there. But there is also a growing body of less circumstantial evidence that supports this hypothesis, much of it the outcome of an extensive *Newsday* investigation entitled "A World Apart: Segregation on Long Island," published in September 1990.

The practice of blockbusting as it occurred in the Nassau County town of Uniondale is chronicled in the September 24, 1990, edition of *Newsday*. Uniondale's population changed dramatically during the 1980s. In 1980, it was 70 percent white, 26 percent black, and 7 percent Latino. In 1990, the white population had dropped to 45 percent while the black and Latino populations had doubled to 47 percent and 14 percent respectively (*Newsday* March 8, 1992). White homeowners received alarming letters from realtors stating, among other things, that an agent "'will be contacting you from time to time regarding something new happening in our local real estate market'" (*Newsday* September 24, 1990). One white resident who has fought to maintain a racially mixed town described the pressure from agents as "'getting to the point where real estate agents don't even have to steer. People are leaving on their own. I am beginning to feel that my ideal of people living interracially together is nothing but a pipe dream'" (ibid.).

Racial steering is also alive and well on Long Island even though such discriminatory policies have been officially banned by New York State law since 1958 and by the Federal Fair Housing Act enacted in 1968. Extensive interviews with brokers by *Newsday* and the *New York Times*, as well as a series of lawsuits filed against several brokers, substantiate claims of unfair housing practices made by many African-American and Latino Long Islanders. In 1992, state officials sued two Nassau County brokers and accused a third of contempt of court for practicing racial steering. The suit was based on investigations conducted by black and white testers sent to seek housing. The results revealed that testers were shown properties exclusively in neighborhoods whose inhabitants' race matched their own (*Newsday* February 21, 1992). Most recently, the state attorney general sued an apartment referral service in East Meadow. The owner "was accused of programming his company's computer to indicate the ethnic background of prospective tenants and landlords, along with the biases of the landlords" (*New York Times* February 15, 1994).

Documents in the 1992 suit point to a common response made by brokers when discussing racial steering and other discriminatory practices. Agents claim to be pawns of white landlords who will not negotiate with minorities. Some even asserted that they were threatened by other brokers and homeowners when they brought nonwhites into white neighborhoods (*Newsday* September 24, 1990). Black brokers declare that white owners will deal with them over the phone but reject them at the door when they see that they are black (*Newsday* March 25, 1989). A *Newsday* poll suggests the reason why: 58 percent of whites and 50 percent of blacks say that housing values decline when blacks move into neighborhoods. Thus, tactics employed by whites to preserve the equity in their homes and neighborhoods have resulted in a hyper-discriminatory environment. The poll found that 60 percent of blacks felt that they did not have the same opportunities as whites to buy a house; three-quarters felt that real estate brokers practice racial steering; 20 percent said they had experienced discrimination buying a home, and 40 percent had encountered discrimination renting an apartment (*Newsday* September 17, 1990). Meanwhile, the overwhelming majority of blacks wish to live in integrated neighborhoods (defined by them as 50 percent black and 50 percent white); whites tolerate only 10 to 15 percent black neighbors before moving out (ibid.).

Several of my informants believed that discrimination affected their ability to obtain housing. Margarita, a Salvadoran woman with a young son, commented that the discrimination practiced is two-pronged. Landlords, she argues, dislike Latinos, particularly those with children. "In the case of housing here in [my town], if you go to a real estate office looking for an apartment, they first ask you which country you are from. They don't ask you for a deposit or for their payment; rather, they ask you, 'Where are you from? Are you Salvadoran? Peruvian?' Then they say, 'Oh, no, there are many problems with the Hispanics. We don't want to rent to you.' This is how they begin to talk. They don't want to rent to Hispanics. . . . Here [white] Americans are preferred. In the first place because Americans have small families. They ask you if you have children. Children are not appreciated. This is very bad. That's why I haven't had another child because I know I won't be able to get another apartment." Landlords regularly discriminate against families with children, regardless of race, but Margarita's experience also suggests that racial steering may still be active on Long Island.

Prejudice is not limited to the realtors; frequently recent immigrants are met with direct hostility from the mainstream society, as happened in Glen Cove. When many Central and South American immigrants (most of them undocumented) started moving into the Glen Cove area, the homeowners became concerned that the town was going down and that their property values would fall as a result. They pressured the mayor to do something about the situation, and he subsequently ordered the INS to raid immigrant areas, making it known that Glen Cove did not welcome these people.[3] In the town of Syosset, neighbors of Salvadorans who had rented a house there for $1,200 per month contended that this house and some ten others were being crammed full of too many people. They complained that this taxed the water system and other services and insisted that their motives were not racist (*Newsday* July 15, 1990). "'I see both sides of [the conflict],'" argues a building inspector in Manorhaven, another embattled community. "'Would you want an eyesore reeking of beer next door to you if you invested your whole life savings into your home?'" (*New York Times* September 15, 1991). Opposition to illegal apartments resembles opposition to homeless shelters; homeowners are driven by a desire to preserve the equity in their homes.

Finally, there is some evidence of discriminatory bank lending practices that make it more difficult for Latino and black loan applicants to finance their homes. Redlining, the common term for these practices, originated in the 1930s under the auspices of the Home Owners Loan Corporation (HOLC), and it has served as an effective mechanism for segregation (Jackson 1985; Massey and Denton 1993). Under the practice of redlining, government officials labeled neighborhoods according to their desirability and stability: blue for excellent, yellow for passable but often transitional, and red for undesirable. The labels determined the government's willingness to back mortgages and became key to banks' willingness to lend to prospective buyers. Minority neighborhoods were always labeled red (ibid.). Redlining has been shown to be on the rise on Long Island while it has declined in neighboring New York City (*Newsday* August 26, 1993; September 6, 1993).

Long Island's Minority Pockets

Segregation on Long Island is so obvious that one does not need surveys to find it, only good observational skills. There are areas of the island where minorities represent nearly 100 percent of the population, sometimes labeled "pockets of poverty," which have existed since at least the 1960s and have not changed significantly over the years (Zschock 1969). South Shore towns such as Hempstead, Freeport, Roosevelt, and Wyandanch have been populated by African Americans for several decades. Puerto Rican concentrations have been noted in Brentwood, Central Islip, Glen Cove, Huntington Station, and several other towns. With the possible exception of Roosevelt, these are all prime areas of new Latino immigrant residence (see table 8.1).

In many cases, merely a street divides white middle-classdom from minority pocket. Wheatley Heights is adjacent to Wyandanch in Suffolk County and used to belong to it. If you approach Wyandanch from exit 50 of the Long Island Expressway and drive through Wheatley Heights, you experience one of Long Island's starkest juxtapositions. Huge sin-

TABLE 8.1
Selected Long Island Communities by Ethnicity and Race
(population by percentage of total)

	Latino	Black	Asian	White
Nassau County				
Freeport	20.3	32.4	1.5	56.5
Glen Cove	10.4	7.8	3.2	86.2
Hempstead	18.5	59.0	1.4	32.4
Long Beach	10.4	7.5	1.7	87.3
New Cassel	18.6	66.1	1.5	27.3
Roosevelt	8.2	89.6	0.5	7.9
Uniondale	13.7	46.6	2.2	44.7
Suffolk County				
Brentwood	34.7	13.3	1.8	73.1
Central Islip	26.2	24.9	1.7	62.6
N. Bay Shore	36.7	14.7	0.5	69.5
Huntington Sta.	11.7	12.4	1.9	82.0
Wyandanch	14.8	83.5	0.3	9.4

Source: U.S. Bureau of the Census, *Census of Population and Housing* (1990).

Note: Latinos may be of any race, so percentages do not add up to 100 percent. "Other" race category is not listed.

gle-family mansions set back from the street by terraced and landscaped lawns line your journey through Wheatley Heights. A stop sign next to the neatly groomed elementary school signals that an abrupt change is coming up. The blinking red light on Main Street at the classic red firehouse begins the transformation. Cross this road and the vehicles take a step backward in time. Homes are surrounded by weeds and strewn with old cars and children's abandoned toys. There is no town center, only the principal artery, Straight Path, blazing a trail to the nearest highway. Wyandanch has no supermarket; it is home to a few gasoline stations, a struggling health clinic, a bodega, and several fast-food restaurants. But more significantly, every face is black or brown; I was invariably the only white person on the street whenever I visited.

The situation in Glen Cove is different but only in degree. African Americans live almost exclusively in two areas of this middle-class bedroom community. One is the government-built public housing project on a hill near the center of town; the other is the Orchard, a small neighborhood traditionally inhabited by immigrants. The Orchard greeted Italians at the turn of the century, and now a few Italian landlords rent most of the poor housing stock out to blacks and Salvadoran and other Latino immigrants. Tucked away from the commuters' view, the Or-

The immigrants' view of suburbia. Photograph by Susan Calvin

chard has achieved and maintained a strong sense of community over generations—but this is largely because its inhabitants know they are excluded from the rest of town.

Glen Cove, especially the Orchard, is a good example of how immigrants tend to follow the paths laid down by earlier migrations of Italians, Puerto Ricans, and blacks. They occupy marginal, poorer, fringe neighborhoods, communities, or even buildings (but undocumented immigrants do not qualify for public housing and therefore are not concentrated there). Since immigrants often provide services to the middle and upper classes, they also find it convenient to live as close to them as possible. As a result, they tend to form another residential pattern: clustering in substandard, although not necessarily cheaper, housing on the margins of more affluent communities such as Great Neck, Port Washington, Glen Head, Manhasset, Oyster Bay, Huntington, and Westbury on the North Shore. Typically only live-in domestics live in Anglo neighborhoods, but—as I shall illustrate shortly—a few rent illegal apartments from whites who need the cash to hold on to their houses.

Of course, the introduction of new immigrants into minority areas, although often profitable, is frequently fraught with tension. Latino-black relations are particularly strained in communities such as Wyandanch and Westbury. In Wyandanch, my informants were so afraid of being robbed that they never left their homes at night unless escorted by at least one other person. Westbury's traditionally black neighborhood,

New Cassel, has witnessed a steady stream of Salvadorans and Haitian immigrants. The newcomers are drawn in by slum landlords, according to church workers who minister to the poor there, and the diversity has resulted in new antagonisms. Animosities run very high between the African-American and Salvadoran groups; these hostilities are duplicated all over the island. Salvadorans complain that they are assaulted and robbed by the blacks. Because they are physically small and because (lacking easy access to banks) they are known to carry money on their persons, Salvadorans are common targets. Blacks, meanwhile, complain that Salvadorans receive favorable treatment from the U.S. government and from charitable institutions such as the Catholic Church. They feel that the Salvadorans are being helped up the queue, taking their jobs and leaving them behind.

Sharing neighborhoods with U.S. minority populations only adds to immigrants' perceptions that they are isolated, culturally as well as physically, from the mainstream. Much as Massey and Denton (1993) describe for Chicago, there are many opportunists—natives and immigrants alike—who exploit and even exacerbate the tight housing market for their own gain.

THE HOUSING CRISIS: PROFITS FOR MANY

The aggregate effects of blockbusting, racial steering, discrimination in bank lending, and redlining on Long Island have resulted in its being one of the most segregated areas in the United States. Other forces contributed to the formation of a lucrative, illegal housing market that came to be exploited by a whole host of profiteers, from large landlords to homeowners to immigrant renters. The booming real estate market of the 1980s drove home values higher and higher, increasing the equity at stake and the desire by homeowners to safeguard it. However, as equities rose, so too did tax assessments based on property values. Some families, particularly those on fixed incomes, found themselves "house rich but pocket poor." As tax burdens rose, through both higher assessments and greater overall spending, homeowners began to find difficulty in meeting their tax obligations and/or in selling their homes. The dearth of young families whose incomes could support mortgage payments for Long Island homes helped fuel a slump in the real estate market. Meanwhile, the demand for affordable housing continued to climb, fostering the growth of an illegal rental industry.

The quest for affordable housing stimulated different sectors of the population to explore newfound opportunities for profiting from the crisis. Absentee and slum landlords managed the housing market in the traditional minority pockets; white middle-class homeowners squeezed by taxes and with space to spare carved illegal apartments out of their homes; and immigrants instituted a system of subletting space in rented properties that profited the leaseholders—the encargado system.

Absentee and Slum Landlords Profit

The scarcity of housing opens fertile ground for entrepreneurs of all descriptions, but absentee and slum landlords profit particularly well. They exact high prices for substandard housing commonplace in minority areas. In an old Italian community located on the North Shore of Nassau County, I walked into Yanira Palacias's apartment and almost fell through the exposed floorboard. As roaches skittered along the floor, I noticed that the ceiling had collapsed over the hallway and that there was a persistent drip from the bathroom. Yanira, an undocumented immigrant from El Salvador, took me inside to show me the nonfunctional shower. Water dripped from the ceiling and had smeared wet plaster all over the shower floor. Yanira had asked me to come by when she heard that I worked with lawyers. She was being evicted—purportedly because she had two small children there, including an infant suckling at her breast. Soon after she and her family of five moved out and occupied a room within another Salvadoran apartment, I learned that the apartment was rented to an African-American family with three children. Their rent was subsidized by Section 8 housing—the federal subsidy for low-income families. Apparently the landlord, a descendant of Italian immigrants, could reap more income through Section 8 than the $800 he charged Yanira and her family. In another incident I witnessed, a black landlord in Wyandanch was negotiating the rental of a very dilapidated apartment to the Peruvians Manuel and Berta. He asked $700 for the apartment but wanted an extra $200 when he found out that there would be three Peruvians living there. He also had the basement rented out to Salvadorans at $300 per room. The Peruvians knew the price was exorbitant. But, with few options in the tight housing market, they agreed to the deal.

An effective slumlord tactic is to take advantage of the immigrants' language and cultural differences. Edmundo was charged by his landlord for an inside parking space even though he had no car. Edmundo and his common-law wife, Altagracia, are a young couple from El Salvador. After they had lived as boarders in several locations, Edmundo was able to rent a one-bedroom apartment for $750 in a building run by a notorious slum landlord in Nassau County. He, Altagracia, and their infant son lived in the bedroom, and they rented out the living room to five boarders. Edmundo insisted that they all divide the rent equitably, but when his lease came up for renewal, he was shocked to find it had increased to $938. After investigating the paperwork, we realized that

the landlord had slipped a separate sheet (which resembled the rent renewal form) into the same envelope with the renewal. This other sheet
was a request form for the parking space. Edmundo and his wife do not
read English and inadvertently signed the parking space authorization
only to find their rent hiked $100 for the privilege. The landlord had
targeted Spanish-speaking families with this trick, and about a dozen
had signed the forms without knowing what they were doing. With help
from a local organization they took the landlord to court. In the meantime, the landlord sought Edmundo's eviction on grounds of overcrowding the apartment and won. The family had to move into a room
in a friend's apartment. So after nearly a decade in the United States
Edmundo had raised himself to a degree of independence only to be
knocked down again.

Patterns of tenant abuse by large property owners are not uncommon
on Long Island. Some cases involve overcharging on security deposits
and illegal evictions, while others entail sharply raising rents when tenants vacate apartments. In one case filed against landlord Arthur Mott
by the New York State Division of Housing and Community Renewal in
1993, when an apartment in Hempstead was vacated in 1989, the rent
charged to the new tenant jumped from $361.91 to $748.50 per
month. The majority of the victims named in the case are Latino, indicating that landlords specifically targeted this population of new immigrants, perhaps reasoning that they would be least likely to challenge the
overcharges (Logan 1994).

Homeowners Profit Too

Landlords are far from the only Long Islanders profiting from the lack
of affordable housing. Solid middle-class families and elderly "empty
nest" homeowners who find it increasingly difficult to sustain a single-
family home have likewise contributed to the eruption of a vast illegal
housing market wherein they carve rental spaces out of their homes. The
escalation of property taxes, in particular school taxes, during the 1980s
was a principal driving force in these homeowners' decisions to rent part
of their homes. For example, between 1991 and 1992, school taxes
jumped nearly 27 percent in Hempstead; the average increase on the
island was 8 percent—2.5 times the rate of inflation (*Newsday* December
9, 1991). To offset tax burdens and the general high cost of living on
Long Island, homeowners created some ninety thousand rental units
despite local housing codes under which the units were illegal. Tenants
are not difficult to find owing to the deficit of rental housing on the
island; they include struggling young native workers and families as well
as incoming immigrants.

During times of financial difficulty in the past, families would take in boarders or double up with other families in order to economize on housing costs (Mutchler and Krivo 1989). Boarding was a particularly helpful strategy historically among newly arrived immigrants,[4] including immigrants to Long Island (LaGumina 1988). But this preceded the appearance of zoning laws and regulations that currently limit the flexibility of families to rent rooms, apartments, or houses to nonfamily. Where the need for rental income is strong enough and zoning laws are not enforced, as in many areas of the island, homeowners are more likely to risk fines for renting to strangers. One of many techniques they employ to hide their maneuvers is to renovate their buildings to contain multiple apartments but with one mailbox out front and one main entryway. The buildings appear to be single-family homes when, in reality, several families or a multitude of nonrelated people may be living there. I have documented this in very detailed fashion through my alternative enumeration for the 1990 census (Mahler 1993). In recent years, public concern over illegal overcrowding and its effects on property values, schools, and municipal funding has resulted in increased enforcement of local ordinances. Immigrants have been the principal targets of the enforcement, with many evicted, while the landlords who rent the units have generally not been disciplined.

Immigrants are a particularly vulnerable population in the illegal housing market owing to their ethnic visibility. Homeowners who construct illegal units also risk detection and ostracism by neighbors, especially when they rent to people who stand out because of their race or ethnicity in the neighborhoods. Juanita discovered this when she and her brother rented, for $650 per month, an apartment fashioned out of a basement in a home owned by elderly Italian immigrants. The apartment lacked a stove and a kitchen sink; Juanita had to buy a two-burner electric stove to cook on. The owners were fearful that their neighbors would detect this apartment and required Juanita to cover her windows and be very quiet. But the entrance to the apartment was accessible only when the family's garage door was opened, and within a couple of months the family became so nervous that they asked Juanita to leave. Since she had expected her sister to arrive from Peru and the trip became delayed, Juanita and her brother decided to move to more economical lodgings. Shortly after they did so, the sister arrived and the three spent the next month living in a six-by-eight-foot room rented from another immigrant.

Juanita's relationship to her landlords illustrates a pattern of symbiosis between renters seeking affordable housing and owners in need of added income. It is not always a happy marriage; there are risks and rewards, as I have illustrated above. Owners are in the less vulnerable position because, if fearful of neighborhood reprisals or fines for noncompliance with housing regulations, they can readily evict or lock tenants out, threatening to call the INS.

IMMIGRANTS CAPITALIZE ON THEIR COMPATRIOTS' NEEDS

The housing needs of immigrants vary over the course of the immigrant's stay in the United States. Initially, most of my informants migrated without their immediate family and thus required only minimal housing—a bed and some space to store belongings. Since newly arrived immigrants tend to move frequently to take advantage of job opportunities, they need flexibility in their commitments and responsibilities. As their stays lengthen, they often bring in family members or form new families in the United States, and this changes their housing needs and costs. Accommodating these variables as well as the forces affecting the availability of housing on Long Island in general, immigrants have met the challenge of a tight and exploitive housing market by innovating their own way of matching supply with demand. This structure is what I label the encargado system, and it is the principal avenue by which some immigrants also profit from Long Island's housing crisis. As I shall describe in the pages below, over the years immigrants' need for housing evolves but so does their knowledge of its availability and accessibility. They gain immigrant capital by learning about the complexities of Long Island's housing markets, and with that capital many also find ways to profit as encargados and homeowners.

When immigrants first arrive, they almost invariably live with family or friends, generally those who have sponsored their trip to the United States. Often these homes are "mother ships," homes that serve as way stations for almost every immigrant who arrives in a certain town. Mother ships are also frequently used as mailing addresses and networking centers by immigrants even after they have stopped living in them. During immigrants' first few days they are overwhelmed by the need to find work but are also rapidly acculturated to the differences between residing with one's relatives in the home country and doing the same in the host country. Immigrants told me time and time again that visitors, even nonrelatives, were always welcome and cared for in their own countries. But once in the United States almost everyone feels that their welcome has a time limit. One testimony collected by Ward (1987) from a Salvadoran living in Los Angeles mirrors my informants' experiences:

> Everything is money here. Family members can be worse than friends: if you don't have money and don't work then things are bad. I have family here but for them I don't count. My sister and her husband live here but

it's as though we never were family. They are family in name only. They made things difficult for me. They criticized me for not getting a job and they charged me $150 a month to sleep on a mat in the living room. . . . I think the system here has swallowed [my sister] up. She used to be a student activist for social change in El Salvador, now all she cares about is money. . . . My sister would never loan me money because she and her husband are so materialistic now. (230–31)

What new immigrants realize in their first days is that life is much more expensive in the United States than in their home countries and that the biggest difference is in the cost of housing. They realize that they must look for a place to stay as well as a job. For some this process can be extremely long and painful, particularly if they arrive, as Cándido did, in the fall or winter when jobs are very scarce. He spent five months with no stable job or place to stay. Fortunate in that many members of his extended family live in his town, Cándido would move from house to house staying a few days until he wore out his welcome. It was a very humiliating time for him. Cándido left El Salvador because, after he had served in the army, his life was threatened. "They told me that the United States is really *galán* [nice]," he said. His goal in the United States became to save enough money to buy a house for his family in El Salvador. "I didn't have a house," he lamented. "Only if you are here are you able to buy a house." But for his first four months Cándido lived on the verge of homelessness.

Men like Cándido, who may be married, acompañados, or single, often emigrate alone, leaving their families in the home country. When such "unattached" men arrive in the United States, they focus their concern on providing for their families left at home. They look for the least expensive form of housing through networks of coethnic family and friends. They cannot afford to rent an apartment but rather look for sleeping space, usually a bed for $150 to $250 per month in a room shared by other men in similar circumstances. They are mobile free-floaters who move from one apartment or house to another in rapid succession as they change jobs, find their roommates disagreeable, or locate a cheaper arrangement. Free-floaters may also move from space to space within housing units. Jesús lived in a house with some ten others. During one summer he occupied the basement, creating a modicum of privacy with sheets hung on clotheslines. In the winter he moved upstairs and shared a room with his friend, but the next spring he moved back to the basement because the person in charge, the encargado, rented his room to a couple who desired more privacy.

Since there are fewer immigrant women than men and strong social pressures bar women from sharing rooms with men unless they are related or acompañados, women and men rarely share rooms. Instead, these women tend to be incorporated into relatives' households more readily than men and stay there until they get married or become acompañadas. This is exactly what Ana's sister did when she arrived from El Salvador. She moved into Ana and Jorge's apartment and helped them care for their two children while she looked for work cleaning houses. Many other women work as live-in maids until they marry, which saves them money because they do not have to pay room and board. But they often feel isolated from family and friends. Luz described the life of the interna as "depressing" because "you grew up doing your own things in your house and now you have to go and work as a servant in somebody else's house." Altagracia added, "Many women don't like to be internas because they get bored. It's not easy spending your life slaving to the wishes of your boss." Much as was true in the past, when male boarders move into housing units where there are unattached or even married females, tensions often increase. Sometimes this ends tragically—as it did for a fourteen-year-old high school student in Gold Coast whose story was related to me by her teacher. The girl's mother, a Protestant evangelical who works very long days, rented sleeping space to a twenty-one-year-old man. During the course of his stay in the apartment, and without the knowledge of the mother, he sexually assaulted and impregnated her adolescent daughter. The man refused to take responsibility for the pregnancy and the girl dropped out of school.

Piore (1979:63–64) describes the lifestyle of these unattached individuals as an ascetic existence that is difficult to sustain for long periods of time. This description rather misses the mark for many of the immigrants I have studied because they lived highly "ascetic" existences—at least in terms of material privation—in their home countries. Most peasant Salvadorans had no running water, bathrooms, or even mattresses to sleep on and lived in one-room houses with little or no privacy. By U.S. standards, however, the living conditions of most of my informants are abominable. One night, for instance, I went to visit a group of Salvadorans from Morazán. I drove up to the house, or at least what I believed to be the house—it was completely dark. The encargado greeted me outside and escorted me through the front door and into the living room. The room's floor was bare; its unfinished boards looked as if hundreds of sweepings had worn dirt deep into them. There were a few K-Mart–style couches around and no other furniture visible. A group of men were inside waiting. Their faces were barely visible, illuminated irregularly by a bulb that had been attached to a heavy-duty extension cord and swung from a hook at the far end of the room. The faces were distinctly *campesino* (peasant), and I felt as though I had entered into one of their homes in the far reaches of eastern El Salvador.

For some immigrants on Long Island, generally unattached males, temporary homelessness is an economic strategy. I have seen men living in makeshift shelters in forested areas and in abandoned housing. One forested trail led me to an aqueduct. A cement ledge designed to allow repair workers into the tunnel had become the living quarters for an unknown number of Salvadoran men who ran away as I approached. Informants suggest that these men are homeless during the summer months in order to reduce their housing costs to a minimum. The recession of the early 1990s has taken a high toll on immigrants, particularly since they do not qualify for government assistance, and may be one reason why immigrants become homeless, albeit only temporarily. While some have resorted to living outdoors, others, like Manuel, seek no-cost, alternative lodging. He told me that "at one time I was going to go and live in the car so I wouldn't have to pay rent. The rent is too expensive." Still others face dire prospects after a sudden fall from grace. Evangelina Cardoso, a Salvadoran who once held the lease on an apartment, lost her job owing to the recession, could not make her rent payments, and was evicted along with her husband, infant son, and their sublessees. In one instant, these people slid down the mobility ladder. They were forced to take a room in Amalia's apartment, sharing space with ten other people.

Housing needs change dramatically when family members arrive and join the first pioneers. Immigrants miss their families, and many send for their spouses and older children as soon as they have the money to finance their trips. Salvadorans send for their families to get them out of the dangerous situations that they themselves have escaped; South Americans tend to send for their families when they find they cannot meet their targets on schedule and their stays in the United States must be prolonged. They also realize that they can further their own goals by bringing in siblings and other workers among whom they can distribute remittance burdens and housing costs.

As the family expands, however, the free-floating model is no longer an option. At this point couples or men with their grown sons look for rooms to rent. This dramatically increases their rent burden as well as other expenses. Jesús, for instance, told me that he had not sent for his family because "I think that it's hard to have a family here—paying rent, paying for food and everything. Maybe with some people who have a place where they can stay, things change. Maybe they have more family members or more possibilities. But for me to bring my family here I'd have to have more money because it costs a lot. If I had the money maybe I'd bring the oldest one up so that he could learn English and other things. But there aren't the resources for this." If they are lucky, a family group will be able to rent a room for a fixed price and fill it with as many people as they want to, each paying a portion of the room's cost. Rooms rent for between $250 and $500 per month. But the encargado generally prefers to rent by the individual.

Increased expense is not the only problem immigrants face when they have to house their families. Don José had been sharing a room with two other men; when his wife and young son arrived from El Salvador, he moved into another room in the same apartment. But this arrangement created severe problems for his wife because the three of them shared the room with another Salvadoran woman and her newborn baby. Not even a curtain separated their space from hers. Don José looked for an affordable room to rent but could not find one. In the meantime relations with his wife became increasingly strained, he said: "She is tremendously jealous. So when she found out that other women lived in the same place as I did, she didn't like it. Secondly, she found out that I was living in the same room [as another woman]. She's used to living in a house only for ourselves, one with a living room, kitchen, dining room, and three bedrooms. We always had servants too; I lived in one room, she in another, and the servants in the third. She has always had a lot of room. But here! [She found herself] in a tiny room that is divided with my bed here for us and our son, and the other woman there with her baby. She felt very bad. . . . We couldn't continue to live where we were living because she couldn't live in the environment. She is a person who likes her privacy when she undresses; she doesn't like to undress in front of me even. She likes to be alone. And since we were living with other people it was very hard for her." Don José's wife was used to a solid middle-class lifestyle in El Salvador and could not bear the asceticism in the United States. Her dissatisfaction soured relations with the remaining half-dozen roommates, and Don José and his family were asked to leave. At this point, José's wife decided to return to El Salvador; since then there has been little communication between her and José. Their experience illustrates the effect housing has on relationships of various kinds. It also highlights, once again, the importance of class background in the immigrant experience.

Benjamín's experience illustrates the fact that few families can afford to live by themselves until they contain some three or four workers. After several years of laboring as a roving construction worker in Texas and New Jersey, he moved to Long Island and lived in a boardinghouse. When his sister and her deaf son arrived from El Salvador, they all moved into a two-bedroom apartment but rented one bedroom to Juanita and her brother, the Peruvians. Juanita was asked to move out when Benjamín's sister's husband arrived from El Salvador and they needed more space for the couple. Soon after, two more brothers arrived and later a third. They still live in the same apartment, and the financial pressure is finally abating for Benjamín.

Chavez (1990), studying Salvadorans in Los Angeles, has observed a similar need to share the rent burden as well as other domestic duties. He argues that having family members cohabit has alleviated the "sadness and loneliness" they felt before they came (51). But Chavez also contends that as their residence in the United States lengthens, undocumented immigrants' households generally come to resemble nuclear family units. While this is true to some degree on Long Island, the very expense of housing there tends to keep housing arrangements in flux such that they do not resemble the classic "settling" phase of migration as described by Piore (1979). In almost every case a minimum of an extended family is required to rent and maintain an apartment or house.

The Encargado System

Up to this point I have described the housing dilemma largely as an equation whose only variables are policies, landlords, and roommates. In reality, the lessee is pivotal. As the "encargado" or "person in charge," this individual (or family) bridges the gap between the property owners (who are primarily from the United States although many are older immigrants) and their immigrant tenants. In return, encargados wield tremendous power within the units they control. Renting an apartment or house requires the outlay of large amounts of capital. Usually from two to four thousand dollars, and sometimes more, is needed to cover the security deposit, first month's rent (often the last month's rent as well), and a broker's fee to the rental office. These expenses are added to any costs incurred in moving. Newly arrived immigrants do not have this type of capital readily available; on the contrary, they are already heavily in debt from their journeys. They are therefore in no position to rent their own units, and they need to economize. "If you want to live in a house by yourself," Berta explained, "or, in our case, in a house for us and a friend who lives with us, then you would have to go to a real estate office where you need a lot of money because they ask for a lot of money. If it is a basic house you have to give two to three thousand dollars down, for the first month and the security. But if we have come here with the idea of saving money, we have to find a cheaper house and not pay all that money."

The prohibitive costs of renting act as a screening process and, as a consequence, the encargados are almost always older immigrants who have saved some money or can pool resources with family or friends and rent the apartments. They do not view this as a service, however, but as an investment. And they want a return on their investment. Thus, their objective is simple: lease a house or apartment at a fixed rent (plus utilities) and sublet space in it to enough people so they can turn a profit. At a minimum, encargados wish to cover the rent and utilities expenses so that they, and perhaps their family, can live for free. Juanita boarded in a number of places over the early years of her life in the United States and has seen the system very clearly. "I have heard about rooms with eight beds in them and the beds are so close together that there's no place to move in," she recalled. "And they pay $200 per person. . . . Even in a jail or basement people don't sleep like this. I have been in poor houses [in my country] and the people don't [sleep like that]. . . . [These people here] pay $200 just for the space and they don't have room for anything. What [encargados] do is 're-rent.' For example, I rent an apartment for $600. I put ten people there; in just the living room I would put the ten and I would keep my own room. And if everyone is paying $200—you make the calculations! Ten people at $200 each is $2,000. Two thousand dollars. The $600 that I pay [the owner] plus the electricity and water is about $900 total. So I make a profit. It's a business. The Hispanics are doing business with housing. . . . And how often are we [tenants] at home to enjoy it? Almost never. You only want to have a place to rest your bones at night when you come home tired and want a place to relax. But here they've made it into a business and they make very good money. [The encargada where I live] is living for free. In the other room the girls there pay her $400 between the two of them. . . . We pay $250. That's $650. And she pays $675 for the apartment. So she only pays $25 toward rent and has the biggest room and everything! You see?"

Note the tinge of resentment in her words. She goes out of her way to say that "*Hispanics* are doing business with housing." She places the blame for her feeling of being exploited squarely on her coethnics' shoulders. She never mentions the structural causes of the crisis—the lack of investment in low-cost housing and residential segregation, to name just two. Nor does she speak of profits reaped by the building's owner. The main culprits are vindicated while the small ones are vilified.

The strategy Juanita describes is particularly useful to women leaseholders. Juanita's encargada at this time was a Mexican woman with small children separated from her husband. She had been in the United States for ten years, cleaning houses part-time for a living. This income did not cover her expenses, so she rented out two bedrooms in her apartment. For two months, Juanita lived there with her brother in a room the size of a large closet. Another woman I met in the New Cassel neighborhood of Westbury lived entirely off her income as an encargada. Relatives of hers, taking pity on her as a single mother of two small children, had paid the security deposit and first month's rent on her apartment. She sublet the bedrooms to boarders and lived in the living room with her children. The surplus income from the rent they paid provided the cash she needed to buy food and take care of her other needs.

Finally, in a few cases the encargado system is employed merely to cover the expenses of homeowning. Only rarely do immigrants buy their own homes; when they do, they generally meet their mortgage payments by subletting space much as if they were merely renting the units. For homeowners, the encargado system is indispensable because even a family with two wage earners will not be able to buy and maintain a house if their salaries average only $250 per week each. This is the situation in which Carmen and her husband now find themselves. Carmen came to the United States in early 1990 and joined her husband in the house where he had rented a room. But Carmen felt miserable there because another tenant, a woman who Carmen suspects had a relationship with her husband, would inform him about all her activities. She felt incarcerated in her own home and pressured her husband to move them to the house that her husband's brother (a legal permanent resident) was buying with a subsidy from the U.S. government. They moved from Brentwood to a nearby town and into the small house. Now there are ten adults and two babies living there. The extra bedrooms are rented to Carmen and her husband and another couple at $300 each. Another room holds four boarders. Since the mortgage is $1,200, the owners, Carmen's in-laws, cover most of the payments through the rent they collect. Everyone must share the kitchen and small bathroom but each group cooks separately and keeps its food labeled in the refrigerator. The three women in the house take care of the cleaning.

Unlike their subletters, encargados do not see themselves as exploiters. They do not feel that they live for "free" since they are responsible for collecting rents, maintaining the property, and so on. Sometimes they have to cover for tenants who cannot pay the rent when they are unemployed, run low on cash, or move out suddenly. They feel that their boarders benefit a great deal from the relationship because they do not have to pay a security deposit, are not locked into a lease, and are more free to move when opportunities arise than are the encargados themselves. Encargados also must be responsible for paying bills and for shouldering the consequences if they are not paid. Often it is the encargado, for instance, who installs the only phone in the unit and is pressured into lending it to the tenants. This phone sharing almost always results in the suspension of service when the bills arrive and no one owns up to making the calls. The tension between the encargados and their sublessees is apparent though often subtle. When I interviewed Isabel, the Peruvian woman who lost her chance to get illegal papers because of her pregnancy, she had just become an encargada in association with her compañero. Obviously nervous about her new role after being a renter for some time, she artfully deflected my questions about how much rent she was paying and insisted, "Well, you have to take into account the cleaning and maintenance we do." I knew that she felt uneasy, and I also knew that in her house her compañero had set up a job wheel to rotate cleaning chores each week. The cleaning excuse was weak, but it illustrates the strain between encargados and tenants. Tenants believe that the encargados profit by overcharging them; encargados, answerable to owners, resent tenants' disregard for the property.

Don Federico is the encargado of a small, ramshackle three-bedroom house in a Suffolk County town that is home to the makeshift car-repair business described previously. On approaching the house one's first impression is that it serves merely as a centerpiece for the numerous junked cars that nearly encircle it. For a long time a motley dog whose coat was nearly eaten away by a flea-borne infection would greet you when you walked through the gate. The "living room" has never had a couch; its furniture has varied from two to three single beds separated from the entrance by a "world map" shower curtain. The beds have been accompanied by ragtag dressers and are now ringed by several free weights and an aged black-and-white television set. In the kitchen, the linoleum is nearly translucent from wear, the walls are covered with spatters of grease, and the stove is always busy. The garage doubles as living space for Vidal, the mechanic. Heat is sporadic, the water is occasionally turned off owing to nonpayment, and the cesspool backs up.

Don Federico has weathered some eight years in the United States, about half of them in this house. Many tenants have come and gone, but there is a core who were there for the duration of my fieldwork. He describes his role as a "headache" and told me that he hated having to collect rent each month as well as worrying about the house's services. In the meantime, one of his tenants described the arrangement from the tenants' viewpoint. "[Don Federico] rents our house for $800 but he says he has rented it for $1,200. This means that there is a difference of $400 which he makes off of it. He doesn't pay to live in this house. He lives for free. And he probably makes some money on it too. This is life here, there is no justice. It's not that we rent a house together; rather, the person who is in charge of the house takes advantage of it to make some money. He treats it like a business, not as a way of sharing housing. This makes things get more expensive. *We* are making life more expensive, we immigrants. Not the North Americans but they are also learning." Once again, blame is placed on the immigrants, and not on the larger housing crisis and its levels of profiteers, for the high cost of housing. Since it is Don Federico's face that this tenant sees each day, it is logical that he is the object of his rancor. But the man's words are illustrative also of immigrants' transition from home country ways and expectations of others' behavior, such as reciprocity without personal gain, to the host country's mores. Immigrant physical and cultural isolation only hinders this process, fostering resentment toward those closest—particularly those who appear to be getting ahead by riding on the backs of others.

Doña Rosa Cifuentes is the most imaginative—and one of the most profiteering—of the encargados I met during my research years. She is also perhaps the most despised. Rosa owns three buildings, including a boardinghouse in a mixed immigrant neighborhood, and provides most of the housing available to undocumented immigrants there. She is a South American immigrant who has lived in Gold Coast for about thirty years. She began her immigrant life as a factory worker, but after inheriting several properties from her ex-husbands, she turned to renting space to immigrants. This was about fifteen years ago—precisely when Salvadorans began arriving in town. Since then, nearly every Salvadoran who has come to this area has either stayed in one of her houses, most often the boardinghouse, or has known someone who lives there. She is a local institution.

Doña Rosa occupied the ground floor of her house but rented out two of its three bedrooms to a Salvadoran and a Colombian. Rosa allowed them to use her phone but charged them for incoming as well as outgoing calls. One of her daughters lived in one room on the second floor, next to the small apartment my husband and I occupied during my fieldwork. Rosa arranged the electric bills so that I would have to pay for her daughter's electricity. The basement of this building was crudely carved into four rooms and a tiny bathroom. The only entrances to the basement were a small door onto a rickety ladder and, from the outside, the heavy metal cellar door. Lacking heat, the basement inhabitants depended on the boilers for the first and second floors to heat their rooms. This was not an adequate solution since Rosa always kept her heat at sixty-five degrees or lower.

Many different people occupied these rooms while we were there, but one family's plight is the most memorable. This family lived in one dark room with no ventilation in the basement. They consisted of Amalia, her husband, and their two children, ages two and four. Doña Rosa did not want to rent the space to them because, she said, she does not like children. She agreed only on the condition that the children always stay outside and that Amalia not use Rosa's kitchen, even to store milk for the children. She also forbade the family to buy a refrigerator, claiming it would waste too much energy. Since Amalia and her family did not have a car, I would offer them rides to doctors' appointments and the like. This angered Rosa tremendously since she also ran a taxi service. On one occasion, Rosa wanted to charge Amalia forty dollars to take them to an interview to qualify for the Women, Infants and Children (WIC) supplemental food program. At that price, most of the monetary benefit the children, all U.S. citizens, were entitled to would have been spent on the transportation. Rosa would also arrange to take groups of immigrants in her aging station wagon to the INS to apply for work authorization when she knew that they would be denied unless they applied for political asylum. For this "service" she charged each of them seventy dollars although the train fare was only ten dollars. In order to recruit passengers, she would invite herself to social functions such as baptisms and parties.

Doña Rosa was infamous, however, for her boardinghouse. According to my count, approximately thirty people resided there at any one time. Some lived in the two separate apartments on the first floor and paid their own utilities. But the basement and upper floors were inhabited by people who paid forty-five dollars per week for the privilege. Many windows in the building were broken; during my first visit, in March, the rooms were freezing. Tenants reported that heat was provided only intermittently and they were not permitted to have space heaters—or any other electrical appliances—because Rosa wanted to minimize her electric bills. Even radios were prohibited. She installed only fifteen-watt lightbulbs in the hallways. In the narrow passage leading to the third-floor rooms there was no light at all and tenants had to feel their way down in the darkness. To enforce her rules, Rosa enlisted informers and, according to rumor anyway, reduced their rents in return for information.

Rosa never stopped complaining about her tenants and the cost of living. She would rise on rainy mornings in a foul mood and curse everyone who came her way, then turn to going over her accounts. She complained bitterly that the Salvadorans never paid her on time and that they did not appreciate the fact that she had many bills to pay. Although she was known to have large deposits in her bank accounts, Rosa would always protest that she was low on money. I learned much about Rosa through Teofilo Gómez, a Salvadoran Catholic lay church worker who lived in her boardinghouse but ate in her apartment. Because he commiserated with the other boarders yet was privy to Rosa's finances, he proved to be a key informant about Rosa and the encargado system in general.

Admittedly, Doña Rosa represents an extreme case of landlords who take advantage of their tenants. Rosa has come to make her entire living off these immigrants and depends on the steady appearance of new arrivals to prey upon. As these people become more savvy about the ways of life in the United States, they move to less exploitive situations. Cándido, for example, resided temporarily at Doña Rosa's after being homeless for months. He stayed there only a short time because Rosa forbade him to prepare food in his room or use any electrical appliances. "Doña Rosa's place is the worst," he confided. "We only stay there if we have nowhere else to go. But as soon as we can, we leave."

In conclusion, the encargado subletting system is an immigrant-generated innovation born of a tight, expensive, and racist Long Island housing market. The encargado system thrives parallel to, but on the margins of, the housing market open to natives, particularly whites. It permits a few immigrants to rise above the rest and thus contributes to the growing stratification and heterogeneity of the immigrant population on Long Island. Without the encargado system immigrants might not be able to obtain housing at all and more might join the ranks of the homeless. But immigrants rarely feel beholden to encargados for this; rather, they feel used by their coethnics who serve as encargados. They target their anger at the encargados because they feel that these people are profiting while they, the renters, forgo remittance payments to pay their rent.

Although coethnic encargados bear the brunt of the resentment, they are hardly the only players to profit from the game. Mainstream middle-class families participate in growing numbers, as do real estate brokers and large property-holding corporations. But they, and even slumlords, are not chastised in the same way as immigrant encargados. This narrow attribution of culpability is, I argue, the manifestation of immigrant marginality to the mainstream. Lacking contact with it, they cannot comprehend it or its relationship to their lives. What immigrants see and understand best is their estranged world. Perhaps blame is easily placed on ecargados' shoulders too because renters know that as time goes by, they also will learn the system, gaining immigrant capital, and pass from temporary inhabitants of mother ships to free-floaters to encargados. At that third stage they can prey upon the next wave of immigrants who will also learn the ropes in time.

Chapter Nine

IMMIGRANTS AND THE AMERICAN DREAM

THE TITLE OF THIS BOOK is *American Dreaming* but nearly all of my informants say that they have not found the American dream they longed for. Most lament their decisions, indicating that had they known better what life would be like in the United States prior to emigrating from their homelands, they would never have made the journey. "No, I wouldn't have come," Eugenia said, "because when you come here what you do is begin to regret it. Life [in El Salvador] is slower. You live more relaxed than here. Here life is very fast because you only live to work. . . . Over there you're free. Maybe you're in a bad situation, but you're happy because you are in your country." A few individuals have indeed returned home but with only pennies in their pockets—little to show for their years away from their families. And, over time, most of these people have returned to Long Island, implying an incipient transnational, circulatory migration pattern. Overall, they offer profoundly pessimistic evaluations of their careers as immigrants. Probably most readers would concur that these people have not been impressively successful, that the American dream has eluded them.

I would temper this evaluation. That is, despite their average $250-per-week salaries ($12,000 annually), mountains of debt, severed social relations, and transnational obligations, immigrants demonstrate remarkable success in that they have survived a multitude of adversities. But they have not just subsisted, they have also constructed a world for themselves on the very foundation of their exclusion from mainstream society. And within this world, they have paved avenues that serve as conduits—for a few seasoned immigrants—to the American dream.

One reason my informants are unhappy with their experiences in the United States is that they emigrated with the notion that earning a living would be easy, that jobs would be plentiful, and that they would be able to save up a nest egg fast enough to return home in a few years. Though within weeks, if not days, following their arrival most found their vision of "streets paved with gold" an illusion, they still retained the belief that they could enjoy more opportunities in the United States than in their home countries. This transnational outlook has been linked by many researchers to immigrants' tangible achievements, more substantial than those of nonmigrant minority populations (Ogbu 1990; Suárez-Orozco 1989; Gibson 1988; see also Jacob and Jordan 1993).

At the altar of American dreaming: nostalgic reminders of home and
consumer gratifications of life in the United States.
Photograph by Susan Calvin

More important, the dim prospects for success among these migrants—and by success I mean principally improvements in their socioeconomic status—are the product of structural forces that marginalize
them and that lie almost entirely outside their control. The obstacles
they face include undocumented status, language and cultural differences, residential segregation, constricted employment opportunities,
and outright prejudice and hostility. These immigrants integrate into a
bottom rung of the American dream, the working poor. They lack access
to society's safety net—often because they have been denied legal status
as asylum seekers or refugees—and they find that they are excluded
from many of society's institutions. The world they come to inhabit
does not embrace them, but they rarely blame it for their problems.
This should not be surprising; it is difficult to perceive the core from the
periphery.

While the greater society is sheltered from the brunt of their antipa-
thies, immigrants launch their antagonisms at each other. Why? How
can we comprehend the anger and hostility immigrants projected on
each other in the statements I quoted at the beginning of the book? Why
were "jealous," "competitive," and "egotistical" the adjectives most
commonly used by immigrants to describe their compatriots? The outlook they convey is antithetical to the notion that immigrant groups exhibit "bounded solidarity" or ethnic cohesion.

One approach to an explanation would be to hypothesize that the antagonism immigrants express is the inevitable outcome of modernization, the disenfranchisement of the peasantry and their consequent rural-to-urban migration. There is a significant historical literature that documents how home country social norms and roles are challenged in the new society (e.g., Warner and Srole 1945; Thomas and Znaniecki 1984 [1918]; Handlin 1951). There is even some evidence that migrants, liberated from the watchful eyes of a small town, exploit each other in ways inconceivable in the home country. For instance, in his autobiographical account of Jewish immigrants in New York in the early decades of this century, Michael Gold (1930) writes about how his father's cousin cheated his father out of a venture they had operated together. One day his father went to work and discovered that his cousin had absconded with the business.

But this approach is problematic. There are numerous studies of rural-to-urban migrants who are hastily inaugurated into modernity but do not manifest a breakdown of rural norms, particularly the practice of reciprocity (Lomnitz 1977; Roberts 1973; Sánchez-Korrol 1983; Trager 1988). Indeed the ethnic solidarity school argues that the migration experience does not lessen but heightens immigrants' reliance on each other. According to Alejandro Portes and others, the ethnic enclave offers a haven, a respite from the strife immigrants encounter in the greater society. Excluded from access to the majority society's resources, ethnics cooperatively tap resources within their own community (see Portes and Bach 1985; Portes and Zhou 1992). One such asset is capital generated through rotating credit associations (e.g., Light 1972; Hendricks 1974; Lomnitz 1977; Bonnett 1981). The existence of these associations—which function on trust, not written contracts—is often cited as a key to immigrants' achievements and native minorities' deficiencies.

My informants, on the other hand, clearly indicate that the norms of reciprocity of their homelands have been suspended in the United States. I suggest that this lies at the heart of their disillusionment but is virtually unavoidable given the conditions they face and the objectives they are expected to fulfill. In the eyes of these immigrants, the pursuit of the almighty dollar has twisted social conventions to the point of pitting each migrant against the other. I argue that this occurs primarily but not exclusively as a consequence of their isolation from the mainstream. Finding their greatest opportunity for socioeconomic mobility within their ethnic group, they learn how to squeeze profits out of their communities as informal entrepreneurs providing services and products to coethnics. Where the greater society fails to meet the needs of immigrants at affordable prices and with a modicum of convenience, immigrants step in to meet their own needs. In so doing, they generate institutions largely parallel to the mainstream society's where a small group of entrepreneurs can profit. When immigrants discover, for instance, that they have to pay rent in the United States, an expense they may never have faced in their homelands, they devise ways to sublet housing to minimize their payments; in some cases, they actually make money off the rental. When they discover that private cars are essential to transportation on Long Island, they offset the maintenance costs by using these vehicles as informal taxis for fellow immigrants. From a more macroeconomic perspective, these activities signify a trend in the immigrant community toward the informalization of enterprise, a trend previously observed largely in the inner cities (Sassen 1988, 1991) that I note here in the suburbs.

These strategies have not evolved into ethnic enclaves or business niches in the mainstream, a development that would support the models of Alejandro Portes and Roger Waldinger discussed in chapter 1. This metamorphosis may occur in the future, but it appears to be hampered by the scarcity of capital—primarily monetary but also human capital (the latter is especially problematic among peasants). As I mentioned before, I have encountered almost no rotating credit associations, and my informants, particularly those who are undocumented, have little if any access to other sources of capital such as banks. Thus, while there is some evidence of ethnic succession occurring on Long Island—a few immigrant landscapers and cleaners have formed their own companies that are competing with older Italian and Cuban firms, for instance—it is occurring slowly. And the livelihoods of these small firms may owe more to the overall shifting demographics on Long Island than to mere ethnic succession.

In the context of the immigrants' construction of their own institutions, we begin to understand why my informants hold their coethnics in low esteem. People came to the United States with the expectation that they would encounter social relations among their migrant friends and family that mirrored those in their homelands; namely, relations of mutual assistance, or what anthropologists refer to as "balanced" or "generalized" reciprocity. They also arrived, however, with a mandate to generate an income over and above that needed to sustain themselves in the host country. Most hoped to save a nest egg and return home when the social, economic, and political climate improved there. They did not anticipate that this mandate would interfere with their social relations because they expected that opportunities in the United States would be bountiful enough to accommodate them all, for each to scoop dollars up off the streets. In my opinion, few come to recognize the connection between the need for surplus income and the deterioration of home county mores. They only perceive that in the United States relations which in their homelands were reciprocal have become commodified. A car ride must be paid for, "guests" are expected to pay rent (at least after a short while), and baby-sitting is performed for a fee. It is the clash of expectation against reality that fosters immigrants' sensation of being taken advantage of, particularly as greenhorns. Over time, they acquire "immigrant capital," including the knowledge of how to extract income from the immigrant sector. As immigrants learn that their likelihood of meeting their financial obligations and goals exclusively within the extraimmigrant sector is very low or would take too much time and effort, they increasingly turn to intraimmigrant niches to exploit. For example, the kind of investment required to start up a small enterprise in the larger economy, such as when Marco and Patricia leased a van for their ill-fated cleaning company, commits them to a longer and less assured trajectory in the United States than the investment an encargado makes in renting an apartment. Marco and Patricia learned this the hard way, sacrificing thousands of dollars in the process. Recently, Marco followed the other pathway, opening an office in Queens where he prepares immigration cases. Although he has training in this area from a previous job, he has no license and does not work under the supervision of an attorney. This way, however, all the profits are his.

There is an added dimension to my explanation of these immigrants' blaming each other for their disenchantment. This is the personal dimension; macrostructural forces are so faceless, while immigrant faces (and actions) are all too familiar. It is family and friends who pull the welcome mat out from under the feet of greenhorns shortly after arrival, not a bureaucratic paper shuffler. And the person who sponsored an immigrant's trip turns into the first person to take advantage of her in the new country. These experiences leave deep imprints on my informants' minds because they occur at transitional, vulnerable times and because they break with culturally embedded expectations for behavior. It takes only a few of these shocks for people to conclude that "folks change here."

The linchpin of my theory is the immigrants' responsibility to produce surplus income. This is the prime mover toward their perceived suspension, not maintenance, of solidarity—reciprocity, nepotism, communitarianism, and the like. This approach is substantiated by literature on reciprocity among poor populations that documents how difficult it is to appropriate a surplus for oneself without cutting off reciprocal relations to others. In the classic studies of Carol Stack (1974) and Larissa Lomnitz (1977), these researchers record how poor people circulate the limited available resources among networks of kin, friends, and fictive kin such that they are redistributed evenly. This system of mutual assistance is enforced largely through social ostracism of anyone who seeks to hoard or extract resources instead of recirculating them. Such interchange fosters as much economic security as can be expected among the poor but at the cost of stifling socioeconomic mobility for a few. People who aspire to better their status must extricate themselves from the network's tentacles, forsaking its social security. They are punished for extracting income, and hence security, from the others. Similarly, drug pushers in many contemporary urban communities—though idealized by those who yearn for the material rewards pushers alone enjoy in these areas—are condemned for extracting resources from their communities and contributing to their blight.

My informants find themselves in the unenviable position of having to restrict the reciprocity they engage in with coimmigrants in order to fulfill transnational obligations. Often this results in an ironic situation. Migrants may have to restrict assistance to their housemates and relatives in the United States in order to send money home. These transnational relatives, in turn, are often called upon to redistribute their remittance wealth among local networks—networks that are very likely to include the kin of the spurned immigrants. The evidence I have of these pressures is very preliminary and is being pursued in follow-up research, but conversations I conducted with several informants indicate that this phenomenon is pervasive. Altagracia's experience was the most direct. She emigrated from El Salvador in the late 1980s and had received remittances from her sister in the United States for several years prior to that. During a conversation, she described to me how knowledge travels the airwaves in El Salvador very quickly and how the recipients of remittances find innumerable *vecinos* (neighbors) who are willing to siphon off some of the riches.

"There are people who say, 'Did you know that so and so has a son in the United States and she just got a package? Let's go and visit her.' It's to bother her: 'Señora, could you possibly lend me five colones?' It's not jealousy, it's that they found out money has arrived and they go after you for a loan."

"And is it necessary to lend money if you have it?" I queried.

"It depends, it depends on where your heart is, as we say. It depends on how well off economically the receiver is and how much money has been sent. But in my case, when my sister would send me money people would find out and say, 'You know, [Altagracia], couldn't you help me out with twenty-five colones, God will pay you.' And because it didn't cost me anything I found that it's hard to have money in your hands. In those days I was less mature and would say, 'Take it as a gift.' . . . But it didn't bother me because they were people who were really needy. . . . It wasn't that they were jealous of you; they would just ask you to lend them money. Since the money didn't cost me any work, I would simply give them the money. But, as I told you, it didn't bother me because they were very poor people."

"Who were the people who would arrive at your doorstep, well-known or not so well-known?"

"Medium-known," she responded. "Something like people whom I would see when I was going to school and they would call to me to say, 'Have a good day' or something like that. And after hearing so many 'Have a good day's, you get used to the person and you get to know what economic situation they're in. Ah, poor woman. . . . I remember one woman who had about eighty kids and she worked doing wash for other people. Her children would be happy to see me: 'Here comes [Altagracia]. Here comes [Altagracia]!' they'd say when they saw me. And it was through her children that I would see the woman and would say, 'Friend of God, fare well,' and she would say, 'Excuse me for bothering you. . . .' She'd say that because she could see that I had my wallet out. And I would tell her to come by later [and I would give her a little money] because I still hadn't cashed the check. 'Okay, very well.' There are many people like her, many friends of mine."

And then I asked her, "Of a hundred dollars how much would you give away?"

"You know I had to pay for our food and everything. I was living with an uncle and I used to take care of his living costs. Out of every hundred dollars, depending on how I was at the moment, I would give away maybe five, six, or seven dollars—depending on how much I had left. About fifty colones was what I would give away to people . . . about ten dollars, but sometimes it was less depending on how many people came by. I had an agreement with my close relatives, my cousins, to give them a colón or two and that would make them happy. This is my personality but it never weighed on me."

Altagracia's testimony helps illuminate the importance of transnational links. Ironically, while the generation of remittances may undermine immigrants' construction of community, their distribution in the home country can help stabilize that local community. Even if only five to seven of each hundred dollars that immigrants send is disseminated this way, as with Altagracia, the fallout to recipients' networks cannot be viewed as insignificant when total remittances to El Salvador are estimated at $500 million to $1 billion.[1] It should be noted as well that Altagracia had few immediate family members to whom to redistribute the remittances, far fewer than many of my informants.

In contradistinction to the portion of remittances that is recycled locally and appears to contribute to steadying people's economic situation, a phenomenon which would lessen certain pressures to outmigrate, most remittance monies are consumed by recipients, foster socioeconomic inequality and jealousy, and indirectly contribute to migration flows. Information from a variety of countries indicates clearly that the greater part of remittances is spent on day-to-day necessities, but some is also spent on enhancing the social status of the recipients. These expenditures include physical improvements of properties such as land and homes, importation of expensive goods, hiring of labor to perform agricultural work, and participation in patronage networks (Montes Mozo and Garcia Vasquez 1988; Georges 1990; Rhoades 1978; Pessar 1982b; Dinerman 1982; Trager 1988). The latter investments serve as stimuli to chain migration, fostering the "Keep up with the Joneses" discussed earlier. That is, when people who do not receive remittances evaluate the status of families that do receive and have made improvements to their home, diets, and so forth, this stimulates these individuals to emigrate in order for their families to enjoy the same benefits. In sum, transnational linkages affect both home country and host country social relations, the latter perhaps suffering in order that the former may be enhanced.

Although I may appear to be arguing that my informants sacrifice ethnic solidarity as the cost of producing a surplus, I must emphasize again that this is a question of perception and degree, not an absolute. Several times I have stated my observations that immigrants *do* assist one another on a regular basis. They loan each other money; they share food, chores, information, and the like; and they can often be relied upon during emergencies. Theirs is not a situation of pure individualism, reminiscent of Colin Turnbull's *The Forest People* (1972), but rather a perception that social relations in the United States represent a deterioration of those which characterized the immigrants' homelands. What I have been trying to do is explain why they feel this way.

ANOMIE, SOLIDARITY, OR WHAT?

This leads me to a theorectical quandary, the degree to which my informants' case study is applicable to a broader understanding of immigrant populations and their experiences. Disillusionment with life in the United States is a fairly common theme in the literature on immigrants; however, disillusionment with one's fellow immigrants is much more rarely reported. If immigrants in general are pressured with producing at least some type of surplus income, then why do they not express the same enmity that I heard from my informants? My answer to this question is complex. First I will argue that immigrant populations and the contexts they migrate under and live in are so different that it is not reasonable to expect them to react identically—either in culturally continuous or discontinuous ways. Some migrants arrive as sojourners expecting to return home, others are determined to settle; some enter inner-city neighborhoods, others filter into the suburbs and rural areas; most come indebted, but some owe years of labor to their smugglers (e.g., the $30,000 typical indebtedness of undocumented Fuzhounese Chinese immigrants in New York City); and migrants arrive with different levels of transnational obligations. On top of this must be added the variation in human and monetary capital that migrants exhibit and the types of societies they have left. With this degree of diversity, it seems unlikely to me that there will be one pathway adopted by all groups.

Consequently, I will offer several historical particularist reasons for why the immigrants I studied seem to stand closer to the anomie side of the solidarity-anomie continuum. I will suggest first several reasons specific to the Salvadorans and then to the South Americans, followed by arguments more general to these groups. Finally, I will examine the likelihood that immigrant solidarity is at least partially the product of romanticism and outsider analysis.

Among Salvadorans, there is a notable consistency between their perspective on the causes of their suffering during the civil war and that experienced on Long Island. In both cases, they overwhelmingly blame localized, personalized factors over higher-level sociostructural factors. There are two ways to interpret this: either as their inability to understand these higher-level forces (perhaps owing to social isolation), or as the imposition of lessons learned during the civil war onto life in the new setting. Unfortunately, because there is no detailed ethnography of prewar Salvadoran campesino social structure and life, it is very difficult to assess the impact of the war on social relations, particularly on trust and reciprocity. The oral histories I presented at the beginning of this book suggest, however, that the war turned neighbors and even family members against one another. This signifies that social solidarity among Salvadorans had been undermined *prior* to migration. I also observed the further impact of the war on my informants' relations on Long Island in joking behaviors and their reticence to address their participation in the conflict openly, except to identify themselves as innocent victims. On the other hand, some ex-military men have internalized their training and try to maintain authority over their fellow countrymen, particularly in the workplace. In short, though they were removed from the war, its imprint was still vividly apparent.

If the civil war continued to divide Salvadorans in the United States, and they maintained a level of uneasiness and suspicion from it, then this effect was exacerbated by their rapid incorporation into the core from the periphery. As previously discussed, most Salvadorans on Long Island had been semiproletarianized peasants who supplemented their subsistence activities with seasonal migratory labor within El Salvador. In less than a month, and in some cases in a matter of days, they migrated from the extreme margins of the world system into its center. They became fully proletarianized in a highly restructured, postindustrial economy where their skills in agriculture were obsolete. This type of radical rural-to-urban migration is rare nowadays; most contemporary migrants' parents or grandparents made the transition to modernity, not they themselves. Or if they were born in rural areas, they first step-migrated to urban zones in their respective countries and then migrated abroad. The dislocation experienced by my informants is difficult to assess independent of other factors. But they make it very clear that in their minds "people change here" in ways that are fundamentally antisocial. Perhaps if they had been more fully integrated into a market economy wherein social relations are highly monetized prior to migration, they might have depicted social relations among coethnics on Long Island in less hostile terms. This same argument cannot be presented to explain South Americans' disenchantment with their compatriots, however, since they were not peasants in their homelands.

Lastly, the impact of these dislocations upon the Salvadorans might have been mitigated by a gracious welcome from their selected country of refuge. But the U.S. government refused to acknowledge them as refugees and therefore deprived them of the benefits of social welfare programs official refugees enjoy. The repercussions of this denial cannot truly be calculated in human terms, but it is a price that the Salvadorans will be paying into at least the next generation, children who are now growing up in poverty and isolation. Their condition virtually guarantees that they will be angry, but this time their anger may join in the chorus of the "culture of resistance" sung by many other minority youth.

South American enmity toward their countrymen and women stems, at least in part, from sources different from those characterizing the Salvadorans. The South Americans experience downward mobility—generally from the middle class to the working poor—in the United States, and this fall from grace angers them. They are aware of their drop in social status and occasionally blame the larger society for their fate. But because they are principally driven by their target-earning goals, they tend to accept their position because it is temporary (at least theoretically) and because it is a means to an end—the financing of middle-class status for their families and for themselves when they return home. The South Americans' dreams for short-term success are thwarted by their

miscalculation of their earnings' power and by the structural conditions
I have discussed throughout this book. They react primarily by investing
themselves into the immigrant informal economy where they can exploit
their class advantage over other groups, the Salvadorans in particular.
This strategy pits them against compatriots and coethnics; success in this
arena is evaluated antagonistically as the outcome of a few individuals
who exploit the majority.

This brief discussion of factors leading to anomie specific to the main
groups I studied leads me directly to my overarching argument. I have
contended that the limited opportunity structure provides few avenues
to socioeconomic mobility. This is not so different from the environments many other new immigrants encounter. But I have found that the
greatest source of economic mobility among my informants is the exploitation of each other's needs, and that this has serious negative consequences for their construction of ethnic solidarity and community. By
extension, the more advantaged an immigrant group is, the more likely
its members are to access mainstream jobs, resulting in less conflict
among compatriots. This is one reason why I appeal to researchers to be
sensitive to intraethnic class cleavages and the processes at play that promote further fissioning.

Another crucial factor affecting these immigrants on Long Island is
the fact that, by and large, they do not migrate as families. Most of the
children of my informants were left, at least initially, in the home country when their parent(s) migrated. This kind of sojourner pattern is typical of labor migrations characterized by men who migrate first and then
send for their families if their stays are prolonged. Even though most
Salvadorans migrated as a direct consequence of the war and therefore
do not constitute a classic labor migration, they exhibit the same male-
first pattern. This is a repercussion of forced recruitment by the military
and the guerrillas in their country. Such birds of passage tend to be less
vested in the host country than migrations with a high percentage of
families. In my follow-up research I have noted an increased stability
among my informants who have either reunited their families in the
United States or have started new ones. As compared to their unattached counterparts, these people are much more likely to live in the
same location.

This leads me to a corollary hypothesis that my informants' discon-
tent may also reflect the common immaturity and return orientation of
their migrations. Nearly all of the Central and South Americans on Long
Island have arrived there from abroad within the past fifteen years. This
means that they have enjoyed little time to establish their own institutions, and that the second generation, those born in the United States,
is small. As their stays lengthen and their children grow up, the first generation is likely to see itself more vested in staying and therefore more

likely to invest even scarce resources in community development. In the short run, however, the desire to return—shared by nearly every immigrant except the youngest—places added stress on new immigrants to maximize the surplus they generate. Target-earners like Alfredo exemplify this competitive strain. They are more interested in extracting income quickly than in investing in schemes that will take years to turn a profit. The immigrant sector provides the easiest access to such profits, outside of illicit activities, but also bears the reputation of being most exploitative. My informants had passed through the greenhorn stage when I interviewed them; they had acquired sufficient "immigrant capital" to comprehend and critique this opportunity structure. Migrants who do not desire to return to their homelands, or who have abandoned this goal as they have had children and settled in the United States, tend to seek opportunities more in the mainstream than before (e.g., Piore 1979; Gibson 1988). As they move into the mainstream, they are more likely to shift their criticisms in that direction.

Finally, the notion of ethnic solidarity must be criticized. As I mentioned in the Introduction, it is a term used widely but rarely operationalized. What is meant by ethnic solidarity, even if we accept that it is the product of immigrants' exclusion from the mainstream? Does it exist behaviorally or does it exist largely within the minds of immigrants or researchers? Do immigrants *believe* they are a community? Scholarly models and public opinions can easily omit the perspective of the people they are describing; an exhaustive study by Zenner (1991) suggests that when researchers "find" solidarity, it may not exist in the eye of the insider:

> Outsiders rarely enter into the internal bickering of an apparently closed minority group. Outsiders do not distinguish between the small-group solidarity, which maintains family firms, from the large, but often weak, communal structures. Even if some of the internal factionalism is known, it is ignored. (102)

This is a deficit I have addressed in this book. My informants certainly do not see themselves as united. I have used their firsthand testimonies extensively to illustrate their point. In most texts on immigrants, however, readers are privy only to the author's analysis; testimonies are much rarer. This leads me to suspect that portrayals of solidarity may reflect a romanticization of the immigrant experience. Much of the literature on turn-of-the-century immigrants (e.g., Ewen 1985; Handlin 1951; Sánchez-Korrol 1983), especially autobiographies such as Gold's (1930), Mangione's (1972), and Jastrow's (1986), depict everyday immigrant life as full of mutual assistance among coethnics and much less frequently offer examples of exploitation. Public life, particularly Tammany Hall politics, provides a backdrop of coercion and exploitation, but family and neighborhood life are characterized mostly by ethnic solidarity. The cooperative theme is central to contemporary accounts of immigrants as well (e.g., Gibson 1988; Chen 1992; Chavez 1992; Zhou 1992; Corcoran 1993; Gold 1994; Stepick and Grenier 1993; Kim 1981; Bonacich 1973), suggesting that this characterization may have become conventionalized.

A few scholars have raised concerns about the applicability of the ethnic solidarity model and point to the existence of coethnic exploitation (e.g., Sanders and Nee 1987; Aldrich and Waldinger 1990; Li 1977; Kwong 1988, 1994; Siems 1994). Sanders and Nee argue, for example, that solidarity theorists fail to distinguish between immigrant entrepreneurs and paid employees when analyzing the benefits of participating in an enclave economy (1987:762). Their analysis clearly shows that entrepreneurs profit, drawing on "ethnic solidarity to enforce and maintain sweatshop conditions, including low wages and closure to union organizing," while workers in the enclave fare worse than their compatriots outside the enclave (ibid.: 763). Li's study of a Chicago Chinese enclave (1977) documents how paternalistic ethnic "assistance" can hinder immigrants' success by entangling them in a web of obligations that stifles their own pursuits. Finally, I have also noticed that in case studies where coethnic exploitation is mentioned, it is not developed but glossed over such that it appears to be far more the exception than the rule (e.g., Corcoran 1993:62; Siems 1994:97).

In his foreword to Zhou 1992, Alejandro Portes argues that portrayals of ethnic communities wherein "poor newcomers, ignorant of the language and their labor rights, are mercilessly exploited by fellow nationals" represent, "in modern academic garb," a continuation of the anti-immigrant literature characteristic of the turn of the century (Zhou 1992:xiii). I agree with Portes that prejudices affected many such writings, but I am concerned that biases—albeit in the opposite direction—may also discolor contemporary portraits of immigrants. Certainly there has been an enormous shift in the tenor of research on migrants. In the first half of the twentieth century, scholars studied assimilation and the breakdown of the traditional; in recent decades this has been reversed. Cultural continuity and resistance to the forces of assimilation are now much more in vogue. Researchers need to be wary of overcorrection.

THE CULTURAL CONSTRUCTION OF THE IMMIGRANT

The centrality of immigrant ethnic solidarity is part of a much broader cultural construction of immigrants. "America" is a quintessentially immigrant nation, and therefore it should not be surprising that the image of the immigrant is inextricably linked to Americans' image of themselves. There are, of course, many Americans who do not trace their roots to immigrants and may be less vested in the immigrant legacy, but there is no denying that the classic American image is one of tremendous ethnic diversity.

Immigrants hold an equivocal status in our society, however. They are identified both with natives (as their ancestors) and against them (as foreigners). They are both a boon to the nation's self-image—the millions who seek their American dreams in the "land of milk and honey"— and a threat to it. The influx of so many foreigners sends fear into the hearts of natives who wonder how their promised land can accommodate so many people, and so many divergent customs, without forsaking America's unique character and promise to all. This anxiety has surged and ebbed throughout the history of the United States; tolerance has battled intolerance even though the nation declares *E Pluribus Unum* as a fundamental creed. The current multicultural movement and its backlash serve as examples of this trend. Proponents of multiculturalism celebrate diversity, while critics warn of "the disuniting of America" and call for strengthening commonalities (see Schlesinger 1992).

Given this history of malleability, the public image of the immigrant plays a crucial role in determining social opinion. If the image associated with immigrants is full of positive qualifiers such as "hard-working," "community-minded," and "mutually supportive," it serves to identify them most strongly with the ideal American temperament. When unflattering qualities—"stupid," "lazy," "dirty," "backward," "childlike"— are attributed to immigrants, a wedge is driven between them and natives. As several authors have masterfully argued, image construction is directly linked to dominant-subordinant relations (e.g., Takaki 1979; Pike 1992). Groups that oppress others, particularly to benefit from their labor, invariably justify this through images. Thus, Asian immigrants were labeled the "yellow tide," and Latinos became "spitfires" and "wetbacks." Over time, negative stereotypes may evolve into more positive ones, a transformation that I argue is the principal outcome of immigrants' ascension into the mainstream. Currently, the most widely denigrated immigrant population is Mexicans, a group highly associated with poverty, manual labor, low education, and dirt. They are the "other," the mojados who have the furthest to travel on the road to middle-classdom. Similarly, Haitians have been stigmatized as collective carriers of AIDS and quarantined from seeking asylum in the United States despite their country's legacy of brutality. On the other hand, "successful" contemporary immigrant populations such as Cubans and Koreans enjoy a much rosier public image, one much more closely aligned with the ideal American character. They are popularly heralded as "model minorities." I do not find it surprising that their success is largely ascribed to ethnic solidarity.

I suspect that within the ethnic businesses that form the backbone of these latter groups' economic opportunities, there is a great deal of exploitation, both intra- and interethnic. There may be cultural rules against airing this perspective that only a few have dared to disobey (e.g., Kwong 1994, 1988), and it may be true that for some people ethnic enterprise provides a "more personalized and human environment than the highly alienating working conditions confronted in comparable outside employment" (Portes and Zhou 1992); but it may also be true that there is pressure to construct and preserve a public image palatable to everyday Americans. This reinforces the common notion, albeit not a theory, that people's success in the United States derives from their exercising the "right" values over and above any other contributing factors such as monetary and human capital. Many immigrants come to the United States seeking to overcome obstacles that precluded success in their own countries—class, surname, title, affiliation, and so forth. Feeling that the playing field is more level in their adoptive country, they become evermore committed to effort as the key to success.

The sense that they are the authors of their fate predominates among my informants even though they have enjoyed comparatively little socioeconomic success. This has major implications for predicting their role in the coming century. I believe that they will be a largely conservative force because they hold minimal expectations of society. Since they are isolated from the mainstream society and its institutions, they are inwardly focused, most intimately knowledgeable and critical of the immigrant's parallel world. "Hispanics are doing business with housing," they complain. "Too many have come and now there are no jobs left," they add, placing the blame for difficulties they meet on coethnic shoulders, particularly on those of people who have gotten ahead. Although exploitative American bosses are objects of disdain, the most despised people are not Americans but compatriots—nobodies in their home countries who have achieved success in the United States. They are believed to have risen by climbing on top of everyone else. "People who come here change," Sonia told me. "Before they come here they're naive, fools as we say, but they change once they come to this country. When they come here they become big shots, as if they were children of the wealthy when they're really the children of poor folk." Though immigrants long for the freedom from obstacles to success pervasive in their own societies—class, familial, and political obstacles, for example—they invoke home country attitudes when condemning those who, in the United States, have broken free.

The fact that my informants burden themselves individually and as a group with their destinies in the United States absolves the greater society from taking much, if any, responsibility. They are perhaps the firmest believers in the ideal that hard work, perseverance, and sacrifice—albeit not solidarity—will yield success. This is the image they have of themselves: workhorses who contribute to America's bounty. As Manuel laments, "Here life is very fast. You go from the house to the job, and after the job you eat and sleep. We are, how can I put it? *Herramienta de trabajo* [workhorses], nothing more. Eat, work, and sleep, that's it." Immigrants also enjoy little of the bounty they create because a few coethnic scoundrels strip them of their hard-earned income.

Immigrants acquire voices of the status quo because, although they occupy the bottom of the social ladder, they aspire to higher positions. And as proponents of self-reliance (even at the cost of communitarianism), immigrants subtly back a laissez-faire politics: look not to the state to help you but take care of yourself. They believe firmly that hard work is the single most important factor in the success equation, not unlike former president George Bush who argues that "'opportunity, hard work, faith, vigor and dedication will allow every American to achieve their God-given potential'" (*Sacramento Observer* October 21, 1992). Indeed, immigrants have been shown to be more politically conservative than natives (de la Garza et al. 1992; Cain, Kiewiet, and Uhlaner 1991).

What I found during my research was that not only do immigrants believe in the individual effort formula for success, but they also project this perspective onto others. Residential and occupational segregation (into unskilled jobs) brings my informants into daily contact with various native minority group members. Since they see greater opportunities in the United States than in their homelands and assume that hard work will earn them socioeconomic mobility, they reason that people who continue to occupy low status in the United States do so because they have failed to work hard and make sacrifices. This understanding is applied to low-income native minorities—African Americans and Puerto Ricans in particular. Immigrants accuse these groups of orchestrating their fate by being lazy and selfish. Not surprisingly, they do not suspect that extrapersonal factors might explain their predicament. Unsavory depictions of these populations were often the topic of conversation during informal bantering; similar denigrations were observed among Salvadorans in Los Angeles (Chinchilla, Hamilton, and Loucky 1993). According to my informants, the animosity stems in large part from their having been victims of robberies. For example, Gilberto told me, "Two times I was beaten up by blacks. In front of the house where the cars are they beat me up. They robbed me, took my money. If you don't give them money they'll kill you. They leave you for dead because I was left like that. . . . They attack you because they think that you have money on you. They know you work, so on weekends they know that you have money on you. They don't work so they know who is working.

They are *de valde* [unemployed] and don't work so they control you. Since they all look alike you can't tell who it is [who attacks you] . . . so I didn't take them to court. The second time they robbed me of six hundred dollars . . . I was coming back from work. That night they got me, they hit me. They left me *botado* [lying on the street]. . . . What they do is to hit you first. If they asked you for money first it would be different. But what are you going to do because they are so big and they also go around in groups of five, six, seven, eight and you're alone. I don't go out much now. Sometimes I go out but if I see them I walk over to the other side of the street. Now I have room for running!"

It is difficult to assess whether people bring negative stereotypes of blacks and other minorities with them when they migrate or acquire them through postmigratory experiences. But the hostility is thick, particularly because the groups tend to live and work in close proximity. First-generation immigrants portray themselves in terms that are directly opposed to the characterizations they offer of their minority neighbors. The immigrants believe that they will improve their lives over time, but view minorities as a stagnant, parasitic population:

EUGENIA: The blacks should be fined, they shouldn't hang out but should find places to entertain themselves and not abuse Hispanics—beating them up. The police don't pay attention when the Hispanics are beaten up. . . . And the problem with the blacks is that the government helps them, giving them almost everything, and it's because of this that they are always in the streets. It would be good if the mayor [of my town] would approve a law that would fine drunks found in the streets. Because these are the ones who cause the most problems and get into fights.

ALFREDO: The Latin American is a person who comes here to dedicate himself to working and he dedicates 100 percent of his time to his job. So, of course, he has to make money. On the other hand, the blacks only spend their time relaxing, they waste their time. So at this time they are probably buying beer, liquor, and many are drunk. Men and women are selling cheap jewelry, deceiving people that it is real gold or silver. Others sell drugs. This is what the blacks do. I think that there is a rejection, a rejection. I thought that they rejected us because we took their jobs from them, but it doesn't seem to be this. It's not this. Because the black seems to be a bit *ocioso* [lazy]. You have to push him so that he works; if you don't push him he doesn't work. It's like they have some latent inheritance from slavery.

DON JOSÉ: I don't know where this negative impression blacks have of Hispanics comes from. Some say it's because the Hispanics come here doing any job and they take jobs away from blacks. Some others say no, it's because the blacks don't want to work. The government supports them, giving them food and everything else since they were children. And so the blacks spend their time doing drugs and trafficking drugs and other things. They don't like to work. The Hispanic says that he has come here to work and works hard. He is attacked because they know that he always has money on him. They know that every time they attack a Hispanic they are going to get money out of him because he has money. There is a whole host of versions, and I don't know which one is right because I have never talked to blacks and I don't know what they think. On the other hand, I know the perspective of Hispanics very well. So I don't really know why the blacks don't like the Hispanics; whether it's because of money, because they are jealous that their jobs are taken, or some other reason.

BERTA: I would say to you that Puerto Ricans, based on their having free entry here, believe themselves to be superior to us, with more rights, with more rights to look down on us, to look at us differently. They act as if they were born here. They can come in and leave this country [but we can't]. So, when they know that we are from other countries and don't have the rights that they have, they look at us with indifference. Like the blacks too. The blacks who were born here, they feel that they are above us. They are protected by this government.

MANUEL: I think that there is racism. Sometimes I see [reason to say so] and it's not because of demagoguery. Sometimes the North Americans marginalize the black race. But the blacks are very lazy, they don't like to work. They like the easy life. Why? Because I see that when we work we have to pay many taxes. And these taxes go to the people who don't work. But they are very physically fit; the blacks are very strong. When they see a demanding job they leave it. Why? Because they know that they can collect [unemployment]. They work a while and they live a life; they are interested in living in the present and nothing more. . . . The Hispanics work like *burros*. They are the ones who work and work hard.

These immigrants view native minorities as architects of their own demise because even as citizens, with all their rights and advantages, they have not pulled themselves up by their bootstraps. In formulating this opinion, immigrants take a step that brings them perhaps the closest they will ever get to the mainstream. Writer Toni Morrison, among other black intellectuals, has observed similarly that immigrants' assimilation is only completed when they have mastered the "lesson of racial estrangement." "It doesn't matter anymore what shade the newcomer's skin is. A hostile posture toward resident blacks must be struck at the Americanizing door before it will open." "In race talk the move into mainstream America always means buying into the notion of American blacks as the real aliens. Whatever the ethnicity or nationality of the immigrant, his nemesis is understood to be African American" (Morrison 1993:57). Her words, coupled with my informants' opinions, do not foretell a future of harmonious interethnic relations in the United States.

Finally, immigrants contribute an important role in the cultural repro-duction of the American dream, an ideal held close to the hearts of na-tives and immigrants alike. My informants contribute to its reproduc-tion though they have achieved barely a foothold in it. This is because, while relegated to the bottom of the status hierarchy, these people are not locked in an undifferentiated underclass. There is mobility among them, albeit modest, and heterogeneity. They can point to some accom-plishments. These rarely reach the level of their aspirations, but their efforts are not meaningless. This sense of accomplishment is reflected in Berta's words when I asked her if migrating to the United States was worth the suffering she had expressed to me. "What we are doing is not in vain," she responded. "It's not been lost in nothingness. We have come, we have seen nice things and unpleasant things. We have helped our family and not just our children, but our mothers and sisters and people who were in need. This is something that we would not have been able to do if we had been in my country, to help these people out economically." Thus, even among what might be an "unsuccessful" im-migrant group, one in which most families fall into the category of the working poor, there is some socioeconomic mobility. I argue that this helps keep the American dream alive, however unintentionally.

Contemplate for a moment the popular images of immigrants that have permeated our elementary educations and you will find metaphors for the American dream: Horatio Alger stories of immigrants scrambling from rags to riches; sweaty ragamuffins sneaking over the U.S. border from shantytowns in Tijuana; passenger boats teeming with women hugging babies sailing into harbors in New York or Miami; men waiting in lines at Ellis Island, their heavy, dark garments chalked with health evaluations by overworked inspectors; black-and-white photographs of grim children toiling at machines many times their size; refugees cramped in makeshift tents along the Thai border—and the list goes on. What story does each image tell? It is the parable of the American dream.

The contribution of immigrant populations to the perpetuation of the American dream, and therefore of the notion of America as a land of opportunity, should not be underestimated although it has been under-researched. This is particularly critical as the American dream for many native-born has become imperiled. Over the past twenty years or so, working-class and middle-class families have experienced declining for-tunes. Their loss of buying power results from a combination of many factors, chief among which are deindustrialization and global economic restructuring (Bluestone and Harrison 1982; Sassen 1988). Some 50 percent of new jobs created in the U.S. economy pay very low wages and offer little if any possibility for advancement. Thus, the United States is producing a lackluster future for its citizens, one in which the coming generations are unlikely to attain to the lifestyles enjoyed by current Americans (Newman 1993). In the midst of declining opportunity and the rise of the "underclass," a few immigrants arrive penniless and become millionaires. "Rags to riches," they remind us; the American dream is alive! The dream thrives among immigrants because of their transnational perspective. Even those who achieve modest success know that in their home country, such accomplishments would be nearly impossible. In the words of one Polish immigrant to Long Island, "'I can be whoever I want to be here . . . I just have to work for it. In Poland there are limits'" (Singer 1990:59).

Thus, immigrants—legal or not—breathe new life into an American dream that has proven elusive to many native-born. The transformation of successful immigrant groups into "model minorities" goads Americans in general, and less successful minority groups in particular, into believing, much as immigrants do, that success is more the product of individuals' hard work and sacrifice than of differences in their levels of education and economic resources. Imported rugged individualists and American dreamers, immigrants buttress the foundational ideology, the primal myths of Americana. In sum, though they are often accused of alien beliefs and practices, they fundamentally contribute to the nation's cultural reproduction.

NOTES

CHAPTER ONE
INTRODUCTION

1. An undocumented immigrant (frequently labeled "illegal alien," a term I prefer not to use) is one who lacks the legal authorization to be in the United States and to work there. U.S. citizens and legal permanent residents (LPRs), the so-called green card holders, may legally reside and work, as can certain other categories of nonresident immigrants who have been granted permission by the Immigration and Naturalization Service (INS). Tourists are permitted to stay in the country for given periods of time but are barred from working. People become undocumented principally by crossing the border without authorization or overstaying their tourist visas.

2. I place quotation marks around this word because, as some informants reminded me, they too are from America. However, in their colloquial usage, "America" was used to designate the United States of America.

3. In order to protect my informants' confidentiality, I use pseudonyms throughout the text. Hereafter, each informant will initially be identified by a first and last name, and subsequently with a first name only. No first name is used for more than one individual; for those married individuals who in real life share the same surname I will continue this convention in the text.

4. There are several Catholic parishes on Long Island that offer mass in Spanish. I attended one parish in Gold Coast regularly and visited others occasionally. Although there have been attempts to involve the Salvadorans in a leadership capacity in these parishes and in the masses themselves, my observations suggest that it is the Puerto Rican and South American parishioners who predominate. In contrast, Salvadorans figure much more prominently in the organization and leadership of evangelical groups, most particularly in the church *Apóstoles y Profetas*. This Protestant denomination has several locales on Long Island and is increasingly popular in the sending communities of El Salvador.

CHAPTER TWO
LEAVING HOME

1. The 1990 census recorded 565,000 Salvadorans but this figure is deemed too low. Funkhouser (1991) compares two surveys of emigrants and arrives at a figure of 658,000, some 12 percent of the Salvadoran population. Other clues to the exact number exist. For instance, during the 1980s legal migration to the United States nearly tripled, from 4,479 residency visas in 1979 to 12,045 in 1988. But these numbers reflect only a trickle of the largely undocumented actual flow. Apprehensions also skyrocketed from 4,365 in 1977 to 16,953 in 1990 (Stanley 1987:135; INS personal communication). Another 168,000 were legalized under IRCA (the Immigration Reform and Control Act of 1986); 134,000 of these had entered the United States illegally. Finally, 187,000 Salva-

dorans received Temporary Protected Status (TPS) in 1991 (terminated in December 1994) and are therefore legally residing in the United States. (This is discussed further in chapter 7.)

2. In 1971, when the last agricultural census was taken, 21.8 percent of the agriculturally active population in El Salvador was completely landless and another 29 percent was living on less than one hectare of land (Durham 1979:47). By 1975, the proportion of landless agriculturalists had risen to 40.9 percent (cited in Hamilton and Chinchilla 1991:90). Land concentration became so severe that by 1971 *minifundias*, tiny farms of less than one hectare, accounted for only 10 percent of total land under cultivation, though they constituted 70 percent of all farms, while large landholders, who numbered only 1.5 percent of all farmers, controlled some 50 percent of the land (Pearce 1986:28).

3. The economic disadvantage of living in the cities is confirmed in Segundo Montes's survey (1979) of 310 households in San Salvador. His data show that few urbanites own the property their houses stand on, and most spend over 50 percent of their incomes on food alone, a poor diet that Montes concludes is the cause of much sickness.

4. The FDR-FMLN is the designation most commonly used for the Salvadoran Left during the civil war. FDR stands for Frente Democrático Revolucionario or Democratic Revolution Front, formed in April 1980 as a moderate to left-wing political and diplomatic organization. The FMLN or Farabundo Martí National Liberation Front is the collective label for some five guerrilla factions that coalesced in November 1980. (See Armstrong and Shenk [1982] for details.)

5. This is confirmed by other sources (Americas Watch 1987:153). Americas Watch also reports that the Armed Forces used children as young as thirteen as informers to point out suspected subversives. This violates Protocol II, Article 3, of the Geneva Convention (ibid.:19).

CHAPTER THREE
THE TRIP AS PERSONAL TRANSFORMATION

1. Szajkowski documents how consuls at the U.S. embassy in Warsaw routinely discriminated against Jews seeking admittance to the United States. One wrote that they should be excluded because they respect only Jewish law and do not live in sanitary conditions. Another letter noted that many Jewish immigrants received money from relatives and friends already in the United States to finance their trips; this, in the writer's view, was proof that they were "incapable of self support, [and therefore] they will not become self supporting in a strange land" (1974:6). Recent reports at U.S. consulates show how visa granting is still very discretionary (*New York Times* August 8, 1990).

2. Dinerman (1982:73) suggests that Mexicans from the province of Michoacán, Mexico, pay between $250 and $300 to migrate to the United States. Crane et al. estimate the cost for Mexicans of reaching the U.S. border at a mere $30 (1990:13). Every Central and South American I interviewed, except one, paid far more.

3. The fact that this figure is similar to the Salvadorans' probably reflects two phenomena. First, the number of undocumented Colombians who responded to this question in my survey is 18, versus 149 for the Salvadorans. This may yield an unrepresentative average response. Second, Colombia is the South American country closest to Central America, and it has an island territory, San Andrés, off the Nicaraguan coast. The cost for Colombians to travel to the United States should therefore be lower than what other South Americans pay.

4. There are only 1,500 official Federal Judicial Police in Mexico—a force similar to the U.S. FBI, but each federal policeman is reported to have a private paramilitary group working with him (USCR 1991). This makes it difficult for migrants to distinguish who are federales. One informant told me that they can be distinguished by dress; most informants used the term *federales* generically for anyone who bribed, threatened, or beat them even though abuse is widespread among the narcóticos and inmigración as well.

5. Edgar's story is substantiated by a report in a Mexican newspaper that recounted how sixty Central Americans were riding in a truck carrying bananas when the platform protecting them broke and six were crushed to death. Two weeks later Mexican immigration officials found another such group—nearly asphyxiated inside a truck (USCR 1991:14).

6. This means more than physically entering the country. A person who enters across the border is considered to have entered the country and has full rights to deportation hearings. A person who presents a fake visa to an immigration officer is not considered to have entered if his passport has not been stamped. This person is placed in "exclusion," not deportation, proceedings and has far fewer rights and remedies. Many people in exclusion proceedings, such as some Marielito Cubans (those who entered in 1980 from the port of Mariel), have been held for years in detention centers—virtual prisons—while their cases have lingered with the INS.

CHAPTER FOUR
GREAT EXPECTATIONS, EARLY DISILLUSIONMENTS

1. Migrants who try to discourage others by telling them their stories can actually foster increased migration. This happened when a Korean wrote a story to a local newspaper back home trying to convince people to avoid migration. Contrary to his wishes, the story became a best-seller on how to emigrate (cited in Reimers 1992:97).

CHAPTER FIVE
THE CONSTRUCTION OF MARGINALITY

1. Carmean, Romo, and Schwartz are careful to note, however, that a microelectronics industry has developed on Long Island which is not dependent on the defense contractors. Furthermore, there are large employers such as industrial bakeries, car parts factories, and plastics manufacturers, among others, who produce for non-defense-related purposes.

2. In 1989 the median household disposable income on Long Island was $51,705, compared to $31,750 nationwide, suggesting that Long Islanders were more wealthy than most Americans. However, as Yago, Wu, and Seifert (1987:10) show in great detail, the Long Islanders' income is not even the highest in New York State yet their costs are rising faster than in comparable regions. Thus, an awareness that costs counteract the higher incomes yields a more accurate portrait of Long Island's affluence.

3. Zoë Baird, a corporate attorney, was nominated by President Clinton in early 1993 to become U.S. attorney general. She later removed her name from consideration when it emerged that she had knowingly hired undocumented domestic workers (in defiance of immigration law) and had failed to pay Social Security taxes on their earnings, also required by law.

4. This outcome was predicted by scholars and community organizations advocating minorities' rights. The General Accounting Office (GAO), which was charged by Congress to evaluate whether the legislation would result in a "widespread pattern of discrimination," ruled in its first two reports that no such pattern was detected. Prodded by immigration experts and others, the GAO revised its methodology for evaluation and conducted a survey among employers which showed that some 20 percent of them were unaware of IRCA, more were confused about sanctions, and 19 percent (some 900,000 employers) admitted to starting or increasing discriminatory actions against foreign-looking or -sounding people (US GAO 1990). Surveys conducted by other organizations in California and New York yielded similar results (CHIRLA 1990; NYS IATF 1988). The findings have not resulted in the repeal of IRCA, however.

5. At this time I was the coordinator of a hot line in New York City that was established to accept and document such cases. The dozens of cases I handled resulted in identifiable patterns, some of which are illustrated here.

6. Employees hired before November 6, 1986, the date of IRCA's signing, were "grandfathered" and did not need to produce documentation, although their employment continued to be illegal. Employers were protected under this clause against prosecution for violating sanctions if their employees were hired before IRCA. Unauthorized workers were not protected; even though they would not be required to provide papers to their employer, they would be susceptible to INS raids and deportation.

7. Ethnic firms operate as subcontractors to larger businesses and contribute to the informalization of the economy. That is, larger firms may need services but can save money and headaches by contracting for these services with ethnic firms. Zlolniski (1994) has observed this within the janitorial industry in San Jose, California. This leaves the ethnic firm with hiring, record-keeping, and other responsibilities that the larger firm would rather avoid—particularly with the liabilities of employer sanctions under IRCA. In turn, the smaller firm can exploit coethnics by paying lower wages and thus make competitive bids for the service contracts. They still turn a handsome profit and, despite the wage exploitation, benefit the community by offering employment. If the workers are caught by the INS, neither large nor small firms generally lose: the large firm is not the employer and therefore not liable, and the small firm can disappear overnight.

CHAPTER SIX
MAKING MONEY OFF THE MARGINS

1. The TLC is the New York City Taxi and Limousine Commission police whose job it is to regulate the taxi industry there. "Gypsy" or "livery" cabs is a general term used to describe non–Yellow Cabs; most gypsy cabs operate in the outer boroughs of the city (not Manhattan) and particularly in more dangerous neighborhoods. In the past years most have been regulated and must obtain licenses from the TLC. But these cabs' activities are restricted, and they generally may not pick up passengers off the streets.

2. The village of Hempstead has witnessed a dramatic influx of Salvadorans over the past ten years, although an early nucleus of Salvadorans seems to have formed in the 1970s in one census tract on the north side of town (Kling and Wang 1985). Hempstead hosts the largest concentration of Latino-owned businesses on Long Island, but by rough count this may not surpass 40. In Nassau County, minority businesses numbered 118 in 1982, employing only 836 persons (122 firms and 492 employees in Suffolk County), so Hempstead may be home to a sizable share of those minority firms run by Latinos without approaching the complexity of a real enclave (Regional Plan Association 1988). Furthermore, those businesses run by Latinos are also divided among ethnicities: restaurants are Salvadoran and South American, bodegas are run mostly by Dominicans, and service firms are owned by a mix of Caribbeans and Central and South Americans. If Hempstead approaches the status of an ethnic enclave, then it is one based on Latino identity rather than identity of national origin—the latter is more typical of enclaves described by Portes and Bach (1985) and others.

CHAPTER SEVEN
LUCRATIVE, LIMINAL LAW

1. Ninety-seven percent of all "affirmative" asylum applications filed with district directors of the INS (and now with a separate corps of asylum adjudicators). No statistics are kept regarding "defensive" applications filed within immigration court. The difference between affirmative and defensive applications is discussed later in this chapter.

2. Many, many people and organizations have criticized the legalization program both as stipulated by Congress and as implemented by the INS (e.g., DeWind 1987; Papademetriou 1989). The many drawbacks of the program lie outside the scope of this chapter.

3. Sometimes to no avail in any case: Puerto Rican birth certificates have also been rejected as proof of citizenship because they are in Spanish and because some U.S. citizens do not know that Puerto Ricans are born citizens.

4. In some ways, they were right. However, these opportunities stem from litigated cases involving special groups who might have qualified for legalization except for the very strict interpretations given by the INS in their regulations. One such example is *Perales v. Meese*, a New York class action filed on behalf of those people who did not apply for legalization because their U.S.-born children

were receiving public assistance. These people had to meet all other requirements of IRCA, such as having been present in the country as of January 1, 1982, and so on. However, most individuals who responded to the ads were people who did not meet these stipulations and were only looking for a new angle to obtain legal status—no matter how.

5. In 1989 the INS introduced a program called "family fairness" for immediate relatives (spouses and minor children) of those who were legalized. Initially, these family members had to have been in the United States as of the signing of IRCA to qualify for work authorization while they waited for sponsorship to come through. In late 1991 this date shifted to May 5, 1988, the last day of the legalization program, but many family members still had not heard of the program or did not qualify under it. Participation also entailed admitting deportability, which is a disincentive for many individuals.

6. I also acknowledge that my own ethnicity may have had an impact on what opinions were voiced in my presence. However, I often overheard disparaging comments about the other groups mentioned in casual conversations between immigrants, not just when I interviewed them formally. The only people who spoke consistently against "true" Americans were South American immigrants of middle-class origins, and not all of them did so. These people also spoke poorly of the groups mentioned above, adding in Salvadorans, whom they characterized as uncultured peasants.

7. The other hindrance to Latin Americans' access to refugee visas is the fact that these visas are not only doled out according to geographic quotas, but they are also distributed according to six priority categories. These categories are: (1) persons whose cases evoke compelling humanitarian concern or interest, (2) former U.S.-government employees, (3) immediate family members of refugees already admitted, (4) persons with other ties to the United States, (5) extended family members of refugees, and (6) persons who otherwise should be admitted for the national interest. Critics of the classification system argue that despite its numerical order, the first category actually represents the lowest priority. That is, family unification takes precedence over persecution as a basis for the decision to grant a refugee visa. Some have argued that this weighting makes the refugee flow look like a typical immigration flow. Once a refugee is admitted, he or she may in time be able to bring in family members, and then they, in turn, may bring in other family, and so on (Robinson 1989:5). The problem with this system, outside of the apparent disregard for issues of persecution and the strength of cases, is that available numbers of visas are so quickly granted to relatives of refugees that fewer visas are available to persons fleeing present persecution.

8. News programs including *Sixty Minutes* argued in the weeks after the February 26, 1993, World Trade Center bombing that immigrants entered the United States having been trained to request political asylum. Similar coverage was given to the Chinese aboard the *Golden Venture*, which beached in New York City in June of 1993. It was asserted that these people had been coached by their smugglers to answer "political asylum" when asked why they had come to the United States.

9. For several excellent anthropological interpretations of the asylum setting,

see Kot (1988), Kälin (1986), Schirmer (1985), and my discussion of them in Mahler (1992).

10. Another court case, *Mendez v. Thornburgh*, a class action on behalf of Los Angeles asylum applicants, revealed very damaging information that further exposed the biases against Central American asylum applicants. When attorneys for the plaintiffs conducted depositions of Los Angeles asylum interviewers and adjudicators, they found that *none* of the officers could name the president of El Salvador or the political party in power there. Furthermore, officers testified that they were unaware of highly publicized and significant events in El Salvador such as the 1989 murders of Jesuit priests and the 1980 assassination of Archbishop Oscar Arnulfo Romero. This testimony illuminated the fact that refugee/asylum decisions had been made regardless of the merits of the cases presented and have been conditioned by political forces. As a result, the INS was ordered to provide new asylum interviews for thirty thousand applicants (American Civil Liberties Union, personal communication).

CHAPTER EIGHT
THE ENCARGADO INDUSTRY

1. For instance, in his study of Central Americans living in Houston, Néstor Rodríguez notes that the regional economic downturn suffered in the 1980s resulted in high vacancy rates within housing complexes originally designed for middle-class families. The glut forced landlords to lower rents and forgo security deposits, such that many undocumented immigrants moved in paying rents of only $250 to $400 (AFSC 1988:22). These apartments on Houston's west side were originally built for young urban professionals who were expected to arrive in Houston but failed to come owing to the economic downturn. As a result, immigrants were courted as tenants for these modern, luxury apartments boasting built-in dishwashers and central air-conditioning. Recently, the trend has reversed and immigrants are being pushed out of these buildings to make room for their originally intended occupants (Jacqueline Hagan, personal communication).

2. Abraham Levitt, Levittown's builder, justified his exclusive policy by suggesting that whites would not buy homes in a mixed neighborhood: "The Negroes in America are trying to do in 400 years what the Jews in the world have not wholly accomplished in 6,000. As a Jew, I have no room in my mind or heart for racial prejudice. But, by various means, I have come to know that if we sell one house to a Negro family, then 90 to 95 percent of our white customers will not buy into the community. That is their attitude, not ours. We did not create it, and we cannot cure it. As a company, our position is simply this: we can solve a housing problem or we can try to solve a racial problem. But we cannot combine the two" (*New York Times* June 28, 1992).

3. Rumors also circulated that the school system was checking students' addresses to find doubled-up families. If they found two children with different surnames at the same address, they would investigate, and they began requiring a statement from landlords for renting families to assure that the families were legal renters.

4. Widows or families with grown children were likely to rent an empty bedroom out to a boarder during the nineteenth century (e.g., Thomas and Znaniecki 1984 [1918]: 242; Modell and Hareven 1973; Kessner 1977:99–102). "Few ethnics have bought homes that have not at least two apartments, one of which was to bring a rental return" (Warner and Srole 1945:80–81). But "by the 1880's, family boarding lost both its official use for social control, as well as its middle-class respectability. It became identified exclusively (if erroneously) as a lower-class practice, and was attacked in the context of tenement squalor and the poverty of immigrant life" (Modell and Hareven 1973:478). However, boarding became an essential strategy among Puerto Ricans (Sánchez-Korrol 1983) and African Americans (Massey and Denton 1993) in the twentieth century.

CHAPTER NINE
IMMIGRANTS AND THE AMERICAN DREAM

1. Estimates range from $400 million to $600 million (Funkhouser 1991) to $700 million by the Salvadoran government (*New York Times* March 11, 1992) to $1 billion (Montes Mozo and Garcia Vasquez 1988). Most of the remittances and goods transported to El Salvador via the couriers discussed in chapter 5 would not be detected and therefore counted in the total, however.

BIBLIOGRAPHY

AFSC (American Friends Service Committee). 1988. *In the Shadow of Liberty: Central American Refugees in the United States*. Philadelphia, PA: American Friends Service Committee.

Aldrich, Howard E., and Roger Waldinger. 1990. "Ethnicity and Entrepreneurship." *Annual Review of Sociology* 16:111–35.

Alger, Horatio, Jr. 1985. *Ragged Dick and Struggling Upward*. New York: Penguin Books.

Americas Watch. August 30, 1987. *The Civilian Toll 1986–1987: Ninth Supplement to the Report on Human Rights in El Salvador*. New York: Americas Watch.

Anderson, Thomas P. 1971. *Matanza: El Salvador's Communist Revolt of 1932*. Lincoln: University of Nebraska Press.

Armstrong, Robert, and Janet Shenk. 1982. *El Salvador: The Face of Revolution*. Boston: South End Press.

Bailey, Thomas R. 1987. *Immigrant and Native Workers: Contrasts and Competition*. Boulder, CO: Westview Press.

Barry, Tom. 1987. *Roots of Rebellion: Land and Hunger in Central America*. Boston: South End Press.

Basch, Linda, Nina Glick Schiller, and Cristina Szanton Blanc. 1994. *Nations Unbound: Transnational Projects, Postcolonial Predicaments and Deterritorialized Nation-States*. Langhorne, PA: Gordon and Breach.

Bluestone, Barry, and Bennett Harrison. 1982. *The Deindustrialization of America: Plant Closings, Community Abandonment, and the Dismantling of Basic Industry*. New York: Basic Books.

Bonacich, Edna. 1973. "A Theory of Middleman Minorities." *American Sociological Review* 38 (October): 583–94.

Bonnett, Aubrey W. 1981. *Institutional Adaptation of West Indian Immigrants to America: An Analysis of Rotating Credit Associations*. Washington, DC: University Press of America.

Bouchier, David. 1978. "Over the Border." *New Society* 14 (September): 557.

Bourgois, Philippe. 1993. "Crack in Spanish Harlem: Culture and Economy in the Inner City." In *Talking about People: Readings in Contemporary Anthropology*, edited by Robert J. Gordon and William A. Haviland. Mountain View, CA: Mayfield Publishing Company.

Brody, David. 1980. *Workers in Industrial America: Essays on the Twentieth Century Struggle*. New York: Oxford University Press.

Brown, Susan E. 1977. "Household Composition and Variation in a Rural Dominican Village." *Journal of Comparative Family Studies* 8 (2): 257–67.

Cabarrús, Carlos Rafael. 1983. *Génesis de una revolución. Análisis del Surgimiento y Desarrollo de la Organización Campesina en El Salvador*. Mexico

City, Mexico: Centro de Investigaciones y Estudios Superiores en Antropología Social. Ediciones de la Casa Chata.

Cain, Bruce E., D. Roderick Kiewiet, and Carole J. Uhlaner. 1991. "The Acquisition of Partisanship by Latinos and Asian Americans." *American Journal of Political Science* 35 (2): 390–422.

Calavita, Kitty. 1981. "United States Immigration Law and the Control of American Labor." *Contemporary Crises* 5:341–68.

CARECEN (Central American Refugee Center). Hempstead, New York.

Carmean, Rachel L., Frank P. Romo, and Michael Schwartz. n.d. "Proposal for Research: Plant Locational Decision Making on Long Island." Institute for Social Analysis, State University of New York at Stony Brook.

Castells, Manuel, and Alejandro Portes. 1989. "World Underneath: The Origins, Dynamics, and Effects of the Informal Economy." In *The Informal Economy: Studies in Advanced and Less Developed Countries*, edited by Alejandro Portes, Manuel Castells, and Lauren A. Benton. Baltimore, MD: The Johns Hopkins University Press.

Chavez, Leo R. 1990. "Coresidence and Resistance: Strategies for Survival among Undocumented Mexicans and Central Americans in the United States." *Urban Anthropology* 19 (1–2): 31–61.

——. 1992. *Shadowed Lives: Undocumented Immigrants in American Society.* Orlando, FL: Holt, Rinehart and Winston.

——. 1994. "The Power of the Imagined Community: The Settlement of Undocumented Mexicans and Central Americans in the United States." *American Anthropologist* 96 (1): 52–73.

Chen, Hsiang-shui. 1992. *Chinatown No More: Taiwan Immigrants in Contemporary New York.* Ithaca: Cornell University Press.

Chinchilla, Norma, Nora Hamilton, and James Loucky. 1993. "Central Americans in Los Angeles: An Immigrant Community in Transition." In *In the Barrios: Latinos and the Underclass Debate*, edited by Joan Moore and Raquel Pinderhughes. New York: Russell Sage Foundation.

CHIRLA (Coalition for Humane Immigration Rights of Los Angeles). March 15, 1990. "Employment Discrimination against Immigrants: A Study of the Job-Seeking Experiences of People Who Speak English with an Accent." Los Angeles: CHIRLA Preliminary Report.

Corcoran, Mary P. 1993. *Irish Illegals: Transients between Two Societies.* Westport, CT: Greenwood Press.

Cornelius, Wayne A. 1982. "Interviewing Undocumented Immigrants: Methodological Reflections Based on Fieldwork in Mexico and the U.S." *International Migration Review* 16 (2): 378–411.

Crane, Keith, Beth J. Asch, Joanna Zorn Heilbrunn, and Danielle C. Cullinane. 1990. *The Effects of Employer Sanctions on the Flow of Undocumented Immigrants to the United States.* Washington, DC: Rand Corporation and Urban Institute.

de la Garza, Rodolfo O., Louis DeSipio, Chris F. Garcia, and Angelo Falcon. 1992. *Latino Voices: Mexican, Puerto Rican and Cuban Perspectives on American Politics.* Boulder, CO: Westview Press.

DeWind, Josh. December 1987. "The Legalization of Undocumented Immigrants in New York: A Mid-Program Assessment." Report prepared for the New York Community Trust.

Dinerman, Ina R. 1982. "Migrants and Stay-at-Homes: A Comparative Study of Rural Migration from Michoacan, Mexico." Monograph Series 5. San Diego: Center for U.S.-Mexico Studies, University of California.

Doeringer, Peter B., and Michael J. Piore. 1971. *Internal Labor Market and Manpower Analysis*. Cambridge, MA: Lexington.

Durham, William H. 1979. *Scarcity and Survival in Central America: Ecological Origins of the Soccer War*. Stanford: Stanford University Press.

Ewen, Elizabeth. 1985. *Immigrant Women in the Land of Dollars: Life and Culture on the Lower East Side, 1890–1925*. New York: Monthly Review Press.

Fernández-Kelly, Patricia, and Saskia Sassen. 1991. "A Collaborative Study of Hispanic Women in the Garment and Electronics Industries. Executive Summary to the Ford, Revson and Tinker Foundations." New York: Center for Latin American and Caribbean Studies, New York University.

Fitzpatrick, Joseph P. 1987. *Puerto Rican Americans: The Meaning of Migration to the Mainland*. 2d ed. Englewood Cliffs, NJ: Prentice-Hall.

Foster, George. 1965. "Peasant Society and the Image of Limited Good." *American Anthropologist* 67 (2): 293–315.

Funkhouser, Edward. April 3, 1991. "Emigration, Remittances, and Labor Market Adjustment: A Comparison of El Salvador and Nicaragua." Paper presented to the 15th Congress of the Latin American Studies Association, Washington, DC.

Garrison, Vivian, and Carol I. Weiss. 1979. "Dominican Family Networks and United States Immigration Policy: A Case Study." *International Migration Review* 13 (2): 264–83.

Georges, Eugenia. 1990. *The Making of a Transnational Community: Migration, Development, and Cultural Change in the Dominican Republic*. New York: Columbia University Press.

Gibson, Margaret A. 1988. *Accommodation without Assimilation: Sikh Immigrants in an American High School*. Ithaca: Cornell University Press.

Glazer, Nathan, and Daniel P. Moynihan. 1970 [1964]. *Beyond the Melting Pot*. Cambridge: MIT Press.

Glick Schiller, Nina, Linda Basch, and Cristina Szanton Blanc. 1992. "Transnationalism: A New Analytic Framework for Understanding Migration." In *Towards a Transnational Perspective on Migration: Race, Class, Ethnicity, and Nationalism Reconsidered*, edited by Nina Glick Schiller, Linda Basch, and Cristina Szanton Blanc. New York: New York Academy of Sciences.

Gold, Michael. 1930. *Jews without Money*. New York: Liveright Publishing Corporation.

Gold, Steven. 1994. "Patterns of Economic Cooperation among Israeli Immigrants in Los Angeles." *International Migration Review* 28 (1): 114–33.

Gordon, Milton M. 1964. *Assimilation in American Life: The Role of Race, Religion, and National Origins*. New York: Oxford University Press.

Gordon, Sara R. 1989. *Crisis Política y Guerra en El Salvador*. Mexico City, Mexico: Siglo Veintiuno Editores.

Grasmuck, Sherri, and Patricia Pessar. 1991. *Between Two Islands: Dominican*

International Migration. Berkeley and Los Angeles: University of California Press.

Hamilton, Nora, and Norma Stoltz Chinchilla. 1991. "Central American Migration: A Framework for Analysis." *Latin American Research Review* 26 (1): 75–110.

Handlin, Oscar. 1951. *The Uprooted: The Epic Story of the Great Migrations That Made the American People.* Boston: Little, Brown and Company.

Harvey, David. 1994 [1990]. *The Condition of Postmodernity.* Cambridge, MA: Blackwell Publishers.

Hendricks, Glenn. 1974. *The Dominican Diaspora.* New York: Teachers College Press.

Horowitz, Ruth. 1983. *Honor and the American Dream: Culture and Identity in a Chicano Community.* New Brunswick, NJ: Rutgers University Press.

Immigration and Naturalization Service. 1991. *1990 Statistical Yearbook of the Immigration and Naturalization Service.* Washington, DC: GPO.

Jackson, Kenneth T. 1985. *Crabgrass Frontier: The Suburbanization of the United States.* New York: Oxford University Press.

Jacob, Evelyn, and Cathie Jordan. 1993. *Minority Education: Anthropological Perspectives.* Norwood, NJ: Ablex Publishing Co.

Jastrow, Marie. 1986. *Looking Back: The American Dream through Immigrant Eyes.* New York: W. W. Norton & Co.

Juffer, Jane. 1988. "Abuse at the Border: Women Face a Perilous Crossing." *The Progressive* 1988 (April): 14–19.

Kälin, Walter. 1986. "Troubled Communication: Cross-Cultural Misunderstandings in the Asylum-Hearing." *International Migration Review* 20 (2): 230–41.

Kasarda, John D. 1988. "Jobs, Migration, and Emerging Urban Mismatches." In *Urban Change and Poverty*, edited by Michael G. H. McGeary and Laurence E. Lynn, Jr. Washington, DC: National Academy Press.

Kessner, Thomas. 1977. *The Golden Door: Italian and Jewish Immigrant Mobility in New York City 1880–1915.* New York: Oxford University Press.

Kim, Ilsoo. 1981. *New Urban Immigrants: The Korean Community in New York.* Princeton, NJ: Princeton University Press.

Kling, Sandra Shoenberg, and Patricia C. Wang. 1985. "A Demographic Profile of Hempstead Village, 1960–1985." Hofstra University Center for Community Studies, Hofstra University, Sociology/Anthropology Department, Hempstead, New York.

Kot, Veronica. 1988. "The Impact of Cultural Factors on Credibility in the Asylum Context." Produced by the Father Moriarty Central American Refugee Project. San Francisco: Immigrant Legal Resource Center.

Kwong, Peter. *The New Chinatown.* New York: Farrar, Straus and Giroux.

———. April 26, 1994. "The Wages of Fear: Undocumented and Unwanted, Fuzhounese Immigrants Are Changing the Face of Chinatown." *Voice.*

LaGumina, Salvatore J. 1988. *From Steerage to Suburb: Long Island Italians.* New York: The Center for Migration Studies of New York.

Lee, Jung-Kyu. October 1989. "A Reassessment of the Dual Economy Approach: Centered on the Determinants of Income Difference." (Draft) Paper submitted to the Eastern Sociological Society. Department of Sociology, State University of New York at Stony Brook.

Li, Peter. 1977. "Occupational Achievement and Kinship Assistance among Chinese Immigrants in Chicago." *Sociological Quarterly* 18:478–89.

Lieberson, Stanley. 1980. *A Piece of the Pie.* Berkeley and Los Angeles: University of California Press.

Light, Ivan H. 1972. *Ethnic Enterprise in America: Business and Welfare among Chinese, Japanese, and Blacks.* Berkeley and Los Angeles: University of California Press.

———. 1985. "Immigrant Entrepreneurs in America: Koreans in Los Angeles." In *Clamor at the Gates: The New American Immigration*, edited by Nathan Glazer. San Francisco, CA: ICS Press.

Loescher, Gil, and John A. Scanlan. 1986. *Calculated Kindness: Refugees and America's Half-Open Door, 1945 to the Present.* New York: Free Press.

Logan, John. July 1994. "Black Suburbia: On the Cutting Edge." Paper presented at the World Congress of Sociology, Bielefeld, Germany.

Lomnitz, Larissa Adler. 1977. *Networks and Marginality: Life in a Mexican Shantytown.* New York: Academic Press.

———. 1988. "Informal Exchange Networks in Formal Systems: A Theoretical Model." *American Anthropologist* 90:42–55.

Long Island Almanac. 1989. Long Island, NY: Long Island Business News.

Loucky, James, Nora Hamilton, and Norma Chinchilla. June 1989. "The Effects of the Immigration Reform and Control Act on the Garment, Building Maintenance, and Hospitality Industries in Los Angeles." Final Report to the Division of Immigration Policy on Research, U.S. Department of Labor.

Mahler, Sarah J. 1992. "Tres Veces Mojado: Undocumented Central and South American Migration to Suburban Long Island." Ph.D. diss., Columbia University.

———. 1993. "Alternative Enumeration of Undocumented Salvadorans on Long Island." Final Report for Joint Statistical Agreement 89–46, U.S. Bureau of the Census.

———. March 10, 1994. "No Harmony in Housing: Latino Immigrants and White Suburbanites on Long Island." Paper presented to the Latin American Studies Conference, Atlanta, Georgia.

Mangione, Jerre. 1972. *Mount Allegro.* New York: Crown Publishers.

Massey, Douglas S., Rafael Alarcón, Jorge Durand, and Humberto González. 1987. *Return to Aztlan: The Social Process of International Migration from Western Mexico.* Berkeley and Los Angeles: University of California Press.

Massey, Douglas S., and Nancy A. Denton. 1993. *American Apartheid: Segregation and the Making of the Underclass.* Cambridge: Harvard University Press.

Mines, Richard. 1981. "Developing a Community Tradition of Migration: A Field Study in Rural Zacatecas, Mexico, and California Settlement Areas." Research Monograph 3. Center for U.S.-Mexico Studies, University of California at San Diego, La Jolla, California.

———. 1984. "Network Migration and Mexican Rural Development: A Case Study." In *Patterns of Undocumented Migration: Mexico and the United States*, edited by Richard C. Jones. Totowa, NJ: Rowman & Allanheld.

Mitchell, Christopher, ed. 1992. *Western Hemisphere Immigration and United States Foreign Policy*. University Park: Pennsylvania State University Press.

Modell, John, and Tamara K. Hareven. 1973. "Urbanization and the Malleable Household: An Examination of Boarding and Lodging in American Families." *Journal of Marriage and the Family* 35 (3): 467–79.

Montes, Segundo. 1979. *Estudio Sobre Estratificación Social en El Salvador*. San Salvador, El Salvador: Universidad Centroamericana José Simeón Cañas.

Montes Mozo, Segundo, and Juan Jose Garcia Vasquez. 1988. *Salvadoran Migration to the United States: An Exploratory Study*. Hemispheric Migration Project, Center for Immigration Policy and Refugee Assistance, Georgetown University.

Moore, Joan W. 1991. *Going Down to the Barrio: Homeboys and Homegirls in Change*. Philadelphia, PA: Temple University Press.

Morrison, Toni. 1993. "On the Back of Blacks." *Time* Special Issue, "The New Face of America: How Immigrants Are Shaping the World's First Multicultural Society." Fall: 57.

Mutchler, Jan E., and Lauren J. Krivo. 1989. "Availability and Affordability: Household Adaptation to a Housing Squeeze." *Social Forces* 68 (1): 241–61.

Nee, Victor, Jimy Sanders, and Scott Sernau. 1994. "Job Transitions in an Immigrant Metropolis: Ethnic Boundaries and Mixed Economy." Russell Sage Foundation Working Paper no. 61. New York: Russell Sage Foundation.

Nelson, Eugene. 1975. *Pablo Cruz and the American Dream: The Experience of an Undocumented Immigrant from Mexico*. Salt Lake City, UT: Peregrine Smith.

Newman, Katherine S. 1988. *Falling from Grace: The Experience of Downward Mobility in the American Middle Class*. New York: Free Press.

———. 1993. *Declining Fortunes: The Withering of the American Dream*. New York: Basic Books.

Newsday. March 25, 1989. "Realtors and Racism; Black Brokers on LI Say Some Areas Off-Limits to Them."

———. November 22, 1989. "From Haiti to Suffolk. Journey's End. The Life and Death of Seven Immigrants."

———. December 8, 1989. "Planners Say Long Island Needs Its Illegal Apartments and Must Declare Amnesty."

———. July 15, 1990. "Questions about Neighbors. Town Probes Charge of Salvadoran 'Rooming Houses'; Owners Deny It."

———. September 17–25, 1990. "A World Apart. Segregation on Long Island."

———. March 17, 1991. "New Frontier for Minorities."

———. May 19, 1991. "Long Island: Still the Family Suburb."

———. December 9, 1991. "Leaps and Bounds: School Hikes Anger Beleaguered LI Homeowners."

———. February 21, 1992. "Three Brokers Cited in Racial Steering; Freeport Rights Group Prompts State Action."

———. March 8, 1992. "State: Racial Steering Persists; LI Home Brokers Deny Charge."

———. May 18, 1992. "Pattern of Bias; Study: Segregation Marks LI Housing."

————. August 26, 1993. "Home Loan Hurdles for Blacks."

————. September 6, 1993. "Red, White and Black; It's Shameful. LI Lenders Are Redlining: Denying Mortgages to People of Color."

New York Daily News. November 10, 1989. "Call 'em Vans of the Oppressed."

New York State Business Statistics Quarterly Summary. 1989. Albany: New York State Department of Economic Development, Division of Policy Research, Bureau of Business Research.

New York State Department of Labor. *Annual Labor Area Report: Nassau-Suffolk SMSA.* Fiscal Years 1985, 1987, 1988, 1990. New York: New York State Department of Labor, Division of Research and Statistics, Bureau of Labor Market Information.

New York Times. November 12, 1988. "Aliens' Rail Trips Grow More Perilous."

————. January 21, 1989. "Starting Over, the Ex-Peruvian Way."

————. February 21, 1989. "Latin Refugees to Be Held in Texas."

————. February 28, 1989. "Seventy-Nine Suspected Aliens Arrested on a Jet."

————. March 1, 1989. "Sixty-Nine More Aliens Arrested on Flight from Los Angeles to New York."

————. November 12, 1989. "False Migrant Claims: Fraud on a Huge Scale."

————. March 15, 1990. "Forty-Seven on Plane Arrested as Illegal Aliens in Atlanta."

————. August 8, 1990. "For U.S. Visa, Peruvians Try Lots of Ruses."

————. December 20, 1990. "U.S. Settles Suit on Ousting Aliens."

————. January 7, 1991. "One Last Deadly Crossing for Illegal Aliens."

————. April 14, 1991. "'Underground Helps Find Low-Cost Housing.'"

————. July 21, 1991. "Trade in Fake Documents Thrives in Neighborhoods of Immigrants."

————. September 15, 1991. "Enclave's Old-Timers Upset by Newcomers."

————. December 19, 1991. "Motor-Vehicle Employees Charged in Fake-ID Ring."

————. December 21, 1991. "After Decades of Growth, Long Island Confronts Stagnation."

————. February 19, 1992. "Boom in Fake Identity Cards for Aliens."

————. March 11, 1992. "For Some in U.S., Peace in Salvador Brings Fear."

————. April 7, 1992. "Theft through Cellular 'Clone' Calls."

————. June 28, 1992. "At Forty-Five, Levittown's Legacy Is Unclear."

————. November 20, 1992. "Stealth of Phone Credit-Card Thieves. Shoulder Surfers Swipe and Sell Numbers of the Unsuspecting."

————. April 25, 1993. "Pleas for Asylum Inundate System for Immigration."

————. February 15, 1994. "L.I. Apartment Service Accused of Bias in Rental Offers."

————. March 17, 1994. "Persistent Racial Segregation Mars Suburbs' Green Dream."

————. September 23, 1994. "Northrup to Cut 8,650 Positions. Fifteen Percent Reduction Hits L.I. and California."

————. January 31, 1995. "Peru: On the Very Fast Track."

Nieves, Isabel. 1979. "Household Arrangements and Multiple Jobs in San Salvador." *Signs* 5 (1): 134–42.

NYS IATF (New York State Inter-Agency Task Force on Immigrant Affairs). November 4, 1988. "Workplace Discrimination under the Immigration Reform and Control Act of 1986: A Study of Impacts on New Yorkers."

Ogbu, John U. 1990. "Minority Status and Literacy in Comparative Perspective." *Daedalus* 119:141–68.

Papademetriou, Demetrios G. 1989. "The U.S. Legalization Program: A Preliminary Final Report." *International Migration* 27 (1): 5–25.

Pearce, Jenny. 1986. *Promised Land: Peasant Rebellion in Chalatenango, El Salvador.* London: Latin American Bureau.

Pessar, Patricia. 1982a. "Kinship Relations of Production in the Migration Process: The Case of Dominican Emigration to the United States." New York University Occasional Papers.

———. 1982B. "The Role of Households in International Migration and the Case of U.S. Bound Migration from the Dominican Republic." *International Migration Review* 16 (2): 342–64.

———. 1985. "The Role of Gender in Dominican Settlement in the United States." In *Women and Change in Latin America,* edited by June Nash and Helen Safa. South Hadley, MA: Bergin & Garvey Publishers.

Pike, Frederick B. 1992. *The United States and Latin America: Myths and Stereotypes of Civilization and Nature.* Austin: University of Texas Press.

Piore, Michael J. 1979. *Birds of Passage: Migrant Labor and Industrial Societies.* Cambridge: Cambridge University Press.

Portes, Alejandro, and Robert L. Bach. 1985. *Latin Journey: Cuban and Mexican Immigrants in the United States.* Berkeley and Los Angeles: University of California Press.

Portes, Alejandro, and Rubén G. Rumbaut. 1990. *Immigrant America: A Portrait.* Berkeley and Los Angeles: University of California Press.

Portes, Alejandro, and John Walton. 1981. *Labor, Class and the International System.* Orlando, FL: Academic Press.

Portes, Alejandro, and Min Zhou. 1992. "Gaining the Upper Hand: Economic Mobility among Immigrant and Domestic Minorities." *Ethnic and Racial Studies* 15 (4): 491–522.

Portes, Alejandro, Manuel Castells, and Lauren A. Benton, eds. 1989. *The Informal Economy: Studies in Advanced and Less Developed Countries.* Baltimore: The Johns Hopkins University Press.

Refugee Reports. December 18, 1987; December 16, 1988; December 29, 1989; December 21, 1990; December 30, 1991; December 31, 1992. Washington, DC: Refugee Resettlement Information Exchange Project.

Regional Plan Association. 1988. "Outlook: The Growing Latino Presence in the Tri-State Region." New York: Latino Commission of Tri-State, United Way of Tri-State, and Regional Plan Association.

Reichert, Josh, and Douglas S. Massey. 1979. "Patterns of U.S. Migration from a Mexican Sending Community: A Comparison of Legal and Illegal Migrants." *International Migration Review* 13 (4): 599–623.

Reimers, David M. 1992. *Still the Golden Door: The Third World Comes to America.* New York: Columbia University Press.

Repak, Terry A. 1994. "Labor Market Incorporation of Central American Immigrants in Washington, D.C." *Social Problems* 41 (1): 114–28.

Rhoades, Robert E. "Intra-European Return Migration and Rural Development: Lessons from the Spanish Case." *Human Organization* 37 (2): 136–47.

Roberts, Bryan R. 1973. *Organizing Strangers: Poor Families in Guatemala City*. Austin: University of Texas Press.

Robinson, Court. 1989. "Politics and Principles: U.S. Refugee Admissions Policies in the 1980's." Washington, DC: U.S. Committee for Refugees.

Rodriguez, Clara. 1979. "Economic Factors Affecting Puerto Ricans in New York." In Centro de Estudios Puertorriqueños, *Labor Migration under Capitalism: The Puerto Rican Experience*. New York: Monthly Review Press.

Rose, Peter I. 1985. "Asian Americans: From Pariahs to Paragons." In *Clamor at the Gates: The New American Immigration*, edited by Nathan Glazer. San Francisco: ICS Press.

Rouse, Roger. 1992. "Making Sense of Settlement: Class Transformation, Cultural Struggle, and Transnationalism among Mexican Migrants in the United States." In *Towards a Transnational Perspective on Migration: Race, Class, Ethnicity, and Nationalism Reconsidered*, edited by Nina Glick Schiller, Linda Basch, and Cristina Szanton Blanc. New York: New York Academy of Sciences.

Sacramento Observer. October 21, 1992. "Bush and Clinton Comment on 'Racism': Both Share Views on Controversial Subject."

Salvo, Joseph, and Ron Ortiz. Forthcoming. "Immigrant Settlement Patterns in the New York Metropolitan Region." In *One Out of Five: The New York Region's New Immigrants*, edited by Nancy Foner. Routledge.

Samora, Julian. 1971. *Los Mojados: The Wetback Story*. Notre Dame, IN: University of Notre Dame Press.

Sánchez-Korrol, Virginia. 1983. *From Colonia to Community: The History of Puerto Ricans in New York City, 1917–1948*. Westport, CT: Greenwood Press.

Sanders, Jimy M., and Victor Nee. 1987. "Limits of Ethnic Solidarity in the Enclave Economy." *American Sociological Review* 52 (December): 745–73.

Santana Cardoso, Ciro F. 1975. "Historia Económica del Cafe en Centroamérica (Siglo XIX): Estudio Comparativo." *Estudios Sociales Centroamericanos* 4 (10): 9–55.

Sassen, Saskia. 1988. *The Mobility of Labor and Capital*. Cambridge: Cambridge University Press.

————. 1991. *The Global City: New York, London, Tokyo*. Princeton, NJ: Princeton University Press.

Sassen-Koob, Saskia. 1984. "The New Labor Demand in Global Cities." In *Cities in Transformation*, edited by Michael P. Smith. Beverly Hills, CA: Sage Press.

Schirmer, Jennifer G. 1985. "A Different Reality: The Central American Refugee and the Lawyer." *Immigration Newsletter* 14 (5): 6–9.

Schlesinger, Arthur M., Jr. 1992. *The Disuniting of America*. New York: W. W. Norton & Company.

BIBLIOGRAPHY

Schoultz, Lars. 1992. "Central America and the Politicization of U.S. Immigration Policy." In *Western Hemisphere Immigration and United States Foreign Policy*, edited by Christopher Mitchell. University Park: Pennsylvania State University Press.

Siems, Larry. 1994. *Between the Lines: Letters between Undocumented Mexican and Central American Immigrants*. Hopewell, NJ: Ecco Press.

Silk, James. 1986. *Despite a Generous Spirit: Denying Asylum in the United States*. Washington, DC: U.S. Committee for Refugees and American Council for Nationalities Service.

Simcox, David E. 1988. "Immigration and Social Welfare: The Notion of the Non–Revenue Consuming Taxpayer." In *U.S. Immigration in the 1980s: Reappraisal and Reform*, edited by David E. Simcox. Boulder, CO: Center for Immigration Studies, Washington, DC, and Westview Press.

Singer, Cathy. 1990. "The New Immigrants." *Long Island Monthly* 3 (3): 57–67.

Stack, Carol B. 1974. *All Our Kin: Strategies for Survival in a Black Community*. New York: Harper & Row.

Stanley, William Deane. 1987. "Economic Migrants or Refugees from Violence? A Time-Series Analysis of Salvadoran Migration to the United States." *Latin American Research Review* 22 (1): 132–54.

Stein, Steve, and Carlos Monge. 1988. *La Crisis del Estado Patrimonial en el Perú*. Lima, Peru: Instituto de Estudios Peruanos Ediciones.

Stepick, Alex. 1991. "The Informal Sector in Miami." *City and Society* 5:10–22.

Stepick, Alex, and Guillermo Grenier. 1993. "Cubans in Miami." In *In the Barrios: Latinos and the Underclass Debate*, edited by Joan Moore and Raquel Pinderhughes. New York: Russell Sage Foundation.

Suárez-Orozco, Marcelo M. 1989. *Central American Refugees and U.S. High Schools: A Psychological Study of Motivation and Achievement*. Stanford: Stanford University Press.

Szajkowski, Zosa. 1974. "The Consul and the Immigrant: A Case of Bureaucratic Bias." *Jewish Social Studies* 36 (1): 3–18.

Takaki, Ronald. 1990. *Iron Cages: Race and Culture in Nineteenth-Century America*. New York: Oxford University Press.

Thomas, William I., and Florian Znaniecki. 1984 [1918]. *The Polish Peasant in Europe and America*. Urbana: University of Illinois Press.

Thorp, Rosemary. 1983. "The Evolution of Peru's Economy." In *The Peruvian Experiment Reconsidered*, edited by Cynthia McClintock and Abraham F. Lowenthal. Princeton, NJ: Princeton University Press.

Thruelson, Richard. 1976. *The Grumman Story*. New York: Praeger.

Time Magazine. April 9, 1990. "What Will the U.S. Be Like When Whites Are No Longer the Majority?"

Trager, Lillian. 1988. *The City Connection: Migration and Family Interdependence in the Philippines*. Ann Arbor: University of Michigan Press.

Turnbull, Colin M. 1972. *The Forest People*. New York: Simon and Schuster.

USCR (U.S. Committee for Refugees). 1991. "Running the Gauntlet: The Central American Journey through Mexico." Washington, DC: American Council for Nationalities Service.

US GAO (U.S. General Accounting Office). March 1990. "Immigration Reform: Employer Sanctions and the Question of Discrimination." Washington, DC: GPO.

Waldinger, Roger. 1986. *Through the Eye of the Needle: Immigrants and Enterprise in New York's Garment Trades.* New York: New York University Press.

———. 1989. "Immigration and Urban Change." *Annual Review of Sociology* 15:211–32.

———. 1994. "The Making of an Immigrant Niche." *International Migration Review* 28 (1): 3–30.

Waldinger, Roger, Howard Aldrich, and Robin Ward. 1990. *Ethnic Entrepreneurs: Immigrant and Ethnic Business in Industrial Societies.* Newbury Park, CA: Sage Publications.

Wall Street Journal. July 20, 1990. "The Shining Path Fights On in Peru."

Wallace, Steven. 1986. "Central American and Mexican Immigrant Characteristics and Economic Incorporation in California." *International Migration Review* 20 (3): 657–71.

Ward, Thomas William. 1987. "The Price of Fear: Salvadoran Refugees in the City of the Angeles." Ph.D. diss., University of California, Los Angeles.

Warner, W. Lloyd, and Leo Srole. 1945. *The Social Systems of American Ethnic Groups.* New Haven: Yale University Press.

Weiss Fagen, Patricia. 1988. "Central American Refugees and U.S. Policy." In *Crisis in Central America,* edited by Nora Hamilton, Jeffry A. Frieden, Linda Fuller, and Manuel Pastor, Jr. Boulder, CO: PACCA and Westview Press.

Wilson, Kenneth L., and Alejandro Portes. 1980. "Immigrant Enclaves: An Analysis of the Labor Market Experiences of Cubans in Miami." *American Journal of Sociology* 86 (2): 295–319.

Woodward, Ralph Lee, Jr. 1985. *Central America: A Nation Divided.* 2d ed. New York: Oxford University Press.

World Bank. March 1979. *El Salvador: Demographic Issues and Prospects.* Washington, DC: The World Bank, Latin American and Caribbean Regional Office.

Yago, Glenn, Sen-Yuan Wu, and Charlene S. Long Seifert. April 10, 1987. "Island: Coming of Age in the Twenty-First Century." Long Island 2000: Report on Economic Development. Economic Research Bureau, Harriman School for Management and Policy, State University of New York at Stony Brook.

Zenner, Walter P. 1991. *Minorities in the Middle: A Cross-Cultural Analysis.* Albany: State University of New York Press.

Zhou, Min. 1992. *Chinatown: The Socioeconomic Potential of an Urban Enclave.* Philadelphia, PA: Temple University Press.

Zlolniski, Christian. 1994. "The Informal Economy in an Advanced Industrialized Society: Mexican Immigrant Labor in Silicon Valley." *Yale Law Journal* 103 (8): 2305–35.

Zschock, Dieter K., ed. 1969. "Economic Aspects of Suburban Growth: Studies of the Nassau-Suffolk Planning Region." Stony Brook: Economic Research Bureau, State University of New York at Stony Brook.

INDEX

About the Author

SARAH J. MAHLER is Assistant Professor of Anthropology at the University of Vermont.